Law and Religion in the Early Modern Period
Recht und Religion in der Frühen Neuzeit

Law and Religion in the Early Modern Period
Recht und Religion in der Frühen Neuzeit

VOL. 7

Christoph Haar (Ed.)

Slavery, Law and Religion in the Early Modern Period

BRILL | SCHÖNINGH

Cover illustration: © Evelina Haar

Bibliographic information published by the Deutsche Nationalbibliothek

The Deutsche Nationalbibliothek lists this publication in the Deutsche Nationalbibliografie; detailed bibliographic data available online: http://dnb.d-nb.de

www.brill.com

Cover design: Nora Krull, Hamburg
Production: Brill Deutschland GmbH, Paderborn

ISSN 2629-6926
ISBN 978-3-506-79632-5 (hardback)
ISBN 978-3-657-79632-8 (e-book)

Contents

Acknowledgments

The collection of contributions in this volume is based on the workshop "Slavery, Law and Religion in the Early Modern Period", held at UC Louvain in Louvain-la-Neuve on 8–9 March 2023. Its aim was to bring together an international group of researchers with a particular focus on junior scholars working on early modern slavery across the globe.

The workshop proposal was developed as part of my Marie Skłodowska-Curie Postdoctoral Fellowship (Individual Fellowship) under the European Union's Horizon 2020 research and innovation programme. I would like to thank the European Commission for funding my time at UC Louvain, an institution that offered me an excellent research environment. Most importantly, I would like to express my gratitude to my host professor Wim Decock.

While drafting the proposal formed part of the fellowship, the workshop itself as well as the research for this publication took place after its end date because I took up a position at the University of Würzburg. I therefore wish to thank Prof. Anuschka Tischer at the University of Würzburg for supporting my plan to host the workshop. Moreover, I would like to acknowledge the administrative and catering staff at UC Louvain who helped with the organisation and the carrying out of the event, particularly Sara Wilmet and Sybille Descampe. I would further like to show appreciation to the university for enabling us to hold our presentations and discussions at their wonderful conference venue Louvain House, Espace du Lac. As regards financial assistance, I gratefully mention the generous sponsorship of the Institut Interdisciplinaire en Sciences Juridiques of UC Louvain.

I express my thanks to the editors-in-chief of Brill's Law and Religion in the Early Modern Period series Herman Selderhuis and Wim Decock, to the copy editor for this volume, Martina Kayser, to Anne Konrad who helped prepare the manuscript, and to Rômulo Ehalt who agreed to give the keynote lecture on "Slavery in Captivity: The Society of Jesus and Early Modern Japan". Evelina Haar kindly and expertly provided the conference poster layout and designed the cover illustration.

This volume contains nine chapters that are based on nine of the presentations and subsequent discussions at the event. My final note of gratitude goes out to the authors for their contributions to the workshop and to this publication.

Introduction: Slavery, Law and Religion in the Early Modern Period

Christoph Haar

In the historical disciplines that deal with the sixteenth to the eighteenth centuries, slavery and the global slave trade have received increased attention in recent years. One characteristic feature of the early modern period lies in the fact that these three centuries experienced pivotal shifts in cultural, economic and political life that stood in direct relation to slavery and the slave trade. The period saw a number of developments reach an unprecedented scale, such as the global economic slave system, European colonialism and imperialism as well as racist taxonomies. With this observation on the larger themes in mind, the narratives in the successive chapters of *Slavery, Law and Religion in the Early Modern Period* unfold the variety of ways how historical agents engaged with slavery.

As the field of early modern slavery studies now spreads across an immense disciplinary and geographical breadth, this introduction will not attempt to cover the great diversity of approaches in the research landscape. Instead, it will highlight research strands relevant to the studies presented in this volume to suggest the individual chapters offer fruitful contributions for further debate.

The present volume draws on previously conducted academic investigations that have examined instances of enslavement, slavery and slave trading in a diverse array of settings in the early modern world. In this regard, major research works have made use of the methodological perspective of global history and they have moreover examined the intellectual historical connections between colonial empire and slavery.[1] Furthermore, examining the history of slavery in a wide range of circumstances has permitted, and indeed required engagement with conceptual research. Much debate has concerned the "question of definition", or the meaning of slavery as it appeared all over the globe

1 Blackburn, *The Making of New World Slavery. From the Baroque to the Modern, 1492–1800*; Davis, *Inhuman Bondage: The rise and fall of slavery in the New World*; Zeuske, *Handbuch Geschichte der Sklaverei: Eine Globalgeschichte von den Anfängen bis zur Gegenwart*; Pagden, *Lords of All the World. Ideologies of Empire in Spain, Britain and France c. 1500–1800* (New Haven, 1995); A. Pagden, *The Burdens of Empire, 1539 to the Present*; Reinhard, *Die Unterwerfung der Welt. Globalgeschichte der europäischen Expansion 1415–2015*.

 | DOI:10.30965/9783657796328_002

in the course of history.[2] On the one hand, this topic speaks to the ubiquitous usage of the label as suggestive of a universal applicability of a certain kind of socio-economic relationship, primarily the egregious labour relation of chattel slavery (commonly distinguished from debt bondage or forced labour). On the other hand, it refers to a theoretical task that in the end result seems impossible to achieve because conditions differed greatly across the world during the early modern period.[3]

In fact, narratives on the history of slavery for a long time tended to rely on the most-researched and most-documented slaveries. The distinctions stemming from those studies consequently stood at the centre of attention for a long time. Thus, it has been highlighted that the research revolving around the transatlantic slave trade as well as plantation slavery produced research concepts based mainly on the dichotomy between unfreedom and freedom (in addition to teleological historical narratives sketching advances from the former towards the latter) and that these models provided an inadequate foundation for the analysis of other areas in the world.[4] In order to advance scholarship, it was suggested that the prevalence of the "great" slaveries in history across global-historical academic works should be considered ill-suited to offer conceptual solutions, that the history of slavery should be written as a transcultural history of various agents rather than the history of an institution of slavery, and that it needed to take account of slaveries as identifiable through the moment of violence against human bodies, besides or irrespective of (Western) legal theories about freedom or property.[5]

Fulfilling these research desiderata has concomitantly led to the writing of an early modern history of slavery that addresses the task of "provincializing Europe", including, but not limited to raising awareness as regards the variety of terminological and legal distinctions surrounding the status of slavery.[6] It has further led to the expansion of research from the primary interest

2 Miers, "Slavery: A Question of Definition". For the European legal debate in the early modern period, see Cairns, "The Definition of Slavery in Eighteenth-Century Thinking".

3 Miers, "Slavery: A Question of Definition", 3.

4 Chatterjee, "Renewed and Connected Histories: Slavery and the Historiography of South Asia", 19–21. Eaton, "Introduction", 1f.

5 Zeuske, *Handbuch Geschichte der Sklaverei*, 63–70, 76, 84. For a critique of slavery as a universal concept, see Rômulo Ehalt's chapter in this volume.

6 For "provincializing Europe" representing a project that regards European thought "at once both indispensable and inadequate" to explaining non-Western modernity, see Chakrabarty, *Provincializing Europe. Postcolonial Thought and Historical Difference*, 16f. Relating this methodological approach to the history of slavery, Chatterjee, "Renewed and Connected Histories", 21f, and Zeuske, *Handbuch Geschichte der Sklaverei*, 64.

in the Atlantic slave world to covering Africa, Asia and the Indian Ocean regions.[7] Increasing the geographical range of case studies to hitherto widely neglected times and places moreover has involved research on slavery within territories of early modern Western Europe. For example, recent scholarship has highlighted in conceptual terms the moment of purchase and sale to identify practices of enslavement in contrast with other forms of bondage in the European, particularly the German-speaking, context.[8]

On the whole, a systematic theorisation that accounts for the complexity of the structure as well as the dynamics of slavery when looking at wide chronological and geographical horizons remains a work in progress.[9] In one current effort to address this issue, the Bonn Centre for Dependency and Slavery Studies has been developing a model of "asymmetrical dependency" in the attempt to categorise coercive social relations and broaden out the conceptual toolbox beyond the confines of the "slavery" label, with the aim to encapsulate various social formations as well as terminological manifestations of dependency and servitude.[10] This agenda encourages research unrestrained by geographical limits or specific historical periods to examine relations of debt bondage, convict and tributary labour, servitude, serfdom, domestic work and some forms of wage labour as well as patronage (chiefly through praxeological as well as comparative methods).[11]

Slavery, Law and Religion in the Early Modern Period seeks to enhance the research field that addresses the perspectives of law and religion to uncover the ways in which local discourse and practice shaped relations of slavery. This research connects empirical case studies with methodological premises centred around the primacy of local settings, especially early modern colonial settings. In the field of legal history, academic work on the basis of such an empirically-oriented approach has emphasised that normative orders in the early modern period routinely developed as responses to specific challenges

---

7 Campbell (ed.), *The structure of slavery in Indian Ocean, Africa and Asia*; Allen, *European Slave Trading in the Indian Ocean, 1500–1850*; Mann, *Sahibs, Sklaven und Soldaten. Geschichte des Menschenhandels rund um den Indischen Ozean*. See also Allen, "Slave, Convict, and Indentured Labour and the Tyranny of the Particular".

8 v. Mallinckrodt, "Verhandelte (Un-)Freiheit. Sklaverei, Leibeigenschaft und innereuropäischer Wissenstransfer am Ausgang des 18. Jahrhunderts", 357; v. Mallinckrodt, "There are no slaves in Prussia?".

9 Allen, "Introduction", 3.

10 Conermann, "Introduction: The Semantics of Slavery and Other Forms of Strong Asymmetrical Dependency in Comparison"; Winnebeck et al., "The Analytical Concept of Asymmetrical Dependency".

11 Winnebeck et al., "The Analytical Concept of Asymmetrical Dependency", 7.

in specific situations rather than by means of authorities systematically applying abstract legal principles to corresponding instances.[12] The research task, in this view, lies in tracing how norms of slavery emerged in specific historical contexts. Scholarship has thus acknowledged a methodological requirement to prioritise the local conditions (and with it, cultural historical analyses), all the while demonstrating how these conditions connected to normative considerations on a global scale – in short, scholarship has acknowledged the need for "glocalised" narratives.[13]

This approach lends itself well to the longer-standing concern, discussed under the heading of legal pluralism, with the various, often competing layers of early modern norms in a given place and time. Thus, it has been noted that research needs to consider the role of political culture (including intercultural relations) and competition for legal authority, i.e. jurisdiction, to comprehend what motivated change in attitudes towards slavery.[14] This approach also fits in with intellectual historical investigations that retrieve the successive correlations between contingent circumstances and abstract narratives. For example, research has traced how various early modern authors articulated colonial conditions as regards social relations or indeed the ownership of property by adopting European legal traditions. Hence, a number of specific social relations were expressed in terms of the classical justifications of slavery in Roman law, predominantly selling oneself into bondage and enslaving enemies in a "just war" undertaken as punishment for crimes, and the concept of *res nullius* (as well as the related *terra nullius*) was implemented to indicate a thing or even a territory supposedly without owner.[15]

Scholarship on religion in relation to slavery has also considered the aspect of norms that stands in the centre of legal historical analyses. However, historians of religion in the early modern period have focused their attention more on the cultural and intellectual foundations of slavery. The present volume supplements the breadth of these approaches by undertaking case studies corresponding to these foundations and relating to different normative levels

12 Duve, "Von der Europäischen Rechtsgeschichte zu einer Rechtsgeschichte Europas in globalhistorischer Perspektive", 49–58.

13 Duve, "Global Legal History: A Methodological Approach".

14 Benton and Ross (eds.) *Legal Pluralism and Empire 1500–1850*.

15 Benton and Straumann, "Acquiring Empire by Law: From Roman Doctrine to Early Modern European Practice". Springborg, "Hobbes, Donne and the Virginia Company: *Terra Nullius* and 'The Bulimia of Dominium'". Pateman, "The Settler Contract". Haar and Kaufmann, *"Gerechter Krieg" und "Niemandsland". Rechtfertigungsideologien für Kolonisierung und Versklavung durch europäische Mächte c. 1500–1800*.

as well as different religious backgrounds. In this field, too, the transatlantic world for a long time served as the main field of empirical enquiry. Hence, to take the example of Christianity in the transatlantic world, intellectual historical research has demonstrated how theological and biblical interpretations of slavery were connected to expressions of racial attitudes.[16] Furthermore, several cultural viewpoints of early modern Christianity and slavery have been reconstructed, such as a culture of Protestant slavery that transformed the dividing line between free and unfree from one of religious affiliation to a racialised line, or practices of Catholic enslavement in which the assumptions of spiritual freedom and temporal servitude coexisted to varying degrees.[17] Methodologically, studies mainly have centred on the processes of interaction and creative adaptation in the formation of religious practice and religious knowledge, and substantively, in the transatlantic case, they have regarded the contexts of Afro-Caribbean religious practice, European mission and colonial activities.[18]

The present book builds on the scholarly foundations described above and adds to current research strands by considering early modern slavery through the lens of law and religion, seeking to understand the discursive and practical contexts in which relations of slavery appeared in different historical settings around the globe. From the point of view taken in this volume, the principal concern lies in unfolding and explaining the circumstances in which the source material invokes relations of slavery. Historical agents shaped the respective instances of slavery by making use of the wide scope of ideas, regulations and practices associated with the concept as well as its oftentimes blurred boundaries to further social relations.

Based on this point of departure, the contributions to the volume are tied together by their focus on a joint agenda. One aspect of this agenda is to continue the research trend that has expanded the geographical scope to encompass any given place on the globe. The individual pieces of scholarship in this volume thus vary across time and space and in this way invite the reader to consider the spectrum of slaveries in the early modern world c. 1500–1800. Particular emphasis is given to the cultural and intellectual settings that informed the production of norms. What legal norms (law codes, conventions,

16 Kidd, *The Forging of Races. Race and Scripture in the Protestant Atlantic World, 1600–2000*.

17 Gerbner, *Christian slavery: conversion and race in the Protestant Atlantic World*. Priesching, *Die Sklaverei im Urteil der Jesuiten*.

18 Gerloff, "The African diaspora in the Caribbean and Europe from pre-emancipation to the present day".

colonial laws based on Roman law or natural law), what religious discourses were connected to the designations of relations of slavery? Besides the intellectual dimension, the cultural and political practices as observable through law courts, political authorities, colonial trading companies and mission stations come into view in this book, as do religious settings of conversion and education.

A second aspect lies in appreciating the significance of microhistorical approaches. The case studies illustrate discursive and practical contexts of slavery and slave trading to pinpoint how the agencies of enslaved human beings, local inhabitants, intellectuals and European colonial agents combined to produce unique situations that need to be understood in relation to the bigger picture of norms and attitudes towards slavery in the early modern world. Among others, the examined contexts revolve around the circumstances of everyday life, working conditions, legal cases, private property and salary, and sexual and marriage relations, as well as philosophical deliberations. The individual chapters are sensitive to the fact that the agency of enslaved human beings – in various social contexts – becomes visible when they are regarded as integrated into the respective social fabric instead of analytically defining these individuals as making up a distinct group within society.[19] One must certainly bear in mind the difficulty of making their voices heard because the relevant source material more often than not is scarce.

Thirdly, the present volume demonstrates the significance of interdisciplinary perspectives in the field of early modern history. Approaches from cultural, intellectual, religious and legal history feature in this volume and enter into discussion. As becomes clear in the introductions to the respective chapters, the approaches taken by the individual contributions are marked by diverse sets of research questions and methodological premises, although they all embark on their analyses from the common starting point mentioned above. They all aim to provide historical case studies that specify how slavery in the early modern period represented a social relation (and typically a legal status) that was highly dependent on the respective context as reproducible by means of the available source material. As a result, one key theme throughout this volume lies in the observation how cultural settings as well as semantic appropriations in relevant discourses resulted in the production of novel normative situations regarding slavery.

---

19 Cf. Hanß, Schiel (eds.), *Mediterranean Slavery Revisited (500–1800) / Neue Perspektiven auf mediterrane Sklaverei*, 201 and passim. For the problems of agency in the context of slavery studies, cf. Johnson, "On Agency".

This interdisciplinary volume brings together an international group of researchers, with a particular focus on junior scholars, who are currently engaged with the topic of early modern slavery in the fields of cultural, intellectual, religious and legal history. Its chapters are organised on the basis of geographical regions and take the readers on a journey from early modern Japan to South Africa and the Gold Coast, Southeast Europe and West Asia (Ottoman empire), South America (Paraguay, Chile) and India.[20]

***

In the opening chapter, *Rômulo Ehalt* considers different research approaches to slavery, law and religion in the sixteenth, seventeenth and eighteenth centuries. While legal historical research often centres on written legislative acts as setting the agenda for the social configurations involving slavery, historians of religion examine the ideological foundations of early modern colonial slavery. However, the perspectives of law and religion offer the chance to examine the history of slavery in another way. By zooming in on the topic of slavery in Japan, Ehalt advances the claim that slavery was not defined comprehensively by legal status or by its universality in practice as a specific, brutal type of labour arrangement. Instead, Europeans deployed the concept of slavery, specifically its rhetorical and normative components, in order to address non-European labour arrangements. To reveal this dynamic, legal and intellectual historians studying slavery need to make use of the methodological tools of legal transfer as well as cultural translation.

Eva Marie Lehner reflects on the Christian and Islamic religious ideas and practices among enslaved, manumitted and colonised people in multireligious Cape Town during the Dutch colonial rule 1652–1795. She argues that religion and slavery were tied together in South Africa during the Dutch colonial period in such a way that religious life shaped the experiences of enslaved as well as manumitted people. Practices included baptism, marriage and burial. Inclusion or, indeed, exclusion from religious life was significant for the maintenance of social groups and networks which in turn could operate by entrenching the institution of slavery or resisting it.

Maximilian Rose centres his attention on the first person of African descent to be ordained in the Anglican church, the missionary Philip Quaque, who was moreover entangled in the Atlantic slave trade as well as Gold Coast slavery

20 For the historicisation of geographical terms, see Chatterjee, "Renewed and Connected Histories: Slavery and the Historiography of South Asia", 23f.

during the second half of the eighteenth century until his death in 1816. Rose argues that Quaque's anti-slavery statements and his own role as a slave owner can be regarded as consistent if one takes into account the plural understanding of slavery in contemporary Gold Coast society: the variety of relationships of dependence allowed for a self-understanding of reformist ideas that sought to emphasise a benign form of slavery.

Early Ottoman chronicles provide the point of departure for *Bahar Bayraktaroğlu* in order to identify the role of *pençik* in the early modern period. In the course of considering its origins, she demonstrates that the concept in the abstract denoted a one-fifth of spoils of war, including captives taken from the opposing powers. In one sense, *pençik* represented a due that was to be spent for purposes of welfare, but in another sense, it came to represent a tax understood as an entitlement of the Ottoman ruler. On this empirical basis of terminological usage, Bayraktaroğlu argues that the character of *pençik* evolved in the Ottoman empire, depending on cultural and political contexts. Its meaning shifted from denoting a conceptual right to indicating a slaving policy as well as a tangible tax, and it would moreover come to serve as a symbol of slave dues as well as a documentation of legal status.

Turkana Allahverdiyeva explores household slavery in the Crimean Khanate in the early decades of the eighteenth century. Specifically, she examines court records to reveal the experiences of the non-Muslim enslaved individuals in such households, centring on the cases of Vasil, Nasta, Konasil and Hasan, who all appeared in court in the years 1701–1706. These two male and two female persons are studied as subaltern slave voices in the early eighteenth-century Crimean Khanate whose gender played a role for discrepancies regarding their agency. The analysis highlights the legal as well as social historical significance of the source material as it illustrates the agency these individuals exercised and shows their resilience in the face of severe systemic constraints to their autonomy.

In the setting of colonial Paraguay in the seventeenth century, *Lionel Mira* examines the Jesuit missionary Nicolas del Techo's work *Historia Provinciae Paraquariae Societatis Iesu*, conceived in Paraguay by 1658 and published in Liège in 1673. In the course of retracing Jesuit criticism of indigenous slavery and the acceptance of African slavery, Mira argues, del Techo pits the missionaries against the Portuguese slavers who according to the Jesuit's narrative hindered the process of evangelisation. This strategy, which involved a pronounced emphasis on the Portuguese slavers' brutality and irreligiosity, was better suited than legal arguments for del Techo's overall aim to raise support for the mission in Europe.

Stefano Rodrigo Torres looks beyond theological and pastoral explanations for the pressure and the violence exercised by missionaries and churchmen against indigenous people in southern Chile to consider social interactions. This brings to light the observation that missionaries infantilised them by assigning childish attributes to them. Following the Dominican scholar in Salamanca, Francisco de Vitoria, who formulated the analogy between indigenous people and children as well as slaves in his *relectio De Indis* of 1539, this view was prominently articulated in the colonial environment by the Jesuit José de Acosta towards the end of the century and by Juan de Solórzano y Pereira in mid-seventeenth century Peru. Written after 1722, the anonymous Mexican instructions how to operate a Jesuit estate, *Instrucciones a los Hermanos Jesuitas Administradores de Haciendas*, consolidate this view: the Jesuit emphasis on hierarchy and obedience is mirrored in the advocacy on a paternalistic basis for physical punishments against servant and slaves, which in this case included Native Americans as well as Africans and Afro-descendants.

In his study of Tranquebar in Southeast India, where the first permanent Protestant mission was set up by German missionaries on Danish colonial grounds in 1706, *Christoph Haar* examines the dynamic transformation of norms regarding slavery and the slave trade that took place during the first half of the eighteenth century. The cultural and political environment drove legal change, Haar argues, based on the interplay between the interests of the inhabitants, the mission, the enslaved and the Danish trading company. In particular, Tranquebar's reputation as perceived by local inhabitants and European and Tamil congregation members motivated the reshaping of the legal framework. The German missionaries for their part deployed European and biblical norms in the course of this process of negotiation.

André Kahl analyses Edmund Burke's (1729–1797) view on empire in relation to the topic of slavery. Burke regarded the developments in India as a threat to the stability of the British empire. As a result, Kahl states, the moral interpretation of Burke's criticism of the British East India Company needs to be accompanied by a political reading of his claims. The analysis of slavery underscores this argument because it offers an explanation why Burke's attitude towards slavery was rather ambivalent: moral, political and economic imperatives concerning slavery stood in tension to each other in ways they did not in his position on India. Throughout Burke's output in the later eighteenth century, three sets of claims can be distinguished: moral criticism of the institution of slavery, support for the slave system on economic grounds, but also disapproval based on further economic considerations.

Works Cited

Allen, Richard B. (2014). *European Slave Trading in the Indian Ocean, 1500–1850*. Athens OH: Ohio University Press.

Allen, Richard B. (2020). "Slave, Convict, and Indentured Labour and the Tyranny of the Particular." *Joseph C. Miller Memorial Lecture Series*, 1–51. https://www.dependency.uni-bonn.de/en/research/publications/bcdsss-publishing-series/joseph-c-miller-memorial-lecture-series (21.8.2023).

Allen, Richard B. (2021). *Slavery and Bonded Labour in Asia 1250–1900*. Leiden: Brill, 1–25.

Benton, Lauren and Benjamin Straumann (2010). "Acquiring Empire by Law: From Roman Doctrine to Early Modern European Practice." *Law and History Review* 28, 1–38.

Benton, Lauren and Richard Ross, eds. (2013). *Legal Pluralism and Empire 1500–1850*. New York: New York University Press.

Blackburn, Robin (1998). *The Making of New World Slavery. From the Baroque to the Modern, 1492–1800*. London: Verso.

Cairns, J.W. (2012). "The Definition of Slavery in Eighteenth-Century Thinking." J. Allain (ed.), *The Legal Understanding of Slavery: From the Historical to the Contemporary*. Oxford: Oxford University Press, 61–85.

Campbell, Gwyn, ed. (2004). *The structure of slavery in Indian Ocean Africa and Asia*. London: Frank Cass.

Chatterjee, Indrani (2006). "Renewed and Connected Histories: Slavery and the Historiography of South Asia." Indrani Chatterjee and Richard M. Eaton, eds., *Slavery & South Asian History*. Bloomington: Indiana University Press, 17–43.

Conermann, Stephan (2022). "Introduction: The Semantics of Slavery and Other Forms of Strong Asymmetrical Dependency in Comparison." Jeannine Bischoff and Stephan Conermann, eds., *Slavery and Other Forms of Strong Asymmetrical Dependencies. Semantics and Lexical Fields*. Berlin: De Gruyter.

Davis, David B. (2006). *Inhuman Bondage: The rise and fall of slavery in the New World*. New York: Oxford University Press.

Duve, Thomas (2017). "Global Legal History: A Methodological Approach." *Oxford Handbook Topics in Law*, https://doi.org/10.1093/oxfordhb/9780199935352.013.25 (21.8.2023).

Duve, Thomas (2012). "Von der Europäischen Rechtsgeschichte zu einer Rechtsgeschichte Europas in globalhistorischer Perspektive." *Rechtsgeschichte – Legal history* 20, 18–71. http://dx.doi.org/10.12946/rg20/018–071 (21.8.2023).

Eaton, Richard M. (2006). "Introduction." Indrani Chatterjee and Richard M. Eaton, eds., *Slavery & South Asian History*. Bloomington: Indiana University Press, 1–16.

Gerbner, Katharine (2018). *Christian slavery: conversion and race in the Protestant Atlantic World.* Philadelphia: University of Pennsylvania Press.

Gerloff, Roswith (2006). "The African diaspora in the Caribbean and Europe from pre-emancipation to the present day." Hugh McLeod, ed., *The Cambridge History of Christianity*, vol. 9. Cambridge: Cambridge University Press, 219–35.

Haar, Christoph and Matthias Kaufmann (forthcoming 2024). *"Gerechter Krieg" und "Niemandsland". Rechtfertigungsideologien für Kolonisierung und Versklavung durch europäische Mächte c. 1500–1800.* Freiburg: WBG.

Hanß, Stefan and Juliane Schiel, eds. (2014). *Mediterranean Slavery Revisited (500–1800) / Neue Perspektiven auf mediterrane Sklaverei.* Zürich: Chronos.

Johnson, Walter (2003). "On Agency." *Journal of Social History*, 113–24.

Kidd, Colin (2006). *The Forging of Races. Race and Scripture in the Protestant Atlantic World, 1600–2000.* Cambridge: Cambridge University Press.

v. Mallinckrodt, Rebekka (2017). "Verhandelte (Un-)Freiheit. Sklaverei, Leibeigenschaft und innereuropäischer Wissenstransfer am Ausgang des 18. Jahrhunderts." *Zeitschrift für Historische Sozialwissenschaft* 43, 347–80.

v. Mallinckrodt, Rebekka (2016). "There are no slaves in Prussia?" Brahm, Felix and Eve Rosenhaft, eds., *Slavery Hinterland: Transatlantic Slavery and Continental Europe, 1680–1850.* Woodbridge: Boydell, 109–31.

Mann, Michael (2012). *Sahibs, Sklaven und Soldaten: Geschichte des Menschenhandels rund um den Indischen Ozean.* Darmstadt: WBG.

Miers, Suzanne (2004). "Slavery: A question of definition." Gwyn Campbell, ed., *The structure of slavery*, London: Frank Cass, 1–15.

Pagden, Anthony (1995). *Lords of All the World. Ideologies of Empire in Spain, Britain and France c. 1500–1800.* New Haven: Yale University Press.

Pagden, Anthony (2015). *The Burdens of Empire, 1539 to the Present.* Cambridge: Cambridge University Press.

Pateman, Carole (2007). "The Settler Contract." Pateman, Carole and Charles Mills, *Contract and Domination.* Cambridge: Cambridge University Press, 35–78.

Priesching, Nicole (2017). *Die Sklaverei im Urteil der Jesuiten.* Hildesheim: Georg Olms.

Reinhard, Wolfgang (2018). *Die Unterwerfung der Welt. Globalgeschichte der europischen Expansion 1415–2015.* München: C.H. Beck.

Springborg, Patricia (2015). "Hobbes, Donne and the Virginia Company: *Terra Nullius* and 'The Bulimia of Dominium'." *History of Political Thought* 36, 113–64.

Winnebeck, Julia, Ove Sutter, Adrian Hermann, Christoph Antweiler and Stephan Conermann (2023). "The Analytical Concept of Asymmetrical Dependency." *Journal of Global Slavery*, 1–59.

Zeuske, Michael (2013). *Handbuch Geschichte der Sklaverei: Eine Globalgeschichte von den Anfängen bis zur Gegenwart.* Berlin: De Gruyter.

Slavery in Captivity: Location, Colonial Slavery and Early Modern Japan

Rômulo Ehalt

There are many studies dedicated to analyzing early modern colonial slavery through the prism of law and religion, particularly Christianity. Often, historical narratives of slavery are built around specific legislation, ranging from restrictions and prohibitions concerning the master-slave relationship to thunderous abolition. Examples abound: the Hammurabi Code, Biblical law, the *Tipitaka*, the *Ritsuryō*, Roman law, canon law, and the *Code Noir*.[1] Slavery laws could be sparse and heterogeneous, such as in the case of Portuguese legislation concerning the enslavement of Black African and Indigenous peoples in Brazil, as well as the legal instruments that defined nineteenth-century abolitionism.[2] The chronological limits of slavery, along with the rights and obligations associated with the *asservicement* of others, are typically perceived through the lens of the timeline of legal restrictions. In recent decades, as studies on slavery in Asia have evolved, lesser-known cases, like slavery in Portuguese India, have similarly been explored, drawing their foundational explanatory models from local and colonial legislation and practices. The enduring concept driving this approach is the belief that law ostensibly establishes the social order that those under its legal authority should follow.[3] In areas where slavery is a less obvious subject of study, such as in Japan, legislation is often cited to construct narratives depicting changes in the social order.[4] Ultimately, slavery, with all its infamy and the consequential scars and unresolved issues it undeniable left for contemporary societies, is commonly perceived through the lens of the binary concept of legality versus illegality.

---

* I want to express my deepest gratitude to Christoph Haar (University of Würzburg) and Wim Decock (UCLouvain), as well as to the participants of the workshop "Slavery, Law and Religion in the Early Modern Period", held in 8–9 March 2023 at the UCLouvain for their comments and the fruitful discussion. Special thanks to Filippo Contarini (University of Paris-Panthéon-Assas) and Jacob Schmutz (UCLouvain).

1 Davis, *The Problem of Slavery in Western Culture*, 60–61.

2 Perrone-Moisés, "Inventário da legislação indigenista: 1500–1800"; Lara, *Legislação sobre escravos africanuos na América portuguesa.*

3 Pinto, *Slavery in Portuguese India (1510–1842)*; D'Souza, "Slavery in Goa: Legal and Historical Perspectives".

4 Maki, *Nihon hōseishi ni okeru jinshin baibai no kenkyū*, 26–81.

 | DOI:10.30965/9783657796328_003

Religion also undeniably influences our perception of slavery. The apparently and seemingly incomprehensible hypocrisy associated with Christianity in its relation with slavery, allowing the perpetuation of this institution for centuries despite the moral principles upon which the religion is founded, leaves the modern observer astonished. The perceived indifference of the church in the face of the horrors of the Middle Passage is viewed either as a form of complicit behaviour or as evidence of the Curia's detachment.[5] Beyond moral judgement, religion arguably served as the stage upon which the ideology of colonial slavery was crafted. Amidst the legal underpinnings of the conquest of the American continent by Spain and Portugal, the writings of Francisco de Victoria, Bartolomé de las Casas, Tomás de Mercado, Luis de Molina and other theologians, canonists, and casuists of early modern Iberia constituted the primary arguments that legitimized slavery in the early modern colonial world.[6] Yet, the intense debates surrounding the enslavement of non-Europeans during this period also highlight the highly particular maner in which legal doctrine—Roman law and canon law within the context of Christianity—was employed in the normativization of labour arrangements. After all, slavery constitutes a form of labour relationship.

The recent increase in projects dedicated to studying the phenomenon of slavery in Asia, particularly under the umbrella of the European colonial empires, has, for the most part, followed the same path laid out by the field of the history of slavery in the US and Brazil. As a result, many histories of slavery are once again defined by colonial regulations, forms of enslavement and, ultimately, abolition.[7] The same holds true for the case of Japan. Despite being a lesser-known topic among most historians of slavery, the study of the enslavement of Japanese by Europeans in the early modern period represents an interesting case for analyzing the process that shaped the idea of slavery during the age of colonialism. Broadly speaking, the history of slavery in Japan revolves around at least three pivotal legal decisions: the 1570–1571 Portuguese royal charter on Japanese slavery, Toyotomi Hideyoshi's eleven-article

5 For a recent treatment of the issue, see Onyemechi Adiele, *The Popes, the Catholic Church and the Transatlantic Enslavement of Black Africans, 1418–1839*.

6 Hanke, *Aristotle and the American Indians*; Davis, *The Problem of Slavery in Western Culture*, 165–96; Pagden, *The fall of natural man*.

7 Klein, *Breaking the Chains*; Campbell, *The Structure of Slavery in Indian Ocean Africa and Asia*; Chatterjee and Eaton, *Slavery & South Asian History*; Alpers et al., *Resisting Bondage in Indian Ocean Africa and Asia*; Campbell, *Abolition and its Aftermath in Indian Ocean Africa and Asia*; Stanziani, *Labour, Coercion, and Economic Growth in Eurasia, 17th-20th Centuries*; Stanziani, *Bondage*; Campbell, *Bondage and the Environment in the Indian Ocean World*; Schrikker et al., *Being a Slave*; Allen, *Slavery and Bonded Labour in Asia, 1250–1900*; Ismard, *Les Mondes de l'Esclavage*; Ekama et al., *Slavery and Bondage in Asia*.

memorandum of 1587, and the 1598 excommunication imposed by the Bishop of Japan against slave traders.[8] Despite the various possible criticisms that can be raised regarding the role and relative authority (*relativer Autoritätsbegriff*)[9] of each of these norms, the reality remains that this multi-layered legislative process was backed by numerous debates concerning slavery in Japan, particularly within the Society of Jesus.

Between the second half of the sixteenth and the first half of the seventeenth centuries, the Japanese archipelago was the stage of Catholic missions conducted by Franciscans, Dominicans, Augustinians and notably, Jesuits. During this period, missionaries encountered a diverse array of dependency and bondage relationships, interpreting them through the prism of slavery. Deriving guidelines from the principles of *ius commune*, they aimed to evaluate the moral and theological quandaries faced by Christians who asserted ownership over others. In essence, they perceived these relationships as both legal and theological concerns, approaching them within the scope of the available legal framework. Consequently, numerous debates took place in Nagasaki, Goa, and Rome concerning the most suitable approach for missionaries to navigate this intricate issue.[10]

This chapter delves into the subject of slavery in Japan, aiming to present an alternative perspective on slavery through the lenses of law and religion. Firstly, I briefly examine the experiences of three Japanese men and their encounters with slavery, emphasizing the dissonant understandings concerning the legal status assigned to these individuals. Next, I critique the universality associated with slavery as both a historiographical concept and analytical tool. This involves a brief discussion of some of the rhetorical strategies used to produce commensurability in the early modern period and the analysis of slavery against this process. Finally, I pivot back to Asia and comment on an understudied debate held in Portuguese Goa in the 1590s where the legal institution (*Rechtsfigur*) of slavery featured as a benchmark to measure and assess labour arrangements in Japan, before concluding with my final remarks. The chapter hopes to demonstrate that the case of slavery in Japan offers a valuable starting point for thinking about slavery not merely as a universal practice but as an idea historically built through its interactions with other designations used by historical actors in shaping labour arrangements.

---

8 Okamoto, "Jūroku seiki ni okeru nihonjin dorei mondai (jō)"; Okamoto, "Jūroku seiki ni okeru nihonjin dorei mondai (ge)", Okamoto, *Jūroku seiki nichiō kōtsūshi no kenkyū*; Nelson, "Slavery in Medieval Japan".

9 Duve, "Mit der Autorität gegen die Autoritäten?".

10 Ehalt, "Goa no iezusukai shingakusha to nihon no doreika mondai".

Violence, Identity, and Memory

In 1613, Hasekura Rokuemon or Hasekura Tsunenaga (1571–1622) set sail from Japan. He had been chosen as the ambassador of Date Masamune (1567–1636), a powerful warlord of Northeastern Japan, for a mission planned by Luis Sotelo (1574–1624), a Franciscan friar. Sotelo's plan was to establish relations between the Date clan with the Spanish crown and the Papacy.[11]

After passing through Mexico, the embassy arrived in Spain in 1614. One of the members of the group was Imaizumi Sakan (dates of birth and death unclear), the captain of the ambassador's guard. In Madrid, Sotelo managed to secure an audience for Hasekura Tsunenaga with the Spanish king, Felipe III. During the meeting, all high-ranking members of the embassy were baptized, including four who decided to stay and enter a Franciscan monastery. Among them was Imaizumi Sakan, now baptized as Tomás Felipe after his godfather, the king. After leaving the embassy and entering monastic life, Felipe disappeared from historical records until 1622 when we find him in Zafra, a city near Seville. There, Tomás Felipe worked for Diego Jaramillo, a local tradesman. One day, a scuffle broke out between the two: the Japanese wanted to be paid for his services, but Diego Jaramillo interpreted their relationship differently. In response to the demands, the merchant branded the Japanese man's face with a hot iron rod. This, in practice, marked Tomás Felipe as a slave, making him recognized as such for the rest of his life. The aggrieved Japanese complained to the local *alcaide* and eventually obtained authorization to leave his employer and the country. Shortly thereafter, Felipe boarded a ship bound to Honduras. Although Spanish sources do not reveal his fate, family records of the Imaizumi clan indicate that Tomás Felipe died in Central America in an uncertain date while attempting to return to Japan.[12]

If Tomás Felipe's enslavement was epitomized by the extremely violent act of branding, Gaspar Fernandes (c. 1574–1642) experience had more to do with his identity. In the late 1580s, the Portuguese merchant Rui Perez hired a boy in Nagasaki to serve him for about a decade. As it was customary at the time, a Jesuit priest recorded a license determining the number of years the boy should serve his buyer after examining the conditions of the kidnapping that led to the sale.[13] Although his Japanese name has not survived the test

11 Ōizumi, *Keichō ken'ō shisetsu no kenkyū*; Ōizumi, *Hasekura Rokuemon Tsunenaga*; Gonoi, *Hasekura Tsunenaga*; Tremml-Werner, *Spain, China, and Japan in Manila, 1571–1644*.

12 For the sources and more information on the cases of Imaizumi Sakan and the other two Japanese men, Ehalt, "Where All Yndios Are Free".

13 Often, children were kidnapped and sold to foreigners in Nagasaki, although there were many poverty-stricken parents who deliberately chose to sell their own children. Hasegawa,

of time, his Christian name has: Gaspar Fernandes. The Japanese grew up in the Perez household, where he closely observed the merchant and his secret Jewish rituals. In the mid-1590s, the Mexican Inquisition caught wind of Rui Perez's religious practices and decided to arrest and bring him to New Spain. The merchant was placed on a ship in Manila bound for Acapulco with all his assets, including several of his employees. However, Rui Perez did not survive the journey, and upon reaching Acapulco, his possessions were confiscated by the Holy Office. Gaspar Fernandes was then assigned to serve a local Spaniard in Mexico City. In 1599, the late merchant's sons decided to sue the Inquisition to reclaim their father's wealth. The young Japanese man was taken to court, where he declared to the judge that he was not a slave and could not be one since, as he said, there was no slavery in Japan. In the end, a rhetorical strategy by Fernandes' defence, who decided in the middle of the lawsuit to ascribe to him the identity of *indio*, allowed the use of the restrictive norms present in the 1542 *Leyes Nuevas*, which forbade the enslavement of *indios*. The plan worked, and the Japanese regained his freedom.

Fernandes's legal use of the *indio* identity associated with his claims of mistreatment by his allocated master was not uncommon among enslaved individuals of Asian descent in New Spain.[14] Yet, a third strategy was available for those at the end of their lives: remembrance. In 1582, Inácio de Lima, the illegitimate son of a noble family from Southern Portugal, was the captain of the trading ship that linked Japan to Macau. In Nagasaki, he purchased a Japanese boy. Again, we don't know his original name, only his baptismal name, Damião de Lima. After taking the child to Europe, the captain financed religious works and purchased several properties in Ajuda, then a town to the west of Lisbon. In 1587, Inácio de Lima made a pilgrimage to Jerusalem, and if we are to believe that the young Damião de Lima went along, he could have been the first Japanese to visit the Holy Land. Eventually, in 1607, the captain passed away, leaving a generous stipend to be paid annually by a local lay brotherhood to Damião de Lima. After a few years, the Japanese decided to return to his native country. He left Lisbon in 1619, passed through India, and upon arriving in Macau, found out that the prohibitions put in place by the Tokugawa Bakufu in 1619 stopped him from going back to Japan. Due to fears of spies and the persecution against Christianity, the Bakufu had imposed

---

"Chūkinsei ikōki no hitouri kankō ni miru dogō no yūzū"; McManus, "'Servitutem Levem et Modici Temporis Esse Arbitrantes'"; Sekiguchi, "Edo bakufu no jinshin baibai kinrei wo megutte".

14 Owensby, *Empire of Law and Indian Justice in Colonial Mexico*, 141–7; Seijas, *Asian Slaves in Colonial Mexico*, 221–7; Van Deusen, *Global Indios*, 89.

capital punishment on all Japanese coming from abroad. Damião de Lima then settled in the Sino-Portuguese enclave, where he lived until 1642. On his deathbed, he reminisced about his origins and the years he spent in Europe. Despite his relationship with the Portuguese captain being quite possibly an instance of enslavement, Damião de Lima chose to describe his affiliation with the late Inácio de Lima in more general terms. In his last will, he described the time spent under the captain's authority as a period of service (*o servi até Deos o leuar*), a description purposefully lacking more compromising legal and theological terms. To further his narrative, Damião de Lima bequeathed large sums to pay the costs of masses, donations, and a procession in Macau after his death, all to consolidate the memory of his life as a Christian benefactor of the city and the local religious orders. The donation of a small image of the Virgin that he brought with him from Portugal to the Jesuit church of São Paulo would be a constant reminder of his life, now rebranded as the past of a page to a member of Portuguese nobility rather than that of a formerly enslaved individual.

These three Japanese individuals had their lives affected by slavery with varying degrees of violence. In the first case, certainly the most violent one, Tomás Felipe had to spend the rest of his days being identified as a slave. Given the practices at the time not only in Zafra but in general, his branding could have been an S with a nail through it, known as "S Clavo" in Spanish, which quite literally meant "slave."[15] In turn, Gaspar Fernandes had to fight in court against the label of slavery while being subjected to actual colonial enslavement in Mexico under the guise of tutelage during the time it took the Inquisitors to decide his fate. Finally, Damião de Lima went through decades of enslavement in Europe and was only able to erase his relationship with slavery through a final act of self-fashioning.

In all three cases, there was a clear line separating slavery from other forms of labour arrangement. In these instances, slavery represented a specific condition against which all of them fought to avoid being associated. Yet, despite their resistance, slavery was the main factor informing social perceptions, expectations, biographies, legal rights, and life possibilities for each one of them. At the local *alcaide*, in the court room, or on their last will—the immense pressure of slavery could be felt even in its silence. But what was slavery for them? Was it the defining characteristic of a certain social group, or the condition of a number of individuals in colonial societies? Despite the many differences in their personal experiences and historical contexts, the legal aspects of slavery were present as a common thread unifying their histories.

---

15 Fracchia, *'Black but Human'*, 39.

A Legal Institution

For jurists, lawyers, theologians, canonists, and confessors, there was no doubt: slavery was a legal category referred to when dealing with difficult situations regarding bondage and labour exploitation. As pointed by the Portuguese historian Antonio Manuel Hespanha, slavery was a legal institution, a *Rechtsfigur*, inherited from and regulated by Roman law. In practice, that meant that all legal principles drawn from legislation and jurisprudence for the legal assessment of labour relations, dependencies and bondage, in the early modern period were taken from the Roman *servitus*. The *servitus* was the only legal matrix available in the areas under the *ius commune* to assess labour relations defined by actual or threatened violence. Not only that, the whole set of legal concepts and images used to justify and ideologically support slavery had a decidedly European origin.[16] It was from this legal institution of slavery that the model of colonial slavery was formed, what Edward Alpers called "the Christian European variety of plantation slavery."[17]

Assuming slavery was a legal institution has direct consequences for the so-called "definitional question." In 1977, Igor Kopytoff and Suzanne Miers drew attention to the difficulty of finding a working definition of slavery for Africa. The problem was that multiple local variations often challenged the most basic assumptions concerning the concept, making slavery inadequate to work in various African contexts.[18] Decades later, Miers once again brought up the problem, now for the Asian context. Since then, numerous scholars working with slavery in Asia have resorted to several different solutions to the issue: some aesthetic, such as the use of inverted commas, quotation marks, and italics; some more conceptual, like the adoption of bondage and other general labels to avoid the political meanings of using the word "slavery." A few have elected to centre their analyses on local terms, although even in such cases one can see the influence of slavery as a conceptual yardstick. Often, scholars choose to redefine slavery based on a shopping list of criteria that a topic needs to fill to be identified more or less with slavery.[19] In that sense, the term remains the universal category to which one refers when examining historical arrangements of labour.

16 Hespanha, "Depois do Leviathan", 65; Hespanha, *Imbecilitas*, 199–231; Hespanha, *Como os Juristas Viam o Mundo*, 209–20; Cuena Boy, "El infierno y las buenas intenciones", 169.

17 Alpers, "Flight to Freedom", 52.

18 Kopytoff and Miers, "African 'Slavery' as an Institution of Marginality", 76–8.

19 Miers, "Slavery: A Question of Definition".

More recently, the Bonn Center for Dependency and Slavery Studies developed an impressive theoretical framework based on the notion of asymmetrical dependencies. Defined as social and economic relationships in which one party has more power, influence, and control over the other, these relationships are characterized by an unequal distribution of resources and opportunities, often resulting in the exploitation of the weaker party. This notion de-centres slavery from its defining role and fosters a more focused analysis on the asymmetries intrinsic to the power struggles present in dependency relations, including slavery.[20] Yet, despite the BCDSS's success in broadening our understanding of labour exploitation beyond slavery and into less explored notions of dependency, forced labour, debt bondage, and indentured servitude, slavery remains a powerful and impactful historiographical and analytical concept.

One issue that should not be overlooked in the study of slavery is its impact on contemporary political discourse, especially in countries whose histories are deeply marked by their slaving past, such as the US, Brazil, and Cuba. Slavery is often attributed to a common human past, a shared heritage that immediately dissolves any responsibility certain groups may have regarding the past enslavement of others. Reparations, Black Lives Matter, racism, affirmative action, all these topics are influenced, to varying degrees, by the recognition or denial of the universality of slavery. This begs the question: is slavery universal? As Alessandro Stanziani put it, if our answer is positive, "then by implication slavery existed before and independently of colonialism." But if the answer is negative, "it means that these forms of dependence and bondage were specific to a particular place and 'imperialist' and revisionist culture would like to call them 'slavery' to minimize the West's 'debt' to the Third World."[21] What one can gather from Stanziani's question is that the problem here is no longer how to define slavery. The study of slavery in Africa and Asia has taught us over the past four decades that there is no safe, fail-proof definition that can be used for all situations while still maintaining the universality of this idea. The conclusion is that the problem here is not just a matter of definition. The problem is of location: what is the place of slavery in the general narrative of human history?

If slavery is a legal institution inherited from Roman Law, it is thus a fundamentally European legal concept. Consequently, its history is intrinsically

20 Winnebeck, "The Analytical Concept of Asymmetrical Dependency".

21 Stanziani, *Labour, Coercion, and Economic Growth in Eurasia*, 2; also, Sajò, *Human Rights with Modesty*.

bound to the history of the development of law in the West.[22] This idea offers, in fact, a powerful solution to the problem of the location of slavery in history. Accepting that slavery is a notion inherited from Roman law prompts a reading of the history of slavery in the early modern world as more than the history of exploitation and suffering under colonialism and imperialism. It becomes the history of how a legal institution was taken overseas by colonial empires and used as the basis upon which norms regulating local relations of labour, coercion, dependency, and bondage were discussed and built. From a legal historical standpoint, it is the history of a legal transfer. From the point of view of intellectual history, it is a history of cultural translation.

Thus, slavery is not universal. It is a historically localized idea with a particular history. This is not a relativized way of looking into the topic; it is an attempt to provincialize slavery. From this perspective, the universalization of this idea came to fruition during the expansion of European colonialism and imperialism and, due to the set of normativities inherited from Roman law that governed this type of human relation, slavery became the main legal institution upon which one could rely when seeking widely accepted arguments for debating novel and unknown labour and dependency relations overseas. Hence, the study of slavery as a legal concept offers a unique opportunity to appreciate processes of cultural translation, legal adaptation, normative enforcement, and knowledge creation. If the history of slavery has often focused on numbers, systems, forms, and resistance, the history of the idea of slavery highlights the intellectual underpinnings of early modern colonialism.

To question the universality of slavery, one can focus on the elements often used to characterize it, the most obvious being violence and the systematic nature of the exploration of the individual through slavery. Discussing different forms of coerced labour arrangements, global labour historian Marcel van der Linden proposed a taxonomy based on what he called the "three moments:" "the entry into the labour relationship, the period during which the worker works, and the end of the labour relationship." His taxonomy analysed various forms of historical arrangements, from chattel slavery to waged labour and everything in between.[23] Yet, despite being presented as a categorization of coerced labour, the Dutch scholar unknowingly introduced a taxonomy of labour where actual or threatened violence was included as one of the elements that defined the relationship. From this angle, slavery becomes a form of labour where social and legally condoned extreme violence determines

22 The particularity of slavery as a Western legal idea is clear in legal history research. See, for instance, Cuena Boy, "El infierno y las buenas intenciones", 164.

23 Van der Linden, "Dissecting Coerced Labor".

all three moments of the relationship (Ehalt forthcoming a). Meanwhile, the disappearance of slavery as a widely accepted labour arrangement can be attributed to nineteenth-century abolitionism not as the result of anti-slavery campaigning, but rather as the result of a concerted effort in removing from labour relationships the element of violence as their defining element in the process of monopolization of violence by the nation-state. From the legal historical point of view, abolitionism took violence out of the equation.

From the standpoint of the history of slavery, the critical junctures discussed by Van der Linden often come up in scholarship translated as forms of enslavement, living conditions of enslaved individuals, and forms of manumission. There is no doubt that these three moments are, since the times of Nieboer, essential to characterize slavery from a systematic point of view.[24] Both elements—the equation "labour + violence = slavery," and the systematic nature attributed to slavery—are what allow this concept to be stripped of any historical context and easily plastered onto different historical contexts as a universal category.

However, the presence of violence in the labour relationship, or the systematic aspects attributed to said relationship, do not suffice to characterize slavery once early modern legal debates concerning the issue are considered. In fact, the "three moments" of Van der Linden's categorization can provide a gateway to a better appreciation of the historicity of slavery, especially when one pays attention to the fact that early modern observers were also attuned to the relevance of at least the first of these moments.

Working in religious schools in Goa, Malacca, Macau, and Manila, casuists analysed dubious moral and legal issues faced by clergymen in colonial settings and missionary frontiers. Their awareness of the multitude of meanings that slavery as a legal institution could assume in the Asian context is outstanding, as evidenced by a long treatise on slavery written by a Jesuit casuist of Goa in the early seventeenth century.[25] In the end, the circumstances of one's enslavement—war, kidnappings, deceit and so on—were decisive when determining the possible legal status that could be attributed to individuals in various forms of dependency and bondage relationships.

Yet, unlike Van der Linden's categories, slavery occupied a very specific place in the early modern taxonomies of labour due to the moral and legal

24 Nieboer, *Slavery as an Industrial System*.

25 Vaz, Gomes, *Disputationum moralium Indicarum*, Biblioteca Nazionale Centrale "Vittorio Emanuele II" (Rome), *Gesuitico* 1441; Vaz, Gomes, *De mancipiis indicis, manumissionibus, et liberta libri quator*, Biblioteca Nacional de Portugal (Lisbon), Cod. 2577. These manuscripts will be further analyzed in a larger project of mine. One of the few studies to use this treatise is McManus, "'Servitutem Levem et Modici Temporis Esse Arbitrantes'".

consequences its use entailed to the individual. Violence was not enough to characterize slavery. Nor was the systematic nature of the relationship exclusive to slavery. Considering the particular place occupied by the *servitus* in the universe of the *ius commune*, how an individual was seen by colonial agents depended not only on violence and systematic abuse but also on a whole range of factors such as local conditions, social expectations, mores, political agendas, and religious backgrounds. Slavery was then but one of the many legal institutions involved in determining the legal capacity of the individual.[26] In the judicial records of the case of Gaspar Fernandes, the Japanese who sued the Inquisition in New Spain, witnesses stated in court that the Japanese had been subjected to a contract of temporary servitude, not slavery.[27] The defence needed to show that, despite the initial understanding of Fernandes's condition as that of an enslaved individual, due to the local pre-disposition to categorize an individual in his situation as a slave, the focus on the contract as a determinant of his status led to his recategorization as an *indio*. The elements that conditioned the moment of entry into the relationship were fundamental to determine the fate of the case, and that was only possible because of the assertion that in Japan there was no *servidumbre*, leading to the conclusion that the category of *servitus* could not be employed.

Indeed, the identification of one's legal status with slavery was a deciding point at certain life-changing moments. Those included the death of the master, matrimony, childbirth, or the transfer of the ownership of an individual to another party. But even in those instances, slavery as a legal institute could be present in a less obvious way: it could influence how relationships were set and how they functioned, without necessarily defining the legal situation of the involved. It does not mean, however, that people were not subjected to slavery. In other words, slavery was, at once, a legal status that could characterize the whole legal existence of the individual, and a legal institution from where normativities were drawn to deal with people that legally existed under different status. The issue is what subjection to slavery meant from a legal and historical standpoint. Cases such as those of the enslavement of Japanese individuals indicate that to be subjected to slavery was a much more complex phenomenon than that of the definition of one's social group.

One example of this complexity can be seen in the testaments of Portuguese merchants in Macau. In 1750, the Misericórdia of Macau, a lay brotherhood

26 As, for instance, in the construction of the juridical *persona* of the *indio* in the Spanish empire (Duve "La condición jurídica del indio"; Garriga, "¿Cómo escribir una historia "descolonizada" del derecho en América Latina?", 348–58.

27 Archivo General de la Nación (México), *Real fisco de la Inquisición*, v. 8, exp. 9, fls. 262–271.

responsible for overseeing the civil, religious, and financial matters of its members, compiled a list of old testamentary passages left by merchants living in the city and their families.[28] The list went back to the 1590s and included numerous instructions on what should be done with young girls and boys born in the merchants' households, men and women serving the deceased, and so on. This is, in fact, a fragmented set of documents that reproduces numerous other non-extant testaments and last wills. The list uses several monikers to refer to these individuals, avoiding the Portuguese word for slave, *escravo*, altogether. The preferred terms were *menino* (boy), *menina* (girl), *moço* (young man), *moça* (young woman), and other similar words that spoke more of the general age group to which the individuals belonged than of their legal status. For the most part, scholarship has interpreted this tendency to avoid the word "slave" in two ways: as an analogy between slavery and childhood, treating enslaved individuals as children due to their deficient legal persona,[29] or as a subterfuge to avoid legal complications that could be caused by royal and ecclesiastical prohibitions against the enslavement of people from certain areas of the continent.[30] However, from a historical standpoint, the use of buffer terms here has nothing to do with possible legal infractions or infantilization. These were, in fact, an effective way to address the perennial tension between the ideal form of the slave, as found in the letter of the law, and the very complicated, messy practices found in everyday life in the various colonial societies under the banners of the Iberian empires. Among these labels, though, there is one that surpasses all others in relevance and frequency: the captive.

Given the Mediterranean past of Iberian slavery, captivity has been often understood as synonymous with slavery. This understanding is still repeated by scholars of colonialism, despite the long debates among historians of Mediterranean slavery about the conceptual limits of the two terms.[31] But, from a legal point of view, there is a fundamental difference between them: while slavery (*servitus*) was a legal institution regulated by Roman law, which carried numerous obligations and duties to the parties involved, captives were a juridically less developed *personae* that referred to a temporary condition of unfreedom that was only possible whenever there was religious difference between the prisoners and their captors.[32]

---

28 For more on this lay brotherhood, see Sá 1997, Sá 2018, and Seabra 2011. The testaments hereby referred are at Macau Historical Archives, *Santa Casa de Misericórdia*, 302.

29 Alberts, *Conflict and Conversion*, 195.

30 Sousa, *The Portuguese Slave Trade in Early Modern Japan*, 5–8.

31 Hanß and Schiel, "Semantics, Practices and Transcultural Perspective on Mediterranean Slavery", 11–23.

32 Calderón Ortega and Díaz González, *Vae Victis*, 21; Cursi, "*Captivitas e capitis deminutio*".

The difference between the slave and the captive was clearly understood and employed by early modern theologians and jurists. In fact, given the temporary situation of captives and the lack of legal tools related to this feeble legal persona, slavery was the main resource employed in determining the uncertainties related to the various forms of dependency and coercion found in the early modern world. After all, captivity was one of the many paths that could lead to enslavement or conditions of bondage or dependency that were regulated by norms derived from the Roman *servitus* depending on the way one was subjected to the relationship. Other ways of enslavement included birth from an enslaved mother (which together with captivity were the only two forms of enslavement with roots in the all-encompassing *ius gentium*) as well as other forms derived from *ius civile*, as how jurists referred to locally specific forms of law.[33] Because of the ambiguous categorization of the *servitus* as a legal institution of both *ius gentium* and *ius civile*, the circumstances of enslavement[34] were dependent on acceptance by royal and ecclesiastical authorities. Particularly significant for these situations was the canonical instrument of tolerance. According to canon law, a priest, confessor, bishop, or any other ecclesiastical representative could overlook a sinful action or a situation that could invite others to sin (what canon lawyers refer to as *scandal*) by tolerating it. Of course, to be able to tolerate legally or for this tolerance to be accepted by higher authorities of the church or the crown, several legal criteria needed to be followed.[35]

Slavery is in the Details

The inherent uncertainty of the slave status in law was taken as evidence of the malleability of the idea in pragmatic contexts. That is the case of slavery in Japan. Due to the subjection of the Bishopric of Japan to the Archbishopric of Goa in the general scheme of the Portuguese empire, legal instruments and opinions generated in India could be employed to assess the situation in the archipelago. The main legal framework for this process was established through the Constitutions of the Archbishopric of Goa, approved in 1568. Despite the questionability of the validity of the constitutions for Christianity in the Japanese archipelago, the text had set standards for the recognition of the

33 Cuena Boy, "El infierno …", 168.

34 Hespanha, *Como os Juristas …*, 209–15.

35 Fedele, "Consideraciones sobre la dispensa y sobre otras instituciones en la ordenación canónica"; Olivero, *Dissimulatio e tolerantia nell'ordinamento canonico.*

enslavement of an individual in the Asian context. The five legal titles delimited by the text served as the basis for discussions concerning regions beyond Portuguese jurisdictions in South Asia. Beyond the traditional *partus sequitur ventrem*, captivity because of just war, the sale of a child in case of extreme necessity, and voluntary slavery, all of which had various criteria defined by canon law, Roman law and theology, the constitutions accepted that people subjected to slavery as a punishment by local, non-Portuguese rulers could also be recognized as slaves. The main criterion for this case was that the laws used to punish the individual should be accepted by Portuguese authorities as just. As a result, labour relations as found in the various Asian contexts could be legally accepted by the Portuguese.[36]

In Japan, the increasingly complex scenario of the 1590s led Jesuits to resort to counsel from outside the archipelago. In 1592, the Japanese leader Toyotomi Hideyoshi invaded the Korean Peninsula. That same year, a group of Spanish Franciscans coming from Manila established a new mission in Japan. These events had a deep effect on the activities of the Society of Jesus in the country. Numerous Japanese Christians were involved in the war waged by Hideyoshi in Korea, a conflict that was seen by Jesuits as deeply dubious in its motivations. The participation of Christians meant they were subjected to morally ambiguous leadership and in dubious acts, such as the capture and trade of tens of thousands of Koreans to Japan. Due to their limited authority in the country, missionaries saw themselves unable to address and properly admonish Japanese Christians.[37] Moreover, the arrival of the mendicants from the Philippines represented a threat to the Jesuit strategy put in place in the country up to that point. Given the geographical position of the islands and the sole presence of the Society of Jesus in Japan, local Christians were in a state of ignorance that exempted them from responsibility due to various morally dubious actions that could result in sin. Jesuit missionaries used this state of ignorance to control the publication of positive precepts of the Church in Japan for decades, thus keeping a delicate balance between ignorance and indoctrination that was eventually threatened by the arrival of the friars.[38] Now, if Japanese Christians needed guidance regarding the ownership of prisoners of war, they could seek alternative views from the Franciscans when Jesuits could not offer them satisfying answers. Jesuits in Japan were then forced to seek higher authority to maintain their primacy in the archipelago.

36 Ehalt, "O Primeiro Concílio de Goa e a releitura da escravidão na Ásia (1567)".
37 Ehalt, "Jesuits and the Problem of Slavery in Early Modern Japan".
38 Ehalt, "Ignorance Lost".

In 1592, a list of 45 questions was sent to Rome by the Japan Jesuit mission. Slavery was among one of the issues included in the questionnaire. The topic became part of the growing conflict between mendicants and the Society of Jesus in Rome, where the fate of the Jesuit monopoly over Japanese Christianity was to be decided.[39] However, definitive answers from Rome could take years to arrive, and the escalating conflict in Korea demanded immediate action. The solution was to ask the casuists of the College of São Paulo, in Goa, to offer temporary guidance concerning the pressing issues of Japan. The undated minutes of the meeting held in India in the mid-1590s to discuss the questionnaire show the difficulties regarding matrimonies, usury, idolatry, and slavery as faced by Japanese Christianity.[40]

The issue of slavery appears under the title *cativeiros* or *captivities*.[41] It is a list of ten different legal titles (*títulos*) of captivity that, according to the document, were gathered following the view the Japanese held of captivity. In other words, local arrangements of labour that were considered in Japan to denote subalternity or inferiority and were informed by the use of violence formed the basis of the debate. That was motivated by the fact that Jesuits were discussing not only the European-Japanese slave trade and the many legal arguments used by Europeans to justify the ownership of human beings purchased in Japan, but also the many reasons that could back Japanese Christian claims of ownership over other individuals. It is clear in this example that there was some distance between captivity and slavery, and that captivity was a general, fuzzy category under which all sorts of labour arrangements marked by inferiority and violence could be gathered. Captivity was a general label used to address the constant tension between ideal models as found in law and the complex practices found in everyday life.

The ten titles discussed were:

- The sale of children by their parents;
- Self-alienation or self-sale;
- Bondage by birth;
- Rescue from death penalty;
- Bondage as legal punishment;
- The bondage of women who take refuge in the local warlord's manor;

39 Uyttenbroeck, *Early Franciscans in Japan*; Willeke, "Biographical data on early Franciscans in Japan (1582–1640)"; Sola, *Historia de un Desencuentro*; Tronu, "The Rivalry between the Society of Jesus and Mendicant Orders in Early Modern Nagasaki"; Bernabé, *Fé e prática entre os Kirishitan*.

40 University of Santo Tomás, Manila, Archivo de la Provincia del Santo Rosário, *Consultas* 2, *Japón* 2, *Miscelanea*, vol. 1, 342v–368.

41 Idem, 345–7v.

- People subjected to bondage in exchange for food and shelter during famines;
- Debt bondage or peonage;
- Bondage of women conscripted by the local warlord;
- and prisoners of war.

A wide variety of arguments was employed to address the cases. Some of the analysed titles were more easily interpreted than others, possibly due to the difference in the origin of the norms—some such as just war and birth had their roots in the *ius gentium*, while others derived their norms from the more specific *ius civile*, thus demanding a more complex level of discussion.[42] For instance, the idea that one could be born into captivity in Japan was promptly accepted by the Goa theologians insofar as it followed the Roman maxim *partus sequitur ventrem*, meaning the child's legal status was defined by the status of the mother. Other cases involving monetary exchange were resolved by the concept of a fair price, meaning that one could be subjected to slavery if a fair price was agreed upon between the parties involved. The decision on the fairness of the negotiation was left to confessors in Japan. In the end, out of the ten titles analysed, seven were considered tolerable forms of slavery: four cases of sales, two of legal punishment, and the passing of the bonded condition from the mother to the child. Moreover, individuals subjected to bondage in exchange for food and shelter, as well as those captured in war, were considered to be in a temporary state: they could be employed as slaves for a limited time, but were not considered to be enslaved.[43] The only case that could not be justified by any means was that of women conscripted by local warlords to serve in their manors.[44]

The meeting results reveal that the plan was not to condemn or suppress the enslavement of individuals by Japanese Christians, nor was it to equate Japanese captivity with slavery. It did not aim at revealing which conditions were analogous to slavery. Rather, they aimed to compile the legal criteria necessary to properly accept and regulate the situation of those who claimed ownership over other individuals in the archipelago. The criteria were gathered from the corpus of norms regulating slavery, but they did not create or reproduce slavery in Japan. The Goa Jesuit casuists found, in the elements

42 Cuena Boy, "El infierno …", 167–8.

43 It was common in early modern legal argumentation to employ legal categories that did not bear direct correspondence with reality when there were not better corresponding categories in the legal doctrine. Garriga, "¿Cómo escribir una historia "descolonizada" del derecho en América Latina?", 356–357.

44 (Ehalt, "Jesuit Arguments for Voluntary Slavery in Japan and in Brazil;" Ehalt, "Goa no iezusukai shingakusha to nihon no doreika mondai"; Ehalt, "Geninka and Slavery".

provided to them by their colleagues in Japan, elements in Japanese captivity that could be associated by analogy to the *Rechtsfigur* of slavery. In the end, the debate reveals that slavery was a legal institution used to regulate different forms of relations between Christians and non-Christians in areas where the assessment of dependencies and bondage was considered challenging, such as Japan.

The use of the legal institution of slavery was possible not because of some arguable stability found in the wide set of normativities, definitions, and debates found in past jurisprudence. Early modern law and theology in general did not employ slavery because it was coherent. Definitions of slavery, from Aristotle to Aquinas, were often contradictory, and there was not a single, clear, and unanimous definition neither in law nor theology.[45] But that was exactly the point. The legal institution of slavery was valuable—and useful—in assessing non-European dependencies precisely because it was ambiguous. Due to its inherent instability, it offered the possibility to be adjusted to the various situations that could be found under buffer and generalizing labels such as *cativeiro*.

Conclusion

The study of slavery from the perspective of religion or law is not limited to the analysis of legal and religious regulations of forms of enslavement, the lives of enslaved people and slave ownership, or manumission. The study of slavery through law and religion offers the opportunity to appreciate the historicity of slavery. The analysis goes beyond demographics, systematic exploitation, trading networks, and other classic topics of the history of slavery. Instead, studying slavery in its relationship with law and religion can help us grasp the role this legal institution had in the larger narrative of modernity.

In this sense, the problem of slavery as history is not a problem of definition, it is a problem of location. Slavery was one of the many elements involved in the complex mix of different historical arrangements of labour defined by the use of violence. By realizing the need to locate slavery historically, it becomes clear that there is still much more to be explored regarding the process of

45 García-Añoveros, *El pensamiento y los argumentos sobre la esclavitud en Europa en el siglo XVI y su aplicación a los indios americanos y a los negros africanos*; Cuena Boy, "El infierno …".

legal transference and cultural translation that involved this specific legal institution. The realization of slavery as an economic system in the eve of abolitionism in the eighteenth and nineteenth centuries, intrinsically associated with racism, the enslavement of Black Africans in the Americas, and the plantation system, was predated by almost three centuries of build-up, in which emerging colonial societies were enmeshed with local and foreign practices of bondage, coercion, violence, and dependency.

The case of Japanese slavery and how it was debated in the sixteenth century is just one example of how slavery offered the necessary rhetorical and normative tools for assessing non-European arrangements of labour. The debate held in Goa was not the Asian version of Valladolid, and the people involved there were not Sepúlveda or Las Casas. This was not a debate on whether people enslaved in Japan had souls or not. This was one of the many instances in which slavery was put to the test, read against what was happening on the ground. In the end, through the process of normativization and the numerous changes in legal discourses and methods of legal thinking, it is possible to see the role of slavery in informing various labour arrangements in the context of European colonialism. It eventually became a hegemonic practice in major colonial societies, coming to epitomize the sort of relationship where violence assumed a defining element. The realization that slavery is not universal, but rather a historically located legal institution used by historical actors to assess ill-defined relationships in various colonial contexts, should suffice to highlight the fact that, despite its universalizing aspirations, slavery only came to full fruition as an actual, concrete system in the context of the violent enslavement of Black Africans in the American continent. That, of course, does not mean European imperialism left no scar in Asian societies. It means, though, that the multitude of issues regarding the historical debt Western societies have towards modern underdeveloped countries cannot be bundled up in a way that is detrimental to the causes of the descendants of formerly enslaved people in the Americas.

Works Cited

Alberts, Tara (2013). *Conflict and Conversion: Catholicism in Southeast Asia, 1500–1700*. Oxford: Oxford University Press.

Allen, Richard B., ed. (2021). *Slavery and Bonded Labour in Asia, 1250–1900*. Leiden: Brill.

Alpers, Edward A. et al., eds. (2007). *Resisting Bondage in Indian Ocean Africa and Asia*. London et al.: Routledge.

Alpers, Edward M. (2004). "Flight to Freedom: Escape from Slavery among Bonded Africans in the Indian Ocean world, c.1750–1962." Gwyn Campbell, ed. *The structure of slavery in Indian Ocean Africa and Asia*. London: Routledge, 52–69.

Bernabé, Renata Cabral, *Fé e prática entre os Kirishitan: jesuítas, franciscanos e as reações japonesas ao cristianismo* (Ph.D. Thesis), São Paulo 2018.

Calderón Ortega, José Manuel and Francisco Javier Díaz González (col.) (2012). *Vae Victis: Cautivos y prisioneros en la Edad Media Hispánica*. Alcalá de Hanares: Universidad de Alcalá.

Campbell, Gwyn, ed. (2004). *The Structure of Slavery in Indian Ocean Africa and Asia*. London: Routledge.

Campbell, Gwyn, ed. (2013). *Abolition and its Aftermath in Indian Ocean Africa and Asia*. London et al.: Routledge.

Campbell, Gwyn, ed. (2018). *Bondage and the Environment in the Indian Ocean World*. Cham, Switzerland: Springer.

Chatterjee, Indrani and Richard M. Eaton, eds. (2006). *Slavery & South Asian History*. Bloomington, IN: Indiana University Press.

Cuena Boy, Francisco (2022). "El infierno y las buenas intenciones: Derecho de gentes y esclavitud (siglos XVI y XVII)." *Anuario de História del Derecho Español* XCII, 159–234.

Cursi, Maria Floriana (2001). "*Captivitas* e *capitis deminutio*. La posizione del *servus hostium* tra *ius civile* e *ius gentium*." *Iuris Vincula. Studi in Onore di Mario Talamanca, II*. Naples: Jovene Editore, 295–340.

D'Souza, Carmo (2007). "Slavery in Goa: Legal and Historical Perspectives." Maria Suzette Fernandes-Dias, ed. *Memories of Slavery: Comparative Perspectives*. Newcastle upon Tyne: Cambridge Scholarly Publishing, 62–75.

Davis, David Brion (1966). *The Problem of Slavery in Western Culture*. Oxford and New York: Oxford University Press.

Duve, Thomas (2003). "Mit der Autorität gegen die Autoritäten? Überlegungen zur heuristischen Kraft des Autoritätsbegriffs für die Neuere Privatrechtsgeschichte." Wulf Oesterreicher et al., eds. *Autorität der Form – Autorisierung – Institutionelle Autorität*. Münster: Lit Verlag, 239–256.

Duve, Thomas (2004). "La condición jurídica del indio y su consideración como *persona miserabilis* en el Derecho indiano." Mario G. Losano, ed. *Un Giudice e Due Leggi: Pluralismo Normativo e Conflitti Agrari in Sud America*. Milan: Giuffrè Editore, 3–33.

Ehalt, Rômulo da Silva (2017). "Jesuits and the Problem of Slavery in Early Modern Japan." Doctoral dissertation. Tokyo: Tokyo University of Foreign Studies.

Ehalt, Rômulo da Silva (2018). "O Primeiro Concílio de Goa e a releitura da escravidão na Ásia (1567)." *Lusitania Sacra* 38, 49–78.

Ehalt, Rômulo da Silva (2019a). "Jesuit Arguments for Voluntary Slavery in Japan and in Brazil." *Revista Brasileira de História* 39.80, 1–22.

Ehalt, Rômulo da Silva (2019b). "Goa no iezusukai shingakusha to nihon no doreika mondai." *Kirishitan Bunka Kenkyū Kaihō* 154, 1–14.

Ehalt, Rômulo da Silva (2023a). "Where All Yndios Are Free: Identity, resistance, and dissonant perceptions about the enslavement of Japanese in the Iberian world (16th–17th c.)." Ângela Barreto Xavier et al., eds. *Slave Subjectivities in the Iberian Worlds (16th–19th Centuries)*. Leiden et al.: Brill, 43–68.

Ehalt, Rômulo da Silva (2023b). "Geninka and Slavery: Jesuit casuistry and Tokugawa legislation on Japanese bondage (1590s–1620s)." *Itinerario.*

Ehalt, Rômulo da Silva (forthcoming a). "Whither Slavery? Decentering and conceptual asymmetries in the study of dependencies in early modern Asia." *eJournal of Portuguese History.*

Ehalt, Rômulo da Silva (forthcoming b). "Ignorance Lost: the arrival of Franciscan missionaries and the Jesuit normative discourse in Japan (16–17 c.)." Luisa Stella Coutinho, ed. *Change over time in the Iberian Worlds: stabilising regimes of normativity.* Leiden: Brill.

Ekama, Kate et al., eds. (2022). *Slavery and Bondage in Asia, 1550–1850: Towards a Global History of Coerced Labour*. Berlin: DeGruyter, 215–230.

Fedele, Pío (1947), "Consideraciones sobre la dispensa y sobre otras instituciones en la ordenación canónica." *Revista Española de Derecho Canónico* 2.5, 393–437.

Fracchia, Carmen (2019). *'Black but Human': Slavery and Visual Art in Hapsburg Spain.* Oxford: Oxford University Press.

García-Añoveros, Jesús (2000). *El pensamiento y los argumentos sobre la esclavitud en Europa en el siglo XVI y su aplicación a los indios americanos y a los negros africanos.* Madrid, CSIC.

Garriga, Carlos (2019). "¿Cómo escribir una historia «descolonizada» del derecho en América Latina?" Jesús Vallejo et al., eds. *En Antidora. Homenaje a Bartolomé Clavero*. Pamplona: Arazandi, Thomas Reuters, 325–76.

Gonoi Takashi (2003). *Hasekura Tsunenaga*. Tokyo: Yoshikawa Kōbunkan.

Hanke, Lewis (1959). *Aristotle and the American Indians: A Study in Race and Prejudice in the Modern World.* Chicago: Henry Regnery Company.

Hanß, Stefan and Juliane Schiel (2014). "Semantics, Practices and Transcultural Perspective on Mediterranean Slavery." Stefan Hanß et al., eds. *Mediterranean Slavery Revisited (500–1800)*. Zürich: Chronos, 11–23.

Hasegawa Yūko (2004). "Chūkinsei ikōki no hitouri kankō ni miru dogō no yūzū: seimei iji to mura no naritachi no shiten kara." Fujiki Hisashi et al., eds. *Shōen to mura wo aruku II*. Tokyo: Azekura Shobō, 92–118.

Hespanha, António Manuel (2007). "Depois do Leviathan." *almanack braziliense* 5, 55–66.

Hespanha, António Manuel (2008). *Imbecilitas: As Bem-Aventuranças da Inferioridade nas Sociedades do Antigo Regime*. São Paulo: Annablume.

Hespanha, António Manuel (2015). *Como os Juristas Viam o Mundo, 1550–1750*. Lisbon: self-published.

Ismard, Paulin et al., eds. (2021). *Les Mondes de l'Esclavage: Une Histoire Comparée*, Paris: Seuil.

Klein, Martin A., ed. (1993). *Breaking the Chains: Slavery, Bondage, and Emancipation in Modern Africa and Asia*. Madison, WI: University of Wisconsin Press.

Kopytoff, Igor and Suzanne Miers (1977). "African 'Slavery' as an Institution of Marginality." Suzanne Miers et al., eds. *Slavery in Africa: Historical and Anthropological Perspectives*. Madison, WI: University of Wisconsin Press, 1977, 3–81.

Lara, Silvia Hunold (2000). *Legislação sobre escravos africanos na América portuguesa*. São Paulo.

Maki Hidemasa (1961). *Nihon hōseishi ni okeru jinshin baibai no kenkyū*. Tokyo: Yūhikaku.

McManus, Stuart M. (2018). "'Servitutem Levem et Modici Temporis Esse Arbitrantes': Jesuit Schedulae and Japanese. Limited-Term Servitude in Gomes Vaz's De mancipiis Indicis." *Bulletin of Portuguese-Japanese Studies* series II, 4, 77–99.

Miers, Suzanne (2003). "Slavery: A Question of Definition." *Slavery and Abolition* 24.2, 1–16.

Nelson, Thomas (2004). "Slavery in Medieval Japan." *Monumenta Nipponica* 59.4, 463–92.

Nieboer, Herman J. (1910). *Slavery as an Industrial System*. The Hague: Nijhoff.

Ōizumi Kōichi (1994). *Keichō ken'ō shisetsu no kenkyū*. Tokyo: Kōshindō.

Ōizumi Kōichi (1998). *Hasekura Rokuemon Tsunenaga*. Tokyo: Kōshindō.

Okamoto Yoshitomo (1934a). "Jūroku seiki ni okeru nihonjin dorei mondai (jō)." *Shakai keizai shigaku* 4.3, 247–65.

Okamoto Yoshitomo (1934b). "Jūroku seiki ni okeru nihonjin dorei mondai (ge)." *Shakai keizai shigaku* 4.4, 372–85.

Okamoto Yoshitomo (1936). *Jūroku seiki nichiō kōtsūshi no kenkyū*. Tokyo: Kōbunsō.

Olivero, Giuseppe (1953). *Dissimulatio e tolerantia nell'ordinamento canonico*. Milan: Giuffrè.

Onyemechi Adiele, Pius (2017). *The Popes, the Catholic Church and the Transatlantic Enslavement of Black Africans, 1418–1839*. Hildesheim et al.: Georg Olms Verlag.

Owensby, Brian P. (2008). *Empire of Law and Indian Justice in Colonial Mexico*. Stanford: Stanford University Press.

Pagden, Anthony (1982). *The fall of natural man: The American Indian and the origins of comparative ethnology*. London et al.: Cambridge University Press.

Perrone-Moisés, Beatriz (1992). "Inventário da legislação indigenista: 1500–1800." Manuela Carneiro da Cunha, ed. *História dos Índios no Brasil.* São Paulo: Companhia das Letras, Secretaria Municipal de Cultura, FAPESP, 529–66.

Pinto, Jeanette (1992). *Slavery in Portuguese India (1510–1842).* Bombay: Himalaya Publishing House.

Sá, Isabel dos Guimarães (1997). *Quando o rico se faz pobre: Misericórdias, Caridade e Poder no Império Português, 1500–1800.* Lisbon: Comissão Nacional para a Comemoração dos Descobrimentos Portugueses.

Sá, Isabel dos Guimarães (2018). *O Regresso dos Mortos: Os Doadores da Misericórdia do Porto e a Expansão Portuguesa.* Lisbon: Imprensa de Ciências Sociais.

Sajó, András (2004). *Human Rights with Modesty: The Problem with Universalism.* Leiden et al.: Martinus Nijhoff Publishers.

Schrikker, Alicia et al., eds. (2020). *Being a Slave: Histories and Legacies of European Slavery in the Indian Ocean.* Leiden: Brill.

Seabra, Leonor Diaz de (2011). *A Misericórdia de Macau (séculos XVI a XIX): Irmandade, Poder e Caridade na Idade do Comércio.* Macau et al.: University of Macau et al.

Seijas, Tatiana (2014). *Asian Slaves in Colonial Mexico: From Chinos to Indios.* New York: Cambridge University Press.

Sekiguchi Hiroo (2019). "Edo bakufu no jinshin baibai kinrei wo megutte." *Rekishi minzoku shiryōgaku kenkyū* 24, 231–263.

Sola, Emilio, *Historia de un Desencuentro: España y Japón, 1580–1614,* Madrid 1999.

Sousa, Lúcio de (2018). *The Portuguese Slave Trade in Early Modern Japan: Merchants, Jesuits and Japanese, Chinese, and Korean Slaves.* Leiden: Brill.

Stanziani, Alessandro, ed. (2013). *Labour, Coercion, and Economic Growth in Eurasia, 17th–20th Centuries.* Leiden: Brill.

Stanziani, Alessandro, ed. (2014). *Bondage: Labour and Rights in Eurasia from the Sixteenth to the Early Twentieth Centuries.* New York et al.: Berghahn Books.

Tremml-Werner, Birgit (2015). *Spain, China, and Japan in Manila, 1571–1644: Local Comparisons and Global Connections.* Amsterdam: Amsterdam University Press.

Tronu, Carla, "The Rivalry between the Society of Jesus and Mendicant Orders in Early Modern Nagasaki", in *Agora: Journal of International Center for Regional Studies* 12 (2015), 25–39.

Uyttenbroeck, Thomas (1959). *Early Franciscans in Japan,* Himeji: Committee of the Apostolate.

Van der Linden, Marcel (2016), "Dissecting Coerced Labor." Marcel van der Linden and Magaly Rodríguez García, eds. *On Coerced Labor.* Leiden et al.: Brill, 293–322.

Van Deusen, Nancy (2015). *Global Indios: The Indigenous Struggle for Justice in Sixteenth-Century Spain.* Durham et al.: Duke University Press.

Willeke, Bernward (1990). "Biographical data on early Franciscans in Japan (1582–1640)." *Archivum Franciscanum Historicum* 83.1–2, 169–80.
Winnebeck, Julia et al. (2023). "The Analytical Concept of Asymmetrical Dependency." *Journal of Global Slavery* 8, 1–59.

Religion, Slavery and Resistance in Cape Town during the Dutch Colonial Period (1652–1795)

Eva Marie Lehner

In 2003, archaeologists discovered over 2,000 human remains in Cape Town, revealing an unmarked burial ground used by the eighteenth-century "underclass" to bury their own dead. It included niche burials, where the body is oriented towards Mecca, reflecting Islamic cultural traditions from South and Southeast Asia, and culturally modified teeth through filing, which refer to religious and cultural practices from Tanzania and Mozambique. There were also coffin burials and coins placed over the deceased's eyes that were typical Western and Christian burial styles.[1] This multireligious burial ground outside the city is a testament to different religions and belief systems coexisting and interacting in early modern Cape Town.[2]

During the time of Dutch colonial rule from 1652 to 1795, Cape Town experienced settler colonialism, which involved high mobility, slavery, and violence. The city was unique among early modern colonies as it had a diverse population made up of people who migrated from various European countries and others who were forcibly moved from Africa and Asia. This diversity resulted in different religions being practiced. Enslaved individuals from Mozambique and Madagascar, for instance, were practicing various African religions. Moreover, Muslim leaders who were exiled from other Dutch colonies in South and Southeast Asia brought their Islamic traditions to Cape Town, which became significant to the enslaved and manumitted people in the city. However, only Christianity and the Dutch Reformed Church were officially recognized by the colonial government between 1652 and 1795.

In light of these facts, this article explores and examines how different religious ideas and practices influenced the lives of enslaved, manumitted, and colonized people in Cape Town in the seventeenth and eighteenth centuries. It argues that the multireligious setting shaped slavery. The Dutch Reformed Church became an exclusive religion for free people, who were mainly Europeans and a few formerly enslaved women and men from Asia and Africa. On the contrary, Islam became an inclusive religion that benefited the African

1 Finnegan, Hart, Timothy and Halkett, "The 'Informal' Burial Ground".
2 See for the diversity of religions in South Africa: Chidester, *Wild Religion*.

 | DOI:10.30965/9783657796328_004

and Asian enslaved and manumitted people. Their common faith was important in building communities and in their resistance to slavery.

Slavery at the Cape

Otto Friedrich Mentzel, a German from Prussia, came to South Africa as a soldier, enlisted in the Dutch East India Company (VOC), and stayed between 1732 and 1740. After returning to Germany, he published a book about the geography of the Cape of Good Hope and its society, describing the origin of the enslaved population that was transported to the Cape:

> The first slaves were brought to the Cape from Madagascar, but the French afterwards put a stop to this traffic, and importations were made from India and the East Indies, from Bengal, Amboyna, Ternate, Tutegrin, Negapatam, Trincomali, Java, Candia, Surat, Malabar, and also from the Portuguese settlements.[3]

The Cape stands out among early modern colonies because it features a highly complex and mixed population that has been recognized and described by contemporary explorers like Mentzel.[4] In 1652, the VOC established a supply station at Table Bay in South Africa for ships traveling between Europe and Asia. The goal was to secure economic supremacy over England for the Netherlands, as the Dutch economy relied heavily on maritime trade.[5] Although the local South African societies, the Khoi and San, had already established trade relations with European travellers, they did not anticipate permanent settlement.[6] The Cape of Good Hope then began to experience conflict, violence, and wars when the Dutch settled there. The Dutch constructed a fort at Table Bay to claim the land, which led to fierce conflicts with the Khoi and San throughout the century.[7] The VOC established company gardens at the Cape of Good Hope to provide food to their employees and the crews of passing ships. However, labour was necessary for food production. Since the Company forbade the enslavement of people in their conquered territories, Jan van Riebeeck, the first Dutch colonial administrator, requested unfree labour from elsewhere.[8]

---

3 Mentzel, *A Complete*, 125. The German original was published in two volumes in Glaugau 1785 and 1787.

4 See for the diversity of the population and the creolization of people and cultures in early modern Cape Town: Shell, "The Tower of Babel"; Worden, *Cape Town*.

5 Knaap, *Genesis and Nemesis*.

6 Marx, *Südafrika*, 23–42.

7 Penn, *The Forgotten Frontier*.

8 Marx, *Südafrika*, 29.

This led to a slave trade in the Indian Ocean, which lasted from 1658 until the early nineteenth century.

The historian Robert Carl-Heinz Shell estimated that between 1652 and 1808, around 63,000 enslaved people were imported to the Cape from East Africa, Madagascar, South Asia, and Southeast Asia. The number of forced migrants from each region was roughly the same.[9] However, this number varied throughout the period.[10] In the second half of the period, for example, fewer people from Asia and more from East Africa were brought to the Cape. The enslaved individuals were responsible for the vast majority of production and labour, so Cape Town could be classified as a slave or slave-based society.[11] It is worth noting that throughout the entire period, more men were imported than women.[12]

The Dutch East India Company bought enslaved individuals from local traders in their posts around the Indian Ocean and then officially shipped them to the Cape.[13] However, private traders played the most important role in this slave trade.[14] How people were abducted, sold, and enslaved could vary. For example, the Dutch would abduct children playing on the beach and then sell them into slavery, while children could also be sold by their parents into slavery.[15] After abduction or purchase, the people were transported to the Cape, where they were sold. Mentzel characterized this process as follows:

> Burghers and farmers obtain their slaves on the local market. Sometimes an East Indian official makes a private speculative venture and takes a few slaves with him on his return voyage. Such slaves must be sold at the Cape, either privately or by public auction since no one is allowed to land a slave in Holland.[16]

---

9 Shell, *Children of Bondage*, 41.

10 Mbeki and van Rossum, "Private Slave Trade", 98.

11 Lenski, "Framing the Question"; Fourie and van Zanden, "GDP in the Dutch Cape Colony".

12 Worden, *Slavery in Dutch South Africa*, 52–63.

13 Chakraborty, "Slave Trading", 709.

14 Mbeki and van Rossum, "Private Slave Trade".

15 See for cases of abduction and other ways how people were enslaved on the Malabar coast: van Rossum, Geelen, van den Hout, and Tosu, *Testimonies of Enslavement*; Ari van Bengalen told this to the free burgher Jacobus van der Heijden, a former fellow prisoner. When he was trailed before the Council of Justice in Cape Town and charged with arson, Jacobus van der Heijden was examined about him and revealed this story to the judge. CJ 2961 Minuut Justitieële Attestatiën, Actens etc., 1706, ff. 73–76. Translated and edited in Worden and Groenewald, *Trials of Slavery*, 5–9; China of Singaracolla was sold into slavery by her mother as a child: M49: Transfer deeds for China, Serrurier papers, double-folded loose page. Translated and edited for the exhibition and project "Under Cover Darkness. Tracing stories of women in servitude under colonialism: https://undercoverofdarkness.co.za/china/#_edn1 (30.6.23).

16 Mentzel, *A Complete*, 126.

The company claimed ownership over 500 enslaved individuals, including women, children, and men, who were housed in Cape Town's city centre, in a building called the Slave Lodge. This Lodge was situated beside the Dutch Reformed Church and the Christian cemetery.[17] The enslaved individuals were assigned to work in the company gardens, food production, and the hospital, or had to do all kinds of instruction work.[18] Farmers in the hinterlands purchased unfree labourers primarily for agricultural work on their farms. Depending on the size of the farm, only one or up to two hundred unfree labourers worked there.[19] If they worked for the burghers of the city, they served as artisans or household servants in urban production.[20]

The slave trade transported individuals from diverse backgrounds and cultures to Cape Town. People from South and Southeast Asia, Madagascar, and Mozambique often came through abduction and forced relocation, leaving behind their families and social connections in Asia or Southeast Africa. These individuals lived and worked in Cape Town, but what was their religious life like? Religion and slavery were intertwined in South Africa during the Dutch Colonial period, and they shaped the experiences of enslaved and manumitted people. In the following section, I will show how access to the Dutch Reformed Church was restricted for the enslaved people, and how Islam became a crucial alternative belief system that influenced their practices of resistance.

The Dutch Reformed Church at the Cape

In 1609, the States General, the legislative body of the Netherlands, appointed the first governor of the VOC and established its objectives. The primary aim of the VOC was to expand East India trade to benefit the Netherlands financially. Additionally, the company was to promote Christianity and convert "non-believers," thereby enhancing the reputation of the Dutch nation. Dutch expansion, economic gains, and Christianity were to be intertwined.[21] However, the main goal was to further economic interests, with religion playing a subordinated role.

Therefore, the VOC primarily used the clergy of the Dutch Reformed Church to provide religious services to European subjects in its overseas territories. In

17 Groenewald, "Slaves and Free Blacks", 967–8.
18 Schoeman, *Early Slavery*, 127–94.
19 One of the bigger farms was Vergelgen, with around 200 enslaved people living and working there: Markell, Hall and Schrire, "The Historical Archaeology".
20 Groenewald, "Slaves and Free Blacks", 968–70.
21 Groenewald, "Slavery and the Church", 27; Chidester, *Religions of South Africa*, 35.

Cape Town, these subjects were referred to as free burghers, although not all European immigrants belonged to the Dutch Reformed Church and hailed from the Netherlands. There were also Lutheran immigrants from German-speaking areas, Huguenots from France, and Anabaptists like the Mennonites, making the Christian population in Cape Town very diverse.[22] According to the church register of the Groote Kerk, the Dutch Reformed Church in Cape Town, an adult known as Abel, whose parents were Mennonites and had not baptized him, was christened in October 1656.[23] Mentzel also noted that the enslaved individuals who were brought from Portuguese trading posts had already been baptized in the Catholic faith by the Jesuits.[24] Despite belonging to different Christian denominations, people could coexist and participate in the religious practices of the Dutch Reformed Church. Baptism, marriage, funerals, communion, and attending a church service were important aspects of their religious lives as Christians and free burghers.

But what did the religious life of enslaved people look like? While en route to Tranquebar in South Asia, Johann Georg Bövingh, a German-Danish missionary, stopped at the Cape and voiced his concerns regarding the religious state of the enslaved population. He noted that only a small fraction of them had been baptized and added that even those who expressed interest in Christianity were often barred by their owners from converting. This was because the owners were afraid that if their slaves became Christians, they would no longer be able to sell them and would eventually have to set them free:

> Only a few of the heathens [enslaved people] have been baptized. However, a fine congregation could be gathered from these people with little effort since many have already gained a decent understanding from their many years of association and want to become Christians. Still, their masters, as I have heard from many, do not want to admit this because they cannot be sold again if they are baptized, and whatever other reasons may be of interest.[25]

---

22 Witmer, "Between Compliance".

23 https://www.eggsa.org/sarecords/index.php/church-register-transcripts/church-registers/cape-town-baptisms-1653-to-1664 (30.12.2023); a further adult Mennonite was baptized on 20 July 1559.

24 Mentzel, *A Complete*, 126.

25 "Um dieser Heyden Bekehrung aber hat man sich biß daro wenig bemühet: Nur etliche wenige sind getaufft / da doch mit leichter Mühe aus diesen Leuten eine feine Gemeinde könnte gesammlet werden / angesehen viel aus dem vieljährigen Umgange schon eine zimliche Erkäntniß haben und selbst Christen zu werden verlangen: so aber ihre Herren/ wie ich von vielen gehöret / nicht zugeben wollen / dieweil sie / wenn sie getaufft / nicht wieder verkaufft werden können/ und was sonsten vor interessirte Ursachen seyn mögen."

Unlike the Portuguese in South Asia much earlier and the British colonial efforts in South Africa later on, the Dutch Reformed Church did not attempt to convert enslaved individuals to Christianity at the Cape. The only missionary efforts were made by the German Moravian church. They established a mission community in 1737, with the intention of converting the indigenous Khoi and San people. However, these efforts were unsuccessful, as the mission was terminated just a few years later in 1743.[26]

During the eighteenth century in Cape Town, only a few enslaved individuals were allowed to be part of the Dutch Reformed Church. This was due to owners' concerns that those who converted and were baptized would need to be freed and could not be sold.[27] However, there was no law that prevented Indigenous or unfree individuals from becoming members of the Dutch Reformed Church either, but they needed to undergo a conversion process. This process required them to learn about Christian beliefs, the Dutch language, and to receive baptism before being officially accepted as Dutch Reformed parish community members. To baptize a newborn in the Christian faith, the parents and godparents had to pledge to raise and educate the child in the teachings and values of the Dutch Reformed Church. The parents also needed to be Christians, or they would be required to ask Christian intercessors to act as godparents.[28] Certain exceptions were made for children born to enslaved women with European fathers. According to Robert Shell's estimates, out of the 2,543 enslaved people who were baptized between 1652 and 1795, 1,715 were children over whom the Company claimed ownership.[29]

Pieter van der Steal, known as the "sieckentrooster" or "sick comforter" of the Company, was required to provide regular reports to Amsterdam regarding church matters. Between 1652 and 1663, he wrote several letters mentioning the birth of children and the first baptisms that took place at the Cape. On July 18, 1660, he recorded three baptisms, including that of a newborn named Jannetje, whose father was the free burgher Thielman Hendriks (or: Heindricx). The other two children, Pietertje and Reintje, were also baptized. According to the letters, both children had been born out of wedlock, and their mothers were enslaved women. One of the mothers worked in Pieter's household, while the other worked in the household of Jan van Riebeeck, the governor of the

---

Bövingh, *Kurtze Nachricht*, 2–3. For further discussion of Tranquebar in Southeast India, see the chapter by Christoph Haar in this volume.

26 *Bredekamp, "Construction and Collapse".*

27 Shell, "Religion, Civil Status".

28 See for conversion, baptism, and record keeping: Lehner, *Taufe – Ehe – Tod*, 87–156.

29 Shell "Religion, Civil Status", 33.

Cape.[30] Their fathers were not named in the letters but were most likely free European men working for the VOC.

This tradition was later followed for children born by enslaved women at the Slave Lodge. Since the VOC regarded them as "their children" and acted as their Christian "parent," they could be and had to be baptized.[31] During the eighteenth century, the baptisms of these children were registered separately from other baptisms in Cape Town. In addition, these children, who typically had a European father and an African or Asian mother, inherited their mothers' unfree status and were recorded as "halvslag" or "heelslag" in the church register.[32] However, since the children had been baptized, the Company believed it was their duty to offer them a Christian education. To that end, a school was established in the Slave Lodge, where the children were taught about Christianity. The German ethnologist Peter Kolb mentioned the school for children at the Slave Lodge in his published account on the Cape of Good Hope.[33]

Johannes Smiesing was born in the Slave Lodge, where his mother, Manda Gratia, worked as a teacher despite being unfree. His father, a Dutch civil servant, was seldom present as he left the Cape shortly after his son's birth. However, his son was baptized and named after him, received a Christian education at the school in the Slave Lodge, and spoke Dutch. Following in his mother and grandmother's footsteps, he eventually took over the school service at the Lodge and educated the children there himself.[34] We know about him and the education system in the Slave Lodge because he left a notebook with biographical notes and educational materials related to the Slave Lodge's education system. This notebook includes an alphabet chart and a Christian hymn in Dutch and Tamil writing.[35]

There was an interest on the part of the Dutch Company to baptize and educate the children in the Slave Lodge in a Christian way.[36] But even though they had been baptized, children like Johannes Smiesing could not claim any inheritance from their fathers because they were born out of wedlock and were not considered legitimate heirs. And since their fathers were mostly not mentioned

30 Upham, "What Can't be Cured", 55–7.

31 Cravens, "Manumission and the Life Cycle".

32 The baptismal entries for children born in the Slave Lodge can be accessed online: https://www.eggsa.org/sarecords/index.php/church-registers/cape-town-baptisms-1743-1756/338-company-slave-baptisms-1743-1756 (20.7.2023).

33 Kolben, *Caput Bonae Spei*, 330.

34 Dick, *The Hidden History*, 12–29.

35 Dick, "The Notebook".

36 Jarzebowski, "Children".

in their baptismal records, they were difficult to locate. Fathers were often absent, even before the child's birth, as in the case of Johannes Smiesing. Despite being baptized by the Dutch Reformed Church and receiving a Christian education, children born to enslaved women were not entitled to claim legitimate kinship with their European fathers due to their inherited legal status.

Ideally, the conversion to Christianity and baptism should result in manumission. Women should be freed at the age of 22 and men at 25. However, this did not happen in practice. The mortality rate, especially for newborns and children, was very high at the Slave Lodge. Conditions were so terrible that many children born there did not live to see their twenties. Even those who did were often denied manumission.[37] For instance, Johannes Smiesing only received his manumission at the age of 34, three years before his death. It was only during his final years that he could live as a free person in Cape Town. Johannes Smiesing and his partner, Anna van Dapoer, had four children who were born at the Slave Lodge and were baptized. Unfortunately, the rules of the Dutch Reformed Church did not allow enslaved individuals to officially marry, and so he and Anna van Dapoer could not get married as they were considered unfree by legal status.

Belonging to the Dutch Reformed Church required more than baptism and a Christian education. Marriage and the Lord's Supper were also crucial. However, because they were forbidden to marry, it was difficult or impossible for enslaved people to live a Christian life, which included having a monogamous Christian marriage. Therefore, if they lived together as husband and wife, like Johannes Smiesing and Anna, the Dutch Reformed Church considered their union to be sinful since all sexual relations outside of marriage were immoral in Dutch Reformed Christianity. This made it practically impossible for enslaved people to become members of the Dutch Reformed Church, even if it was theoretically possible.

Very similar were the experiences of Adam van Africa, who appeared before the Church Council in Stellenbosch. He had spent his entire life with a woman who was also enslaved, but they could not get married. Adam sought help from the Church Council and requested them to legalize their relationship. However, the council advised him to end his relationship instead. They even barred him from receiving communion in the church if he continued to stay with her.[38] This case exemplifies the difficulties enslaved people faced in leading a righteous Christian life since they were not permitted to marry or form legally recognized family bonds.

37 Shell, "Religion, Civil Status".

38 Groenewald, "Slavery and the Church", 35–6.

The marriage between free European men and manumitted women was an exception. Especially at the beginning of the Dutch colonial period at the Cape, and because of the shortage of women, some enslaved women were manumitted and converted in order to allow them to marry European settlers or Company officials. Catharina Anthonis van Bengalen was the first woman to be manumitted. In 1656, she married Jan Woutersz, a Company official from Middleburg in the Netherlands. In her marriage entry, found in the records of the Dutch Reformed Church from May 1656, the pastor noted the following:

> On the 21st of May, Jan Woutersz van Middelburg is assistant to the council of this fort, married to a young black maid named Catharijna Anthonis van Bengale, may God bless them.[39]

A few years later, her husband was sent to Batavia, and she travelled with him as a free woman and his wife.[40]

The second woman who was manumitted was Maria from Bengal. She was freed in 1658 so that she could marry Jan Sacharias, a free burgher from Amsterdam. He bought her freedom under the condition that she would become his legal wife.[41] The fact that the transaction lists included an entry noting that her free status was conditional to marriage shows overlapping concepts. On the one hand, slavery was conceptualized as ownership over another person. On the other hand, the Christian-reformed theological idea of marriage was constituted as a consensus between two free parties. A free person could then buy or release an unfree person and marry them. Because of the gender imbalance in Cape Town, where there were a lot more men than women, it was common for free male citizens to ransom unfree women in order to marry them, especially at the beginning of the colonial period in the seventeenth century.

---

39 "Den 21:en meij is Jan Woutersz van Middelburch adsistent voor den raet deser fortresse, getrout met een swarte jonge dochter genaemt Catharijna Anthonis van Celagon in Bengale, Godt gelievede zelvige te zegenen." Cape Archives Verbatim Copies VC 603, Nederduits Gereformeerde Kerk, baptisms 1665 to 1696: https://www.eggsa.org/sarecords/index.php/church-register-transcripts/church-registers/cape-town-marriages-1656-1662 (5.7.2023).

40 Böeseken, *Slaves and free blacks*, 78.

41 Vol. I: Schepenkennis, 1652–1662. Edited and translated in: Böeseken, *Slaves and free blacks*, 124.

Access to the Dutch Reformed Church, parish, and burgher community in the Cape Colony was tightly controlled and restricted.[42] The maintenance of regulations, baptisms, and marriages were crucial as these events reinforced hierarchies, dependencies, and privileges. Additionally, colonial burial traditions helped to stabilize social and religious hierarchies and dependencies. Only members of the Christian Dutch Reformed Church or the VOC were allowed to be buried in the Christian cemetery, which was located in the city centre by the Groote Kerk. Christian burials in Cape Town, much like in Europe, came with a cost, and families were responsible for paying a fee for the funeral.[43]

As stated earlier in this article, individuals who were not part of the burgher community and the "underclass" who lacked the financial means to pay for an official funeral administered by the Dutch Reformed Church, which included low-ranking European soldiers and sailors, were buried outside the city in an unmarked and unofficial burial ground.[44] The Dutch Reformed Church was the only officially recognized religion in the Cape Colony. However, it did not actively seek to convert the indigenous population or the enslaved workforce. Only the children of enslaved women and European fathers who were born in the Slave Lodge were baptized and raised in Christianity. Unfree individuals could not legally marry or establish official family ties, making it difficult for them to lead a "Christian" life. Their burials were also separated and had to take place outside the city.

Early modern Cape Town was a place where religion, class, social status, ethnicity, and legal status intersected. The Dutch Reformed Church played a role in maintaining social boundaries and hierarchies alongside these axes of differentiation.

Islam at the Cape

In early modern Cape Town, various religions were present. Christian denominations such as the Methodists, the Moravian Church and the Lutherans from German-speaking territories could be observed. Enslaved individuals who had been baptized in the Catholic faith by Jesuits in Portuguese colonial posts

42 Groenewald, "Slavery and the Church"; Shell, "Religion, Civil Status"; Keegan, *Colonial South Africa*, 15–36.

43 See for the role funerals, marriages, and burials played for the respectability of the burgher community and to stabilize status and hierarchies at the Cape under Dutch rule: Ross, "Status and Respectability", 9–39, 94–124.

44 Finnegan, Hart and Halkett, "The 'Informal' Burial Ground".

in South and Southeast Asia were brought to the Cape. The indigenous Khoi and San communities practiced their religions. Forcefully imported individuals from Mozambique and Madagascar followed their African religious beliefs and practices.[45] However, what stands out at the Cape are the diverse Islamic traditions originating from Southeast and South Asia and the spread of Islam brought about by enslaved individuals and their manumitted descendants from Asia and Africa.[46] Various Islamic traditions were brought to Cape Town through the slave trade in the Indian Ocean and the expulsion of convicts from other Dutch colonial posts.[47] Displaced individuals from Muslim areas in South and Southeast Asia as well as East Africa brought their religious practices with them.

According to Georg Forster's publication about his famous voyage around the world with Captain James Cook, the enslaved population in Cape Town appeared to have no religious beliefs (a typical European misperception of non-monotheistic religions) and only acknowledged Islam as a possible alternative to Christianity:

> A few of them [enslaved people] followed the Mahommedan rite, and weekly meet in a private house belonging to a free Mahomedan, in order to read, or rather chaunt several prayers, and chapters of the Koran. As they have no priest among them, they cannot partake of any other acts of worship.[48]

While public Islamic praying was not permitted, private religious practices were allowed at the Cape, as Forster correctly observed. However, in contrast to his interpretation, there were experts in Islamic theology and spiritual leaders at the Cape. The VOC exiled religious and political leaders resisting the Dutch in South and Southeast Asia to South Africa.[49] Despite Islam not being an officially recognized religion in Cape Town, a thriving Muslim community developed there in the seventeenth and especially the eighteenth centuries. For enslaved and manumitted people from East Africa and Asia, it was a welcome alternative to the Christianity practiced by the Dutch Reformed Church, which was highly restricted, as elaborated above.

Mentzel mentions in his publication that some rebellious subjects were banished from Batavia and brought to the Cape.[50] Lists from the Council of

45 Chidester, *Religions of South Africa*, 1–34.
46 Beyers, "Beyond denial", 5.
47 Bradlow, "Islam at the Cape"; Baderoon, *Regarding Muslims*, 1–26.
48 Forster, *A Voyage*, Book I, Chapter III, 48.
49 Ward, *Networks of Empire*.
50 Mentzel, *A Complete*, 125.

Justice at the Cape registered incoming individuals who had been expelled from Batavia and Ceylon.[51] The VOC saw these insurgents as threats to its bases and trade in Asia, thus exiling them to South Africa.[52] Between 1652 and 1795, about a hundred political exiles stayed at the Cape. Among them were political figures and also religious leaders.[53]

Authorities at the Cape especially feared the Makassarese exiles.[54] These were noble leaders of the resistance who were a threat to the Dutch outposts and influence in Sulawesi.[55] Their status, power, and religious expertise made them a menace. At the Cape, some were sent to Robben Island, and others were housed on farms outside the city to minimize their religious influence on the enslaved and manumitted population.[56]

Robben Island was ideal for this purpose because it is close to the coast, but one would need to have a boat to reach land. The island served as a place of punishment and as a prison from the late seventeenth century onwards, and it was used especially for political exiles.[57] These convicts who were sent from South and Southeast Asia to the Cape played important roles in the development of the Muslim community because many were Islamic religious dissidents.[58] They were referred to as "Mohammedan priests" ("Muslim priests") in Dutch sources and European travelogues.

One of the most important exiles at the Cape was the Sufi scholar Abad Allah Abu al-Mahasin al-Taj al Khalwati al-Maqassari.[59] He was referred to as Sheikh Yusuf from Makassar at the Cape and Muhammad Syekh Yusuf Al-Makassari in Sulawesi.[60] Born into the Makassarese nobility, he received an Islamic education, travelled throughout the Near East, studied Arabic and religious science in Mecca, and became part of an 'ulemā network in the Indian Ocean.[61] Later, he became a local leader and helped organize an uprising against the

51 Copies of the sentences of persons banished from Batavia, Ceylon. 1/2 Raad van Justitie (Council of Justice) 1652–1843. Western Cape Archives and Records Service.

52 Ward, *Networks of Empire*, 179–237.

53 Penn, "Robben Island".

54 Ward, *Networks of Empire*, 194–199.

55 Utung Surapati is one of Indonesia's most remembered figures of resistance against the Duch East India Company. Kumar, *Surapati*.

56 Ward, *Networks of Empire*, 194–5, 198.

57 Penn, "Robben Island", 20.

58 Ward, *Networks of Empire*, 230.

59 Steiner, "The Indian Ocean", see for the name and different forms, 172 footnote 1.

60 Ward, *Networks of Empire*, 199–212.

61 His manuscripts are preserved in several archives, including the South Sulawesi Archives and the University of Leiden in the Netherlands.

Dutch colonial powers in Java.[62] In 1683, he was taken captive by the Dutch and was sent to Ceylon. In 1694, he was banished to the Cape along with 49 others, including his two wives, their children, free and unfree servants, and some followers. They were taken to Zandvliet, a farm outside of Cape Town, to limit his influence. Despite this, he continued to hold religious services that freed and unfree Muslims attended.[63] According to Kerry Ward, Sheikh Yusuf's life is a significant illustration of the vast Islamic networks that connected the archipelago of the Indian Ocean to Ceylon, South Asia, the Arabian Peninsula, and ultimately, to South Africa.[64] Sheikh Yusuf was one of the several religious authorities who helped establish Islam as an alternative religion to Christianity at the Cape.

This included establishing an institutional and non-institutionalized Islamic education system. The Auwal Mosque was constructed on Dorp Street in Cape Town in 1794, making it the first mosque in South Africa.[65] Among the first imāms to preach was Imam Abdallah ibn Qadhi Abd al-Salam, known as Tuan Guru (Grand Teacher) at the Cape. He taught boys and girls, both free and enslaved, to read the Qur'ān in Arabic at the first madrasa. This Muslim school served as an alternative, and perhaps even as competition, to the Christian school in the Slave Lodge.[66]

Tuan Guru came from a noble family in Tidore, an Indonesian island. Like Sheikh Yusuf, he was taken as a captive and brought to the Cape in 1780, where he was imprisoned on Robben Island. While in captivity, he authored multiple manuscripts, including handwritten copies of the Qur'ān, a manual on Islamic jurisprudence, and medical treatises that involved talismans for healing purposes.[67] Practicing and converting to Islam took place in the early modern Cape on both the institutional and non-institutional levels. The latter contained verbal communication, cultural traditions, and the writing of religious texts, including mystical talismans for protection.[68]

In Cape Town, Islam was a mixture of different traditions and practices, including Sufi mysticism and even elements of Buddhist and Hindu

62 Beyers, "Beyond denial", 3–5.

63 Dangor, *Shaykh Yusuf.*

64 Ward, *Networks of Empire*, 200.

65 Bradlow and Cairns, *The Early Cape Muslims*. See also: https://www.auwalmasjid.co.za/index.php/history-of-the-auwal-masjid/ (21.7.23).

66 Davids, "Muslim-Christian Relations", 82.

67 Morton, *From the Spice Islands.*

68 Ward, *Networks of Empire*, 233.

traditions.[69] This blend resulted in a creolization of various religions and Islamic currents. Despite the diversity of religious practices by some Muslims at the Cape Colony, the different religious practices inspired by Islam created a spiritual world and faith community alongside the officially recognized Dutch Reformed Church. People legally considered unfree at the Cape could not convert to the Dutch Reformed Church but to Islam, which made the latter more accessible for the enslaved population.

Resistance at the Cape

Some argue that there was little resistance to slavery in Cape Town due to the diverse origins of the population, which made it difficult to build a united community and culture against the colonial class.[70] Despite this, the court cases at the Court of Justice in Cape Town show various forms of resistance to slavery, even if no revolution or bigger uprising was organized by the enslaved and oppressed population in the early modern period. There are cases where small groups of enslaved men ran away and tried to free themselves from enslavement.[71] Running away in order to flee slavery was considered a severe crime at the Cape and was punished very harshly by flogging, branding, or a lifelong sentence in chains.[72]

One of the court cases involved a group of enslaved men who attempted to escape and rebel against their condition by fleeing into the interior regions which were not controlled by the colonists. They attacked a settler household and murdered some of the members, including unfree servants. Eventually, they were caught and executed, and the Dutch authorities made an example out of them. This case is particularly interesting because it also highlights the use of religious practices to unite people from diverse backgrounds and form a community.[73]

---

69 According to Gabebe Baderoon and Robert Carl-Heinz Shell, there is evidence of Islamic influence in South Africa coming with people from South Asia. Baderoon, *Regarding Muslims*; Shell, "Islam in Southern Africa". Frank R. Bradlow suggests that immigrants from Bengal played a significant role in bringing Shafi'I influences to the Cape colony. Bradlow, "Islam at the Cape"; Beyers, "Beyond denial", 5.

70 Ross, *Cape of Torments*.

71 Ekama, "Just Deserters".

72 Nigel Worden wrote about discipline and punishment as part of slavery in South Africa: Worden, *Slavery in Dutch South Africa*, 101–118. See for examples: Böeseken, *Slaves and free blacks*, 41.

73 Parts of the court trial are edited: Criminal Justice 795 Sententiën, 1782–189, ff. 376–406. Criminal Justice 424 Criminele Process Strukken, 1786, deel 2, ff. 699 & 701. Worden and

In 1786, six men between the ages of 25 and 30, who were forcefully brought from South and Southeast Asia to the Cape or were born there as unfree men, managed to escape slavery. These men were August van de Caab (26), Andries van Calkuta (25), Jonas van Batavia (30), Damon van Bougies (28), Saripa van Mandhaar (30), and Welkom van Ternate (27). They fled towards the eastern Cape, seeking refuge in the land of the indigenous Xhosa people to avoid being controlled by the Dutch colonial government.

The group forged strong bonds and a shared sense of dedication. They relied on the help of unaware European settlers, the support of the indigenous Khoi and San people in the area, and individuals who actively aided them during their escape. They were given falsified documents by a manumitted man named Valentijn van Dapoer and a schoolboy called Johannes Jacobus Fabritius, which allowed them to travel. During that time, it was required by law that individuals who were enslaved and were transporting goods or traveling alone needed to have letters or something in writing, so-called "passeerbriefjes," from their owner which indicated that they had permission to do so.

Additionally, a Muslim religious leader named Norman van Marantu, who had been exiled from Batavia to the Cape, gave them a written talisman and charm for protection (azimat or jimat). Their experiences as forced migrants and unfree labourers at the Cape, along with their shared goal of escaping slavery, brought the young men together. Their common religious beliefs and practices, such as taking an oath and seeking assistance from a religious leader, further strengthened their bond.

The men made it as far as the Swellendam district with their forged passports. Once in the Swellendam district, they raided a farm. Several enslaved people who worked there, the "knecht," as well as the housewife and some children, were injured or killed in the violent robbery. The group took some items and food with them. However, the theft caused such a stir that they were caught by a group of Khoi, who were probably used as trackers, and were subsequently handed over to the colonial authorities.

After they were arrested and before their trial, the authorities searched the men and discovered the forged documents and the written talisman, which raised suspicion and concern. Despite having questioned the accused, the court still needed help to determine the exact function and purpose of the writing, as detailed in the court records:

Groenewald, *Trials of Slavery*, 537–556. I am using the English translation by Worden and Groenewald and their additional information in the following interpretation of the case.

> Further, that the third prisoner, Jonas, also took along a small square lead disc, on which were written with a needle some letters, seemingly Malay, and which was provided to the third prisoner, according to his own confession, by the Mohammedan priest Norman, who was banished here from Batavia in the year 1770, without the third prisoner wanting to admit that this might be a charm through which they could remain safe from danger and pursuit, but saying only that he had got this small disc from Norman when he, the third prisoner, was still living with the burgher Elias Voberg, and that such discs are actually charms which protect one from being torn apart by wild animals, and nothing else, while the fourth prisoner says that it is a charm which protects the body, but according to others, that such a disc protects a person from all evil, including being taken prisoner during desertion.[74]

During the investigation, the Dutch authorities discovered a letter on a piece of paper, written with what they presumed to be Malay characters, in the possession of one of the prisoners. However, they were unable to determine the contents of the letter. Following further questioning, one of the prisoners admitted that it was given to them by a Muslim cleric named Norman. The court struggled to determine the exact purpose of the document, as some of the defendants claimed it was a good luck charm that could protect the body from wild animals or even imprisonment. It thus appeared that before their escape, the men had received a written talisman from Norman van Marantu, one of the Muslim imams exiled from Batavia to South Africa. This involvement with the group of runaways made Norman van Marantu suspicious and an accomplice in the eyes of the Court.

What was even more ominous was the fact that the group used the inscribed paper with some powder to create a charm:

> Moreover, that the third, fourth, fifth and sixth prisoners were each provided with a special kind of powder, without, however, their wanting to confess to what end this served, as the one says that it was a kind of incense with which to smoke the aforementioned small disc on Fridays, in order to keep the power of the charm; another that he had taken this along for his health, while the third says that this only served to protect them from any evil, without wanting to acknowledge either the power of the powders or the reason why these were taken along with them, while, notwithstanding this, the fifth prisoner Saripa had even added to the powders a kind of charm on a piece of paper, written upon with Malay characters, which the fifth prisoner says to have obtained from the fourth prisoner Damon, which was also admitted by the fourth prisoner.[75]

74 Worden and Groenewald, *Trials of Slavery*, 549.

75 Worden and Groenewald, *Trials of Slavery*, 549–50.

Four of the detainees were found to have a certain type of powder in their possession. However, the court was not convinced by the information gathered from their interrogations. One detainee claimed to use the powder to enhance the effect of the writing, while another stated that he carried it for health reasons. The third detainee believed that the powder offered protection against evil, and the fourth referred to its magical properties. The court classified the making and handing out of the talisman in combination with the powder and potential religious or magical practices as suspicious and dangerous.

The talismanic writing was linked to a Muslim leader and imam at the Cape and made it an act of rebellion. According to the court, Norman of Marantu was implicated in the escape of the six men that led to the murder of a burgher family, as he supported them by writing them an amulet. Although the accused claimed it was only used as a good luck charm and for health purposes, the court viewed it as a form of resistance.

Written talismans were part of an Islamic tradition of Sufism in Cape Town.[76] They could be used for various purposes: some texts contain medicinal solutions for health problems like headaches. They could be used for spiritual ailments and to speed up plant growth. Some talisman texts also predict the days on which certain activities should be carried out.[77]

What especially alarmed the court was the fact that the different practices, like the written amulet, created a bond between the six men:

> They finally, amongst other things, made a mutual alliance never to leave one another, but to die together, which alliance sworn by them here [i.e., at the Cape] was subsequently confirmed by them with the oath of loyalty as often as they could obtain wine on their way.[78]

According to the court, the men concluded an agreement. They swore an oath not to separate but to die together and then drank to it.

Although the purpose of the written paper was unclear, Norman of Marantu was still sentenced to imprisonment on Robben Island for creating and delivering the talisman that made him part of the rebellious act. Valentijn van Dapoer, who had forged the passes, was punished by being tied to a pole with a sign stating "forger" for an entire day, followed by a five-year sentence on Robben Island.

The six men were sentenced to public execution for murder and theft, and the judge made an example out of the public display. The court case documents

76 Ward, *Networks of Empire*, 230.

77 Koolhof and Ross, "Upas, September".

78 Worden and Groenewald, *Trials of Slavery*, 550.

give a detailed description of their physical punishment and the dishonourable procedure of execution. The men were executed by being broken on the wheel and with their bodies subsequently exposed on the gallows. Nigel Worden and Gerald Groenewald assume that these sentences were the most punitive that the Council of Justice could deliver.[79] The public punishment probably occurred in the city centre in the fort, and the executions outside the city on the gallows. Carl Peter Thunberg, a Swedish scientist who had travelled to Asia and Africa, published an account of his travels to the Cape at the end of the eighteenth century. In his book, he describes two different places of execution that the Dutch authorities used to punish people and also gives examples. One was used for Europeans, and the other for enslaved and indigenous people.[80]

Muslim community leaders at the Cape crafted mystical amulets for their followers. Whether they were used for resisting practices cannot be said for sure by consulting the court records. Still, they were part of cultural and religious practices that created a community other than and distinct from the colonial and Christian settler society.

The Company feared the enslaved running away, forming groups, and opposing their treatment. The court associated these protests with religious practices and a Muslim leader involved in the rebellious act. The brutal punishment and the public display of the bodies of the six men at the gallows outside the city perpetuated religious, social, and ethical boundaries and hierarchies. The punishment thus inscribed these hierarchies and boundaries in the geographical and social landscape of the Cape, such that they could be seen not only by the inhabitants but also by foreign visitors.

Religion, Slavery, and Resistance at the Cape

Christianity and Islam came to South Africa through the VOC in the second half of the seventeenth century. Most of the European settlers brought their Christian faith with them. These included members of the Dutch Reformed Church, Protestants, and Huguenots. During Dutch colonial rule in South Africa, missionary ambitions were extremely limited, and neither the VOC nor the Dutch Reformed clergy undertook systematic missionary efforts. The Dutch Reformed Church and Christianity served in the Dutch Cape Colony by gathering free Europeans and excluding enslaved people from Asia and Africa.

79 Worden and Groenewald, *Trials of Slavery*, 555, footnote 18.
80 Thunberg, *Travels at the Cape*, 153.

Religion helped to stabilize hierarchies, boundaries, and privileges, and with the assistance of religious practices such as baptism, marriages, and burials, family relationships were established and secured. However, enslaved persons were excluded from all these practices. Harsh and public punishment for resisting and fleeing slavery perpetuated these hierarchies further.

In contrast, some of the enslaved persons imported to South Africa came from Islam-dominated areas in South and Southeast Asia. In addition, the political prisoners from VOC areas in the Indian Ocean that had been exiled to the Cape included some Muslim clerics. Although Islam was not recognized as an official religion, it was important for both enslaved and freed people as it was a counterpoint to the Dutch Reformed Church of the colonists and settlers. Islam thus had a community-building function through which resistance could be organized.[81] Religion, in this case, Islam, therefore represented a potential threat to Dutch colonial rule.

In these ways, religion had a dual role at the Cape. Firstly, it was intertwined with slavery and played a part in the formation of social groups by including and excluding individuals. Secondly, it offered individuals practices and resources that helped to build communities and social networks, which could then be used to resist slavery and oppression.

Works Cited

Baderoon, Gabebe (2014). *Regarding Muslims from Slavery to Post-Apartheid.* Johannesburg: Wits University Press.

Beyers, Jaco (2016). "Beyond denial and exclusion: The history of relations between Christians and Muslims in the Cape Colony during the 17th–18th Centuries with Lessions for a Post-colonial Theology of Religions." *HTS Theologiese Studies/ Theological Studies* 71.1, 1–10.

Böeseken, Anna Jacoba (1977). *Slaves and free blacks at the Cape, 1658–1700*. Cape Town: Tafelberg Publisher.

Bövingh, Johann Georg (1714). *Kurtze Nachricht Von den Hottentotten Oder Denen Heyden, welche das äusserste Africanische Vorgebirge Cabo de bona Esperança genannt, bewohnen*. Hamburg: Jahkel.

Bradlow Frank R. (1981). "Islam at the Cape of Good Hope." *South African Historical Journal (Suid-Afrikaanse historiese joernaal)* 13.1, 12–19.

81 Ward, *Networks of Empire*, 233–4.

Bradlow, Frank R., and Margaret Cairns (1978). *The Early Cape Muslims. A Study of their Mosques, Genealogy and Origins*. Cape Town: A.A. Balkema.
Bredekamp, Henry C. Jatti (1997). "Construction and Collapse of a Herrnhut Mission Community at the Cape, 1737–1743." *Kronos* 24, 46–61.
Chakraborty, Titas (2019). "Slave Trading and Slave Resistance in the Indian Ocean World: The Case of Early Eighteenth-Century Bengal." *Slavery & Abolition* 40.4, 706–726.
Chidester, David (1992). *Religions of South Africa*. London/New York: Routledge.
Chidester, David (2012). *Wild Religion. Tracking the Sacred in South Africa*. Berkeley: University of California Press.
Cravens, Mary Caroline (2009). "Manumission and the Life Cycle of a Contained Population: The VOC Lodge Slaves at the Cape of Good Hope, 1680–1730." Brana-Shute, Rosemary and Randy J. Sparks, eds. *Paths to Freedom: Manumission in the Atlantic World*. Columbia, South Carolina: University of South Carolina Press, 97–120.
Dangor, Suleman Essop (2019). *Shaykh Yusuf of Makassar*. Durban: Digniti.
Davids, Achmat (1992). "Muslim-Christian Relations in Nineteenth Century Cape Town (1825–1925)." *Kronos* 19, 80–101.
Dick, Archie L. (2010). "The Notebook of Johannes Smiesing (1697–1734), Writing and Reading Master in the Cape Slave Lodge." *Quarterly Bulletin of the National Library of South Africa* 64.4, 159–174.
Dick, Archie L. (2012). *The Hidden History of South Africa's Book and Reading Cultures*. Toronto: University of Toronto Press.
Ekama, Kate (2016). "Just Deserters: Runaway Slaves from the VOC Cape, c. 1700–1800." Rossum, Matthias van and Jeannette Kamp, eds. *Desertion in the Early Modern World: A Comparative History*. London: Bloomsbury Academic, 161–186.
Finnegan, Erin, Timothy Hart and David Halkett (2011). "The 'Informal' Burial Ground at Prestwich Street, Cape Town: Cultural and Chronological Indicators for the Historical Cape Underclass." *The South African Archaeological Bulletin* 66/194, 136–148.
Forster, Georg (2000 [1777]). *A Voyage Round the World*. Thomas, Nicholas and Oliver Berghof, eds. 2 vols. Honolulu: University of Hawai'i Press.
Fourie, Johan and Jan Luiten van Zanden (2013). "GDP in the Dutch Cape Colony: The National Accounts of a Slave-Based Society." *The South African Journal of Economics* 81.4, 467–490.
Groenewald, Gerald (1990). "Slavery and the Church in the Stellenbosch District during the Eighteenth Century." *South African Journal of Cultural History* 24.2, 25–36.
Groenewald, Gerald (2010). "Slaves and Free Blacks in VOC Cape Town, 1652–1795." *History Compass* 8.9, 964–83.

Jarzebowski, Claudia (2023). "Children. Towards a Global History." Benzaquén, Adriana, ed. *A Cultural History of Youth in the Age of Enlightenment*. London: Bloomsbury Publishing, 215–34.

Keegan, Timothy (1996). *Colonial South Africa and the Origins of the Racial Order*. Charlottesville: University Press of Virginia.

Knaap, Gerrit (2002). *Genesis and Nemesis of the First Dutch Colonial Empire in Asia and South Africa, 1596–1811*. Boston: Brill.

Kolben, Peter (1719). *Caput Bonae Spei hodiernum, das ist: vollständige Beschreibung des africanischen Vorgebürges der Guten Hofnung: worinnen in dreyen Theilen abgehandelt wird, wie es heut zu Tage, nach seiner Situation und Eigenschaft aussiehet ... erster Theil*. Nürnberg: Peter Contrad Monath.

Koolhof, Sirtjo and Robert Ross (2005). "Upas, September and the Bugis at the Cape of Good Hope. The Context of a Slave's letter." *Archipel* 70, 281–308.

Kumar, Ann (1976). *Surapati: Man and Legend: a Study of Three Babad Traditions*. Leiden: Brill.

Lehner, Eva Marie (2023). *Taufe – Ehe – Tod. Praktiken des Verzeichnens in frühneuzeitlichen Kirchenbüchern*. Göttingen: Wallstein.

Lenski, Noel (2018). "Framing the Question: What is a Slave Society?" Noet Lenski, https://www-1cambridge-1org-1000034et0483.erf.sbb.spk-berlin.de/core/search?filters[authorTerms]=Noel Lenski&eventCode=SE-AU and Catherine M. Cameron, eds. *What Is a Slave Society? The Practice of Slavery in Global Perspective*. Cambridge: Cambridge University Press, 15–57.

Markell, Ann, Martin Hall and Carmel Schrire (1995). "The Historical Archaeology of Vergelegen, an Early Farmstead at the Cape of Good Hope." *Historical Archaeology* 29.1, 10–34.

Marx, Christoph (2022). *Südafrika. Geschichte und Gegenwart*. Stuttgart: Verlag Kohlhammer.

Mbeki, Linda and Matthias van Rossum (2017). "Private Slave Trade in the Dutch Indian Ocean World: a Study into the Networks and Backgrounds of the Slavers and the Enslaved in South Asia and South Africa." *Slavery & Abolition* 38.1, 95–116.

Mentzel, Otto Friedrich (2006 [1785/7]). *A Complete and Authentic Geographical and Topographical Description of the Famous and (all Things Considered) Remarkable African Cape of Good Hope*, vol. II., ed. and translated by van Riebeeck Society. Cape Town: van Riebeeck Society.

Morton, Shafiq (2018). *From the Spice Islands to Cape Town: The Life and Times of Tuan Guru*. Johannesburg and Cape Town: AwqafSA.

Penn, Nigel (1996). "Robben Island, 1488–1805." Deacon, Harriet, ed. *The Island: a History of Robben Island, 1488–1990*. Cape Town: David Philip Publisher, 9–32.

Penn, Nigel (2005). *The Forgotten Frontier. Colonist and Khoisan on the Cape's Northern Frontier in the 18th Century*. Athens, Ohio: Ohio University Press.

Ross, Robert (1999). *Status and Respectability in the Cape Colony, 1750–1870: a Tragedy of Manners*. Cambridge: Cambridge University Press.

Ross, Robert (2023 [1983]). *Cape of Torments. Slavery and Resistance in South Africa*. London/New York: Routledge.

Rossum, Matthias van, Alexander Geelen, Bram van den Hout and Merven Tosu, eds. (2020). *Testimonies of Enslavement: Sources on Slavery from the Indian Ocean World*. London: Bloomsbury Academic.

Schoeman, Karel (2007). *Early Slavery at the Cape of Good Hope 1652–1717*. Pretoria: Protea Book House.

Shell, Robert Carl-Heinz (1992). "Religion, Civil Status and Slavery from Dordt to the Trek." *Kronos* 19, 28–63.

Shell, Robert Carl-Heinz (1994). *Children of Bondage. A Social History of the Slave Society at the Cape of Good Hope, 1652–1838*. Hanover/London: Wesleyan University Press.

Shell, Robert Carl-Heinz (1994). "The Tower of Babel: The Slave Trade and Creolization at the Cape, 1652–1834." Elizabeth A. Eldredge and Fred Morton, eds. *Slavery in South Africa. Captive Labor on the Dutch Frontier*. Boulder/San Francisco/Oxford: University of Natal Press, 11–39.

Shell, Robert Carl-Heinz (2000). "Islam in Southern Africa, 1652–1998." Levtzion, Nehemia, Randall L. Pouwels, Nehemia Levtzion and Randall Pouwels, eds. *The History of Islam in Africa*. Athens, OH: Ohio University Press, 327–348.

Steiner, Tina (2012). "The Indian Ocean Travels of Sheikh Yusuf and Imam Ali Ali: Literary Representations in Ishtiyaq Shukri's The Silent Minaret and Achmat Dangor's Bitter Fruit." *Social Dynamics: A Journal of African Studies* 38.2, 172–183.

Thunberg, Carl Peter (1986 [1793–5]): *Travels at the Cape of Good Hope 1772–1775, based on the English edition London 1793–1795*. Cape Town: Jan van Riebeeck Society.

Upham, Mansell (2012). "What Can't be Cured, Must be Endured ... Cape of Good Hope – First Marriages & Baptisms (1652–1665)." *Uprooted Lives is an occasional series published by Remarkable Writing on First Fifty Years:* https://www.e-family.co.za/ffy/ui66.htm (July 23, 2023).

Ward, Kerry (2009). *Networks of Empire: Forced Migration in the Dutch East India Company*. Cambridge: Cambridge University Press.

Witmer, Olga (2022). "Between Compliance and Resistance: Lutherans and the Dutch Reformed Church at the Cape of Good Hope." *The Journal of Ecclesiastical History* 73.2, 326–347.

Worden, Nigel (2010). *Slavery in Dutch South Africa*. Cambridge: Cambridge University Press.

Worden, Nigel and Gerald Groenewald, eds. (2005). *Trials of Slavery. Selected Documents Concerning Enslaved People from the Criminal Records of the Council of Justice at the Cape of Good Hope, 1705–1794*. Cape Town: Paarl Print.

Worden, Nigel ed. (2012). *Cape Town between East and West. Social Identities in a Dutch Colonial Town*. Auckland Park: Jacana Media.

Philip Quaque: An Anglican Missionary Making Sense of Slavery on the Early Modern Gold Coast

Maximilian Rose

The life of Philip Quaque, the first person of African descent to be ordained in the Anglican church, an early Protestant missionary to West Africa, and a historical figure of national importance in modern-day Ghana, is deeply entangled with the Atlantic slave trade.[1] Quaque was born in 1740 or 1741 on the so-called Gold Coast and was raised in the Fante/Fetu settlement Oguaa, which hosted the British slave trading establishment Cape Coast Castle.[2] He enters the historical record in 1754, when the Anglican missionary Thomas Thompson and the Cape Coast power broker Birempon Kojo chose him as one of three boys to be educated in England.[3] Kojo was both a relative of Quaque and one of the most important African allies of the Company of Merchants Trading to Africa (CMTA) under the anglicised name Cudjoe Caboceer.[4]

Quaque spent the years between 1754 and 1766 in London, where he was educated in two private households and ordained as an Anglican priest in 1765. In 1766, he was sent out in a joint venture by the Society for the Propagation of the Gospel in Foreign Parts (SPG) and the CMTA as a missionary, chaplain

1 On the ways in which Quaque is discussed in contemporary Ghana see Holsey, *Routes of Remembrance*, 48, 144, 186–187.

2 On Cape Coast Castle and its relationship with the Fante/Fetu host community see St. Clair, *Cape Coast*. The only means of reconstructing Quaque's year of birth are the "rank lists" of Cape Coast Castle. Quaque was listed as 55 years old in 1795; Rank List 6th February 1795, The National Archives [TNA], T70/1571.

3 Bodleian Libraries Oxford [BLO], Papers of the United Society for Propagating the Gospel [USPG Papers], Journal 12 (170–1752), 391–392; Thompson, *Two Voyages*, 66–67.

4 The most extensive assessment of Cudjoe's role is Deffontaine, "Brɛmpɔng Kojo", 188–213. He asserts that Oguaa elites presented themselves as functionaries of a Fetu kingdom until the mid-eighteenth century and afterwards shaped the settlement into a state in its own right. English language accounts tend to portray Cudjoe as one of several "big men" of the Fante coalition; Reese, "Eating Luxury"; Law, "The Government of Fante". I will use the anglicised name Cudjoe Caboceer since this is the terminology Quaque used in his letters. Quaque is sometimes still called a son of Cudjoe Caboceer; Casely-Hayford, *Genealogical History*, 67, 73–79. Newer studies tend to follow Thomas Thompson's and the SPG's framing as merely a "relation"; BLO, USPG Papers, Journal 12 (1750–1754), 391; Thompson, *Two Voyages*, 67; Glasson, *Mastering Christianity*, 176–177; Andrews, "Black Evangelist", 663–691; Quaque, *Letters*, 6.

 | DOI:10.30965/9783657796328_005

and school master to Cape Coast Castle.[5] As chaplain, Quaque was an officer of the company which operated the infrastructure of the English Atlantic slave trade on the Gold Coast, ranking just below the commanders of the Gold Coast forts and outranking all other administrative staff on the coast.[6] With a short intermission in the early 1780s, Quaque spent the rest of his life at Cape Coast where he died in 1816. Alongside Governor George Maclean and his wife Letitia Landon, Philip Quaque is one of three people who were buried in the castle's courtyard.[7]

Over the course of 200 years of discussing Philip Quaque's life and work, his relationship to the Atlantic slave trade and slavery on the Gold Coast has been subjected to much scrutiny. In addition to pointing out the various ways in which Quaque was entangled with the Atlantic slave trade, scholars have searched the missionary's letters for expressions of sympathy for the enslaved, potential criticisms of the Atlantic slave trade and indicators of abolitionist sentiment.[8] While some of these discussions are more sophisticated than others, they are lacking in two ways. On the one hand, they tend to overemphasise Quaque's anti-slavery sentiment and (covert) complicity with abolitionist arguments.[9] On the other hand, they struggle to reconcile anti-slavery comments made by Quaque with the fact that the missionary was also a slave owner. Drawing on both well-known passages and new archival material, I argue that the apparent incongruencies in the historical materials regarding Quaque's view of slavery fall into place when considering the development of anti-slavery thought over the eighteenth century as well as the plural understanding of slavery which prevailed in eighteenth- and nineteenth-century Gold Coast societies.

The Atlantic Slave Trade

The idea of converting enslaved people to Christianity was controversial in the eighteenth-century Protestant Atlantic world. The religious status of the

5 Bartels, "Philip Quaque, 1741–1816".

6 Rank List 6th February 1795, TNA, T70/1571. On several occasions, he even took interim command of one of the company's outer forts; Glasson, *Mastering Christianity*, 187; Philip Quaque to the Committee of the CMTA, Aug. 10, 1784, London, TNA, T70/1551A.

7 Holsey, *Routes of Remembrance*, 186.

8 Klingenberg, "Quaque"; Priestley, "Quaque of Cape Coast"; Reese, "Anglican Mission", 366; Andrews, "Black Evangelist", 184–188; Quaque, *Letters*, 18–20; Glasson, *Mastering Christianity*, 186–189.

9 A notable aberration from this pattern is Adéẹ̀kọ́, "Writing Africa", 11–13.

enslaved was so often employed in the conceptual justification of slavery that converting an enslaved person to Protestantism seemed to many believers like a contradiction in terms.[10] This conflict often played out in the plantation societies of the Caribbean and North America. Here, missionaries and slave owners fretted over the question of whether or not conversion to protestant Christianity had an impact on the status of slaves and debated if enslaved people should be allowed to congregate for Christian services or learn to read.[11]

Many proponents of protestant mission among the enslaved articulated arguments which fell under the broad umbrella of what Christopher Leslie Brown has called "anti-slavery before abolitionism". Anti-slavery sentiment before abolitionism took many forms but one of its branches entailed emphasising the need to convert the enslaved and harshly criticizing the behaviour of slave owners outside the English metropole. At the same time, these anti-slavery arguments did not question the legitimacy of the slave system on a more fundamental level.[12] Over the course of the eighteenth century, the push for Protestant mission among enslaved populations became inextricably linked to an argument that evangelisation could and had to be reconciled with slavery, both in theory and in practice.[13]

The SPG was deeply involved in this process. Supporters of and missionaries employed by the organisation assured slave masters in North American and Caribbean mission fields that slavery and mission were not incompatible with each other in the hopes of gaining better access to enslaved populations. They continued to promote a kind of reformism which emphasised the moral obligations of Christian slave owners and sometimes left room to criticise especially brutal practices. Nevertheless, the economic interests of the Society became increasingly entangled with those of the Caribbean planter class, especially after it inherited Codrington plantation in 1710. If the SPG preached amelioration in theory, it perpetuated the practices of the West Indian slave regime in all its forms in practice.[14] As Katherine Gerbner has put it, "the Society […] molded itself to the demands of plantation slavery, not the other

10 Katharine Gerbner has called this "protestant supremacy"; Gerbner, *Christian Slavery*, 31–48. The case law on slavery in the British empire reflected this concern with baptism; Wiecek, "Lord Mansfield and the Legitimacy of Slavery".

11 Glasson, *Mastering Christianity*, 76–111; Gerbner, *Christian Slavery*, 31–137; Sensbach, *Rebecca's Revival*, 52–59.

12 Brown, *Moral Capital*, 55–75. See also Glasson, *Mastering Christianity*, 48–55.

13 Glasson, *Mastering Christianity*, 76–171; Gerbner, *Christian Slavery*, 74–196; Hüsgen, *Mission und Sklaverei*, 2016, 28–51.

14 Frey and Wood, *Come Shouting to Zion*, 63–79; Glasson, *Mastering Christianity*, 142–170; Gerbner, *Christian Slavery*, 112–137; Brown, *Moral Capital*, 352–364; Strong, *Anglicanism and Empire*, 87–114. The first articulation of the SPG's ameliorationist position in the 1711

way around".[15] Claus Füllberg-Stollberg has even suggested that, by the end of the eighteenth century, the presence of non-abolitionist protestant missionaries in the Caribbean was regarded by many as a stabilising factor for the institution of plantation slavery.[16]

On a much smaller scale than the Americas, the Gold Coast was seen as a sort of case study for the compatibility of slavery and mission in the eighteenth century. Two of the five protestant missionaries who spent significant time on the Gold Coast in this period published treatises on the subject. The African Calvinist missionary and chaplain Jacobus Capitein published a defence of slavery in 1742, shortly before his departure to the Gold Coast. In this treatise, Capitein argued that slavery as a system was legitimate in the Christian tradition and would not be undermined by proselytizing the enslaved.[17] Scholars have interpreted Capitein's public statements about slavery as a means of popularising the idea of mission among Africans on the Gold Coast to a Dutch Calvinist public.[18]

Thomas Thompson, the first Anglican missionary on the Gold Coast, was similarly sensitised to the discourse on slavery and mission. Thompson was a typical SPG missionary of the Atlantic. He had become interested in working among the enslaved during his tenure in New Jersey between 1745 and 1750, after which he embarked on an SPG sponsored missionary voyage to the Gold Coast.[19] Thompson's work among the enslaved was rooted in a belief that conversion could be reconciled both with the slave status of the converted and the practice of the Atlantic slave trade. In 1772, long after his return from the Gold Coast, Thompson published the pamphlet "The African Trade for Slaves, Shewn to be Consistent with the Principles of Humanity, and with the Laws of Revealed Religion".[20] This essay was conceived as a reaction to the famous Somerset vs. Stuart case of 1772 and became a part of the nascent public discussion about the abolition of the Atlantic slave trade in England as it prompted an answer from the eminent abolitionist Granville Sharp.[21] In the pamphlet, the former missionary admitted that the human suffering of enslaved Africans was undeniable but argued that it was nevertheless acceptable for three

anniversary sermon was a direct reaction to the Codrington bequest; Titus, "SPG and the Barbadian Plantations", 251–252.

15 Gerbner, *Christian Slavery*, 136.

16 Füllberg-Stolberg, "Herrnhuter Mission Sklaverei".

17 Parker, *Agony of Asar*, 64–65.

18 Parker, *Agony of Asar*; Amponsah, "Christian Slavery", 432; Hondius, "Capitein", 136–38.

19 Thompson, *Two Voyages*, 11.

20 Thompson, *African Trade for Slaves*.

21 Glasson, *Mastering Christianity*, 205–207.

reasons. Firstly, Africans traded in slaves among themselves. Secondly, English commerce depended on slave labour in the West Indies and abolition was impracticable. Thirdly, slave owning and trading was permissible in the bible and could be practiced in accordance with what Thompson called the "principles of humanity".[22]

Philip Quaque was generally well informed about phenomena of the Atlantic world and maintained a personal correspondence with Thomas Thompson until at least 1772.[23] The position he articulated on the compatibility of slavery and mission was difficult to reconcile with the line towed by Thompson and many SPG affiliated missionaries. Quaque concluded that the practices of the Atlantic *slave trade* as they manifested themselves on the Gold Coast were a hinderance to Christianity. As early as 1767, he observed in a letter to the SPG that "in these parts [...] the stir of Religion & its Everlasting Recompense is not so much in vogue as the vicious practice of purchasing Flesh & Blood like Oxens in Market Places".[24] He reiterated the sentiment in 1769 when he wrote "that cursed Slave Trade is the only Obstruction to the Minist[e]ring in these desolate parts".[25]

In part, these statements were a condemnation of CMTA employees on the Gold Coast, whom Quaque often portrayed as more interested in vice and profit than Christianity.[26] Quaque asserted that "the Garrison [...] does not approve of [Christian] Service on account of the branch of business which they are obliged to follow".[27] Governor Gilbert Petrie in particular, Quaque argued, "would have no more to do with Prayers while he can purchase slaves at a cheap rate".[28] However, Quaque also aimed to convey the idea that the business of selling slaves could not be reconciled with mission among non-Christians.

The strategy for converting Gold Coast Africans prescribed by Thomas Thompson, which Quaque followed, was built on the idea of gaining the support of exalted Cape Coast personalities like Cudjoe Caboceer who depended on the Atlantic slave trade for their wealth and social status.[29] In a letter from 1782, Quaque gave the assessment: "while Countenance is given to the practice

22 Thompson, *African Trade for Slaves*.

23 Quaque, *Letters*, 99–100.

24 Quaque, *Letters*, 66.

25 Quaque, *Letters*, 77.

26 The other principal vice of the garrison Quaque objected to was the practice of "coastal marriages"; Quaque, *Letters*, 36, 41–42, 67, 76, 81. The practice has been researched for the Dutch and Danish Gold Coast establishments; Everts, "Cherchez la Femme"; Ipsen, *Daughters of the Trade*.

27 Quaque, *Letters*, 94.

28 Quaque, *Letters*, 51.

29 Quaque, *Letters*, 8; Glasson, *Mastering Christianity*, 166–167.

of Slavery, Religion will prove to Us in these Parts [...] a stumbling Block, and to the Heathens who we earnestly wish may become [part of] the Kingdom of God & of his Christ, Foolishness", thereby implying that the Fante, whose livelihood depended on the Atlantic slave trade, had nothing to gain from converting.[30] The same also applied to less exalted personalities of Gold Coast society. Quaque remarked that "Necessity has driven many promising Youths to get their Fortune by such way of Trafick" which made it their "aim & Interest to oppose the means [...] to make Religion flourish & abound".[31]

Quaque's articulation of these opinions was not limited to his correspondence with the committee of the SPG. Philip Quaque was a public figure of sorts in the eighteenth-century protestant Atlantic. His presence in England as well as the ordination were announced to an English-language reading public by two articles in *Gentleman's Magazine* in 1755 and 1765.[32] Between 1767 and 1785, reports of his progress (or the apparent lack thereof) and the occasional abridged version of his letters were featured in the SPG's annual printed reports.[33]

This public exposure to what Edward E. Andrews has called the "protestant international" lead to interactions with a group of North American clergymen with an interest in questions concerning the Atlantic slave trade.[34] Quaque corresponded with the former SPG missionary and intellectual Samuel Johnson, the SPG missionary and future bishop of Massachusetts Edward Bass, the SPG missionary Samuel Fayerweather and Samuel Hopkins, a prominent Rode Island anti-slavery Congregationalist.[35] All of these men knew each other, either personally or through correspondence, and shared information about Quaque.[36] Hopkins in particular presented Quaque to a New England protestant public and, among others, alerted the freedwoman and writer Phillis Wheatley to his existence.[37] This coterie of New Englanders was undoubtedly interested in Quaque as a supposedly "native" missionary

30 Quaque, *Letters*, 161.
31 Quaque, *Letters*, 77.
32 Quaque, *Letters*, 189–191.
33 The first and last report Quaque appeared in were (1767) *A Sermon before the Society*, 70–71 and (1785) *A Sermon before the Society*, 51–52.
34 Andrews, "Protestant International".
35 Quaque, *Letters*, 111–118. On Hopkins' anti-slavery see Kidd, *The Great Awakening*, 228–232; Lovejoy, "Samuel Hopkins", 227–243.
36 Fayerweather had heard about Quaque from Johnson and, in turn, informed Hopkins; Quaque, *Letters*, 99, 110.
37 Wheatley, *The Writings*, 205–206.

to Africa.[38] However, while the SPG reports never mentioned Quaque's comments on slavery, the Americans also saw Quaque as an appropriate informant on the supply side of the Atlantic slave trade.

Samuel Hopkins, who published a pamphlet sharply criticising the Atlantic slave trade and slavery in the Americas in 1776, was particularly interested in this topic.[39] At one point in the early 1770s, Hopkins seems to have asked Quaque about the origins of the trade. Quaque wrote:

> the way in which that horrid, Barbarious and Inhuman Practice became in use was in former Times when but very few Europeans found the Settlement in Africa, […] [the Fante] at last had the Resolution of bringing the head of a Captive Slain to an European commanding Chief at that Time, who accepted it, and in return gave them also a small Present. [B]ut they afterwards making it a common practice, he refused, but desired that [the captives] for the future might not be killed, but be brought him alive, […] [a]nd from this Circumstance it has continued ever since.[40]

This is one of the few comments in which Quaque does not explicitly frame the Atlantic slave trade as a spiritual issue. Instead, he portrayed enslavement as an act of mercy mitigating the barbarity of the African populations of the Gold Coast, specifically the Fante.

This argument was frequently employed by apologists of slave trading in the eighteenth century and was a building block of Thomas Thompson's 1772 defence of slavery.[41] Quaque, however, appropriated the narrative for his own purposes. He enriched the analysis by inserting a degree of local expertise about the ways in which the Fante conducted themselves in war by emphasising the importance of severed heads, which was a topic he was generally interested in and appalled by.[42] The narrative of decapitation and "head taking" had been a staple of travelogues about the Gold Coast in the seventeenth century.

---

38 Quaque, *Letters*, 127. Samuel Hopkins considered Quaque a potential supporter of a missionary project which envisaged sending the freedmen Bristol Yamma and John Quamine to the Gold Coast port of Anomabo as missionaries. Quaque gave some general advice, made some inquiries about the two boys' families and appeared as a "black, and native" testimonial for the feasibility of the endeavour in Hopkins' printed appeal to the public for funding the mission; Styles and Hopkins, *Address to the Public.*

39 Hopkins, *Dialogue, Concerning Slavery.*

40 Quaque, *Letters*, 113.

41 Thompson, *Trade for Slaves*, 19.

42 Quaque, *Letters*, 71. On the importance of severed heads in Gold Coast warfare see Parker, *In My Time of Dying*, 109–110.

Stephanie Smallwood hypothesizes that the shift from killing to selling surplus captives may have had a basis in historical reality.[43]

In Quaque's account of this shift, the coastal Fante populations were the originators of the trade because of their proclivity to violence, duplicity and greed. The continuation of the trade made it difficult to reform the Fante because their economic survival depended on the qualities which had led to the slave trade in the first place and exacerbated them. Quaque commented that currently "they not only dispose of their Brethren as captive slaves taken in War, but make the Practice of stealing and kidnapping their Neighbours, and secretly making away with them".[44] Europeans of the present day, on the other hand, were at fault for continuing the practice of buying enslaved people from Africa even though it was conspicuously amoral.[45]

These assessments do not seem to have influenced Hopkins' thinking on slavery to a significant degree or found a large echo in mainstream abolitionist thinking.[46] Nevertheless, the idea Philip Quaque expressed that the Atlantic slave trade hampered the Christian reform of Fante society tied in well with Abolitionist ideas that the trade corrupted African populations.[47] Quaque's role as an informant to abolitionists on the supply side of the Atlantic slave trade was thus not at an end. In the 1790s, his information appeared in depositions before the House of Commons. In 1790, the abolitionist Alexander Falconbridge testified that Quaque had assured him most Africans were enslaved "by kidnapping" and not as a result of legitimate legal trials.[48] In a similar vein, the Marine Lieutenant John Simpson testified in 1791 that Philip Quaque had informed him about wars "in the interior parts

43 Smallwood, *Saltwater Slavery*, 21–23.

44 Quaque, *Letters*, 113.

45 Quaque, *Letters*, 113.

46 Hopkins' pamphlet on slavery was focused on North America and economic questions. His description of the mechanisms by which Africans were enslaved bears some general resemblance to Quaque's deliberations but differs so much in the specifics that it is doubtful if Quaque was the main informant; "The Europeans, English, French, Dutch, &c. have carried on a trade with [Africans] for above 100 years; and have taken advantage of their ignorance and barbarity, to perswade them to enter into the inhuman practice of selling one another to the European, for the commodities which they carry to them, most of which, they stand in no real need of: but might live as well, or better without them: particularly spirituous liquors, which have been carried to them in great quantities, by the Americans. They by this means have tempted and excited the blacks to make war upon one another, in order to get captives, spreading distress, devastation and destruction"; Hopkins, *Dialogue, Concerning Slavery*, 7–8.

47 For these ideas see, among others, Hopkins, *Dialogue, Concerning Slavery*, 7–8 or Olaudah Equiano's account of Igbo Society; Carretta, *Equiano*, 1–16.

48 (1790) *Minutes, Reported to the House*, 585; Quaque, *Letters*, 20.

of Africa for the sole purpose of procuring Slaves."[49] There is no way to know if Quaque was aware that the information he provided was being used to aid the abolitionist cause or that he consciously provided information to further abolitionism.

In the meantime, the American revolutionary war provoked Philip Quaque's first comment about slavery in the Atlantic world which was not limited to the Gold Coast. Prompted by Edward Bass mentioning the slave trade, he articulated an understanding that the Gold Coast export of slaves was directly connected to American slave economies by accusing his North American colleague of hypocrisy. He exclaimed "[y]ou upon whom the light of the Gospel flourishes and abound[s], [...] find the Hardships of Bondage and Opression! [...] I behold with Sorrowful sighing my poor abject Countryman over whom You, without the Bowels of Christian Love and Pity, hold in cruel Bondage."[50] Quaque expressed outrage at the idea that Americans were oppressed by Britain and contrasted this state of affairs with the oppression experienced by Gold Coast people in the Americas, which he regarded as obvious.

Two things are remarkable about this passage. On the one hand, Quaque once more conceptualised enslavement as a spiritual problem. He positioned the "bondage" in question as analogous to the "wretched state" of heathenism and ended the passage in an exhortation to more missionary endeavour by "encouraging the Heathen World to partake of the brightness of God's Glory and the precious Promises of the Gospel."[51] On the other hand, he proved that he was attuned to the discourses about slavery in the Atlantic world. The irony of North American slave holders using the metaphor of fighting British slavery and oppression to justify their rebellion while enslaving large numbers of black men and women was not lost on contemporaries. While this was sometimes used to discredit the rebellion, North American anti-slavery advocates reacted by attempting to tie criticisms of slavery to the patriot cause.[52] Quaque was clearly aware of the contours of the debate and used it to criticise the hypocrisy of the patriot pro-slavery position but left it up to the reader to decide whether he was sympathetic to a reformist or leaned towards an abolitionist position.

Despite this degree of ambiguity, the sentiment Quaque expressed displayed deep roots in a reformist line of thinking in the mould of British anti-slavery thought before abolitionism. Glasson has suggested that Quaque had

49 (1791) *Minutes of the Evidence before the House of Commons*, 40; Quaque, *Letters*, 20.
50 Quaque, *Letters*, 128.
51 Quaque, *Letters*, 128.
52 Rugemer, *Slave Law and the Politics of Resistance*, 171–212.

been influenced by egalitarian Methodist ideas during his upbringing in London in the 1740s and 50s.[53] This may have been the case but there was also ample Anglican anti-slavery sentiment to draw from. William Warburton, for example, made a forceful reformist argument in the SPG's 1766 anniversary sermon, which Quaque may have read.[54] Similarly, Belby Porteus, the bishop of Chester, had used the 1783 annual sermon to the Society as a platform for positioning the SPG as a leading institution of the reform of Caribbean slavery. He argued that the enslaved were dehumanised in the current system and needed to be treated better in order to give them an opportunity to civilise. This programme would eventually lead to freedom for some of the enslaved but only by degrees.[55] Philip Quaque must have been familiar with Porteus' stance. In 1783 and 1784, he spent several months in London, where he stayed with the Rev. John Moore, the son of his late teacher of the same name.[56] During this sojourn, he must have acquainted himself with the SPG's and other Anglican clergy's newest opinions about Atlantic slavery and witnessed the opening phases of the decades-long controversy over abolition.

This renewed immersion in the controversy about the Atlantic slave trade and slavery in the Americas may be reflected in Quaque's last letter which commented on the subject. In 1786, he described a slave rebellion during which enslaved persons captured the Dutch slaver *Neptunus* while it lay at anchor on the Gold Coast. An English ship trying to recapture the *Neptunus* to reenslave the rebels had fired a shot at the vessel and caused an Explosion in which all but seven of the mutineers perished.[57] Quaque blamed the brutal behaviour of the ship's captain for the incident which he considered illustrative of "the true picture of Inhumanity those unhappy Creatures suffer in their Miserable State of Bondage under the different degrees of austere Masters they unfortunately fall in with in the West Indies."[58] This statement fused the African and American sides of the Atlantic slave trade together by acknowledging that the enslaved Africans were mistreated while they were on the Neptunus in the same way they would be mistreated in the Caribbean. Quaque

53 Glasson, *Mastering Christianity*, 177.

54 Andrews, "Black Evangelist", 686; (1766) *A Sermon before the Society*, 25–6. For Quaque reading the anniversary sermons see Quaque, *Letters*, 108, 120. On Anglican "uneasiness" about the Atlantic slave trade from the 1740s onwards see also Strong, *Anglicanism and Empire*, 96–102.

55 Carretta, *Equiano*, 236; Strong, *Anglicanism and Empire*, 97–98.

56 Quaque, *Letters*, 165–167; Philip Quaque to the Committee of the CMTA, Aug. 10, 1784, London, TNA, T70/1551A.

57 Glasson, *Mastering Christianity*, 189–190. The details of the action are in Postma, *Dutch in the Atlantic Slave Trade*, 167.

58 Quaque, *Letters*, 171.

thus articulated a generalisable critique of slave owners operating within the framework of Atlantic slavery which put the blame at the feet of the analogous personalities of the Captain and the planter.

Slavery on the Gold Coast

Scholars have long wondered how Philip Quaque interacted with the trading society of the Gold Coast, where virtually all people and systems he came into contact with were dependent on the slave trade economically. The eighteenth-century Gold Coast was a slave society in a very different way than the plantation economies of the Americas. Instead of a clearly discernible body of enslaved persons, there were various groups of enslaved and unfree persons: In the European slave forts and factories, the men and women who were sold into the Atlantic slave trade were kept in underground dungeons and separated from the general population as thoroughly as possible.[59] These enslaved persons were provided by vast networks of slave markets and routes which reached far inland.[60]

In addition to the supply networks of the Atlantic slave trade, persons referred to as "company slaves" were involved in the daily business of operating the European establishments as canoe people, carpenters, smiths, labourers and sometimes soldiers.[61] European trading companies claimed ownership rights over these men and women, but they were typically not sold into Atlantic slavery, received wages and formed communities outside the walls of the European forts which has led some scholars to argue that they were a "wage labour 'class' in the making".[62] Another group of enslaved people were owned privately by European traders, soldiers, sailors and craftspeople. It is unclear what exactly the legal status of these men and women was and their number on the Gold Coast is very difficult to determine but they do sometimes appear in narrative accounts of the early modern Gold Coast.[63]

In addition to these groups, both European and African traders on the Gold Coast depended on an elaborate system of pawnship. Pawns were temporarily

---

59 St. Clair, *Cape Coast*, 78–81; DeCorse, "Forts of West Africa", 176–177.

60 Lovejoy, *Transformations in Slavery*, 95–101. For a Gold Coast case study see Perbi and Bredwa-Mensah, "Slave Camps in Pre-Colonial Ghana".

61 Reese, "Company Slaves at Cape Coast Castle". A rough estimate of company slaves on the eighteenth-century Gold Coast is 500 belonging to the English forts, 350 to the Dutch forts and 100–200 to Danish Christiansborg; Shumway, "Castle Slaves", 85.

62 Hernæs, "Fort Slaves".

63 For an example see Ipsen, *Daughters of the Trade*, 108–110.

unfree persons who served as securities for loans. Debtors would typically pawn members of their family to creditors, both as collateral and for their labour force to serve as a sort of interest payment. These men and women were not necessarily reduced to slave status, but they were an important means for Gold Coast traders and slavers to make large amounts of capital available at opportune times.[64] Finally, Fante, Ga and other African elites on the Gold Coast exploited the labour of large numbers of enslaved people. Gold Coast slavery was interwoven with kinship structures and manifestly less commodified than Atlantic slavery. In this system, enslaved people could not be acquired and discarded like chattel but were regarded as members of the household with certain rights and obligations. The Gold Coast system of slavery thus differed from the chattel slavery of the Atlantic in some important ways but the two slave systems also sustained and influenced each other.[65]

Some scholars have suggested that Philip Quaque was personally involved these forms of Gold Coast slavery. One piece of evidence they have pointed to is the fact that Quaque referred to his second wife as "Property of [his] own".[66] Quaque explained that this woman was his late "Spouse's waiting maid giving her by [his] Grand-father Cudjo Cabosheer".[67] In addition to this passing remark, there are indicators that Quaque benefitted from the labour of company slaves, for example a "Chappel servant" named Adjumacon.[68]

There is now also a solid body of evidence which shows that Philip Quaque did indeed buy, sell and own moderate numbers of enslaved people over the course of his life. The first group of sources showing this are the so-called lists of "dead men's effects" which were kept by the CMTA. Whenever an employee of the Company died on the Gold Coast, their belongings were sold to the highest bidder at an auction. The names of the purchasers, the goods sold and the prices paid were recorded in minute detail. In 1785, Philip Quaque bought a "very old woman slave" at an auction at Cape Coast Castle for 2£ 5s.[69] This purchase has previously been reported by William St. Clair and interpreted by Travis Glasson as well as Vincent Carretta and Ty Reese as a possible act of

64 On this system generally and its implementation on the Gold Coast see Lovejoy, "Pawnship, Debt, and 'Freedom'"; Spricksley, "Pawns on the Gold Coast"; Sparks, "Pawning".

65 For the area of modern-day Ghana see Perbi, *Indigenous Slavery*, 4–8, 113–130. For a wider African perspective see Lovejoy, Kopytoff and Cooper, "Indigenous African Slavery"; Lovejoy, *Transformations in Slavery.*

66 Quaque, *Letters*, 89.

67 Quaque, *Letters*, 86. For analyses based on these passages see Quaque, *Letters*, 13; Glasson, *Mastering Christianity*, 182; Adéẹ̀kọ́, "Writing Africa", 13.

68 Glasson, *Mastering Christianity*, 185.

69 TNA, T70/1503.

charity towards an elderly enslaved person.[70] In 1789, Quaque bought another person who seems to fit this pattern. At an auction for dead men's effects, he purchased "an old Man slave (wore out)" for 12£ 11s.[71] In 1795 Quaque purchased three persons which were described as "man slave bricklayers" and went for prices of 21£, 13£ and 4£ respectively.[72] The aim of this purchase was unambiguously economic. Quaque must have hoped to exploit these men's labour, either by putting them to work for wages or by employing them in construction work on the Quaque residence, which had been built in the early 1790s.[73]

Additional information on enslaved persons Philip Quaque claimed ownership of can be gleaned from a will written in 1813. This document details the many unfree and enslaved persons who lived and worked in the missionary's household. Among these were pawns as well as domestic servants in keeping with Gold Coast conventions of enslavement. Quaque recorded his intention of leaving an unspecified number of unfree "Households Servants" to three powerful Gold Coast men.[74] Among these men was Quaque's "nephew" Sam Kanto Brew whom both contemporaries and historians have described as one of the biggest illegal Euro-African Gold Coast slave traders after abolition and the most important middleman between the coast and Asante slavers during this era.[75] Among the household servants, Quaque's will referred to several enslaved persons in particular. He made a bequest of "a small Boy" to "a Mulatto child by name Quashie". To Ambah Sakah, his personal servant and care giver during his later life, Quaque left 4£. To Japah, a cooper, he gave his freedom, thereby confirming that Japah had formerly been enslaved.[76]

At the time of writing the will in 1813, the Quaque household also included a number of "pawns".[77] The presence of pawns suggests that Quaque gave larger lines of credit to Gold Coast traders or may have acted as a broker for transactions between other traders.[78] Another feature of the will which suggests that Quaque participated in coastal trading not only as a petty trader is the mention of Quashie Ansah, whom Quaque referred to as his "gold taker" for many years.[79] Gold takers were middlemen who boarded European ships on the

70 St. Clair, *Cape Coast*, 219; Glasson, *Mastering Christianity*, 189; Quaque, *Letters*, 18–19.

71 TNA, T70/1560.

72 TNA, T70/1504, 55–71.

73 Quaque, *Letters*, 199.

74 Last will and testament of Philip Quaque, June 1, 1813, CCC, TNA, T70/1601.

75 Priestley, *Family Study*, 129–142; Reynolds, *Trade and Economic Change*, 44.

76 Testament of Philip Quaque, TNA, T70/1601.

77 Testament of Philip Quaque, TNA, T70/1601.

78 On the purposes of pawning on the Gold Coast see Spricksley, "Pawns on the Gold Coast"; Sparks, "Pawning".

79 Testament of Philip Quaque, TNA, T70/1601.

behalf of coastal traders and negotiated the sale of goods as well as enslaved people.[80] None of these facts are necessarily indicative of involvement in Atlantic slave trading. They do, however, suggest that Quaque's proximity to the Atlantic slave trade shaped the means by which he ensured his economic survival in ways much more profound than has previously been suggested.

At least in the first half of the eighteenth century, it was not unusual for SPG missionaries to own people personally.[81] The idea of being a Christian slave owner tied in seamlessly with reformist ideas of the mid-eighteenth century SPG. Traces of this ideology are present in the way Quaque wrote about Gold Coast forms of slavery. As we have seen, he sharply criticised the way in which enslaved people were acquired in Fante society, which he associated with the brutalities of warfare and kidnapping. In addition, Quaque made a point of showing his disgust with the practice of sacrificing enslaved people at the funerals of exalted persons which was a part of the ritual repertoire of many West African and Gold Coast societies well into the nineteenth century.[82] Quaque commented on this phenomenon twice. In a description of the funeral of his Fante relative Cudjoe Caboceer in 1778, he lamented:

> the most detestable Scene in all their Actions is the Barbarious and Inhuman practice of Sacrificing innocent Lives as attendences to the Great Folks only in the other World, which Diabolical custom and mistakened vile Notion seems to prevail much with them[83]

In a similar vein, in 1813, Quaque accused a former spouse of "the horrid and detestable crime committed, that of suffering an innocent old Woman to be sold as a Sacrafice to be tortured and masacred to death for a person deceased".[84] Ever since the seventeenth century, the condemnation of human sacrifice in West African societies had been an important discourse for European commentators who used the practice as "an index of African barbarity".[85] In the nineteenth century, the condemnation of the "funeral custom" on the Gold Coast also became a fixture of Euro-African Christian self-representation and the ideologies of Fante elites.[86] By engaging in this discourse, Quaque set him-

80 Sparks, *African Port*, 149–150.
81 Glasson, *Mastering Christianity*, 101–102.
82 Perbi, "Slavery and Social Structure", 164–166; Law, "Human Sacrifice"; Parker, *In my Time of Dying*, 139–154.
83 Quaque, *Letters*, 134.
84 Testament of Philip Quaque, TNA, T70/1601.
85 Law, "Human Sacrifice", 53–56.
86 Shumway, "Anti-Slavery in Nineteenth Century Fanteland". See also the norms collected in Sarbah, *Fanti Customary Laws*.

self apart from non-Christian slave owners on the Gold Coast and projected the picture of a Christian patriarch who abhorred the extremes of non-Christian slave holding.

This attitude also becomes apparent in Quaque's only discussion of Christians owning enslaved people on the Gold Coast. In the same letter in which he described the sinking of the *Neptunus*, Quaque recalled an escape attempt of the fort slaves at Cape Coast Castle. He alleged that it was "easy to conceive that the Evils which they seem to complain of [...] bear an Affinity to the excess of Burden the Children of Israel suffered in the reign of the Pharao".[87] The use of the metaphor of the Egyptian captivity of the Jewish people for describing the plight of the fort slaves leaves room for several interpretations. On the one hand, the Egyptian captivity was a prominent explanatory device for the rejection of the Atlantic slave trade and plantation slavery in the Americas formulated by men such as the Methodist minister Henry Peckwell and especially the North American black missionary David Margrett.[88] On the other hand, it echoed the idea of the "fortunate fall" which interpreted the suffering of enslavement as a comparatively small price to pay for a chance at eternal salvation through Christianisation.[89] Even when discussing Gold Coast slavery, Quaque therefore remained in step with the reformist stance of the SPG. By employing the metaphor of the Egyptian captivity, he declared his sympathy for the enslaved while simultaneously retaining the implication that their enslavement was an opportunity for bettering themselves.

Despite these theoretical discussions of different forms of Gold Coast slavery, Philip Quaque's letters suggest that, like many of his SPG colleagues, he did not see a need, or maybe even a possibility, to discuss the intricacies of his ownership of people with his correspondents across the Atlantic world.[90] With the exception of two ambiguous references to an enslaved spouse, the missionary's letters do not contain any discussions of his personal interactions with

---

87 Quaque, *Letters*, 172.

88 Lockley, "David Margrett", 9–10; Sinha, *The Slave's Cause*, 29; Frey and Wood, *Come Shouting to Zion*, 113.

89 For a discussion of the concept in the writing of Phillis Wheatley and Olaudah Equiano see Carretta, *Equiano*, 171–175 and Andrews, *Native Apostles*, 195–197. The fortunate fall was also central to the public image of Jacobus Capitein and his defence of slavery; Parker, *Agony of Asar*, 47–50, 61. The Moravian church produced a pro-slavery version of the fortunate fall narrative when Nikolaus von Zinzendorf expressed his opinion that the saviour had made Africans slaves before they could become Christians; Müller, *200 Jahre Brüdermission*, 170; Unitätsarchiv Herrnhut, R.2.A.28.A, Barbyer Synodus 1. Quaque sometimes employed a variation of the fortunate fall theme to describe what he portrayed as his own deliverance from heathenism as a small boy; Quaque, *Letters*, 31.

90 Glasson, *Mastering Christianity*, 105.

institutions which a European or North American correspondent would have recognised as slavery. The SPG, in turn, was interested in their only African missionary's involvement in coastal slavery only in so far as they would have seen it as an indicator of his concern with trade in general. Prompted by a 1788 parliamentary inquiry into the slave trade, the SPG secretary William Morice expressed his anxiety that Quaque payed "more attention to the purposes of trade than of rel[igion]".[91]

Nevertheless, some elements of Philip Quaque's understanding of his ownership of people can be reconstructed from circumstantial evidence. Quaque often portrayed himself as a benevolent patriarch who was responsible for the well-being and Christian conformity of his small Christian community. As he grew older, he diligently reported his efforts (and his frequent failure) to protect those entrusted to his care from what he regarded as the double temptations of Gold Coast trading society and heathenism.[92] Quaque explicitly formulated the need to shield young Gold Coast Christians from these influences in his assessment of Samuel Hopkins' plan of sending two African-American missionaries to Anomabo. He wrote "the Nature and Disposition of the Coast […] are such that in a very little Time they would soon lead them to commit such Actions as will entangle them in such Difficulties that they will not easily Eradicate" but implied that he could not fulfil the role of protector.[93] He applied this logic to his own family in particular. Quaque described his third wife as a "tractable" woman and hoped "to bring her up in the Nurture & fear of the Lord", thus laying the foundation for a Christian Household.[94] He hoped to raise his children as Christians in this house and sent them to England to "secure their tender Minds from receiving the bad Impressions of the Country, the vile Customs and Practices".[95]

Quaque tried time and again to mobilise the support of the SPG and CMTA to establish a physical space for this community, household, and family.[96] By the early 1790s at the latest, he had succeeded in establishing a moderately wealthy, Europeanised homestead in Oguaa.[97] Enslaved persons were

91 Privy Council Enquiry re Missions to "The Coast of Africa or to the British West India Islands" Reply, BLO, USPG Papers, C/AFW/1/47, No. 48. The assessment of Quaque's work was printed in (1789) *Report of the Lords*.

92 Quaque, *Letters*, 71, 95, 98, 100, 126–127, 135, 153–154, 174.

93 Quaque, *Letters*, 112.

94 Quaque, *Letters*, 101.

95 Quaque, *Letters*, 154.

96 Quaque, *Letters*, 31–32, 65; Quaque to CMTA, TNA, T70/1551A.

97 Quaque, *Letters*, 199. This household included all the material markers of Europeanised Gold Coast lifestyles. On these lifestyles see Priestley, *Family Study*; Sparks, *African Port*, 68–121. An idea of the items which were present in the Quaque household can be gleaned

explicitly included in Quaque's conception of this household. In his will, he rewarded those "household servants" who had faithfully shown their adherence to his vision of good Christian behaviour with praise and presents and in one case even with their freedom. He then put the remaining enslaved people belonging to his household under the protection of powerful Gold Coast men, at least one of which was a Christian, so "that they not be injured by any soul existing".[98] At the same time, he emphasised that his vision of patriarchal authority encouraged the punishment of deviant behaviour by stressing that in the case that "any of [the household slaves] commit any grievous offence that merits a severe punishment" this punishment should "be inflicted as the nature of that crime deserved".[99]

The ideal of Christian Gold Coast slave holding was not uncommon in the eighteenth and nineteenth centuries. The Basel Missionary Society, for example, established a presence on the Gold Coast in 1828 and became involved in a conflict about the question of whether or not its missionaries should be allowed to own enslaved persons in the early 1860s.[100] In this debate, the Danish-Ga catechist and historian Carl Christian Reindorf insisted that "Christian slaveholders should be seen as a desirable part of African church life. They protect their slaves against the evils of heathenism."[101] This positive assessment of Gold Coast household slavery was often aided by the ways in which slavery in many West African societies differed from the chattel slavery of the Atlantic.[102]

The Akan societies Quaque came into contact with differentiated between various forms of servile and enslaved labourers. The most important Akan words to refer to enslaved people were *akoa*, meaning subject but also enslaved person of Akan origin, *odonkɔ*, meaning a foreign enslaved person, *akyere*, slaves who were subject to capital punishment and *awowa*, referring to pawns held for debt.[103] *Akoa* in particular was a generic term which did not only relate to slavery but described various relationships of subordination and servitude.

from the purchases recorded in the lists of dead men's effects in TNA, T70/1537, 1551A, 1560, 1586, 1596, 1598.

98 Testament of Philip Quaque, TNA, T70/1601.

99 Testament of Philip Quaque, TNA, T70/1601.

100 Haenger, *Slaves and Slave Holders*; Vogelsanger, *Pietismus und Afrikanische Kultur*.

101 Cited in Haenger, "Reindorf and the Basel Mission", 24. Reindorf's slave holding is also discussed in Haenger, *Slaves and Slave Holders*, 77–80.

102 This argument has been made in relation to Jacobus Capitein by Amponsah, "Christian Slavery".

103 Konadu, *Diaspora*, 89; Perbi, *Indigenous Slavery*, 3.

Simply put, *akoa* was not the signifier of a fixed status but a description of a set of relationships of dependence.[104]

Many eighteenth- and nineteenth-century commentators put forward the idea that there was a difference between these relationships of dependence and the Atlantic slave trade. The outspoken abolitionist Olaudah Equiano argued that, in Igbo society, enslaved people in a domestic context were valuable members of the community.[105] Similar arguments were put forward by educated Fante elites in the mid-nineteenth century.[106] The dispute around Gold Coast slavery in the Basel missionary society also unfolded along these lines. Carl Christian Reindorf insisted that household slavery on the Gold Coast was different from plantation slavery in the Americas and questioned if slavery was even the correct term to describe the phenomenon.[107] The missionary Johann Gottlieb Christaller's 1881 Twi dictionary recorded dozens of terms for servile or enslaved roles, with the most important one being *akoa* for subject, slave or servant.[108] Based on observations like these, his colleague Johannes Zimmermann argued that all social hierarchy in West Africa was based on relationships which were regarded as forms of slavery by Europeans. Zimmerman objected to the abolition of these institutions because he regarded them as the only guarantors of patriarchal hierarchy on the Gold Coast and a defence against secular ideas.[109]

While conclusive proof that Philip Quaque fell back on arguments similar to those used by Gold Coast personalities more than forty years after his death is lacking, they may serve to illustrate how a Christian reformist pro-slavery position could be combined with arguments about the relative benignancy of Gold Coast slavery. What is more, the conflict about mission slave holding between the Basel missionary society and its Gold Coast missionaries echoes a dispute about Quaque's slave holding which unfolded in the early years of the nineteenth century.

In the years 1806 and 1807, at a time when the abolition of the Atlantic Slave Trade in the British Empire was becoming a real possibility, John Fountaine, who was employed by the CMTA in the position of writer, was involved in a conflict with the garrison of Cape Coast Castle in general and the chaplain in

104 Perbi, "Slavery and Social Structure", 160.
105 Carretta, *Equiano*, 16.
106 Odijie, "Exploring African Abolitionism", 6–9.
107 Quarterly, *Mission Practices on the Gold Coast*, 146–147.
108 Christaller, *A Dictionary of the Asante and Fante Language*, 42, 269, 449, 501, 502, 629, 663.
109 Haenger, *Slaves and Slave Holders*, 6–10.

particular.[110] Fountaine was intimately familiar with Philip Quaque, both as a fellow employee of the CMTA and as a missionary. He was the son of the Rev. John Fountaine of Marylebone and had spent years on the Gold Coast as a CMTA employee in the 1770s and 1780s. During this time, Quaque and Fountaine had been on good terms with each other. In 1783, Philip Quaque even sent his son Samuel to England under Fountaine's supervision to be educated in the Marylebone parish house.[111]

By 1806, however, the relationship had broken down. Fountaine conceded that Quaque was "universally beloved in the Castle" but explained that the recent conduct of the chaplain and his children had led him to sever all ties.[112] The reasons for the rupture were manifold but one of the strategies Fountaine used to discredit Quaque in the eyes of his CMTA superiors was closely related to the latter man's role as a patriarch and slave owner. Fountaine accused Quaque of neglecting his children whom he thought amounted to nothing more than vagabonds stooping to various forms of petty criminality.[113] He also declared that "two of Mr. Quaques Castle attendants" had been sold off the coast for theft, thereby implying that Quaque was incapable of enforcing discipline among his (presumably enslaved) servants.[114] At the same time, Fontaine painted Quaque as an especially ruthless enslaver. He alleged: "I have known this man to have at the same time a very old man & his Son in Irons in the Slave hole for a demand [...] not exceeding six ackies".[115] He also made much of the allegation that Quaque bought and sold slaves on the sabbath, which he portrayed as the immediate reason for breaking off contact with the chaplain.[116]

Fountaine was not an abolitionist. In a 1789 deposition he had explained that Gold Coast slavery was the worst form of enslavement and that "the purchase of slaves by Europeans preserves their lives and adds to their ease and comfort".[117] Nevertheless, his letters show that, by 1806, accusations related to slave trading and ownership were conceived by some as a potent attack against a Protestant African missionary. This assumption did not always turn out to be correct. Fountaine's accusations were wholly ineffective in the London community of "old coasters": In the deliberations of the London Committee of the

110 Fontaine had lost his wife to yellow fever and was harassed by a group of young Company employees as well as Quaque's son Samuel; Porter and Porter, "An English Family at Cape Coast".

111 Quaque, *Letters*, 165; BLO, USPG Papers, Journal 23 (1782–1784), 196.

112 John Fountaine to the Committee of the CMTA, Mar. 29, 1806, CCC, TNA, T70/1584.

113 Fountaine to the CMTA, TNA, T70/1584.

114 Fountaine to the CMTA, TNA, T70/1584.

115 Fountaine to the CMTA, TNA, T70/1584.

116 Fountaine to the CMTA, TNA, T70/1584.

117 (1789) Number I. Minutes of Evidence, 46.

CMTA, his pleas and complaints featured very rarely and never prompted any action.[118] The accusations may have made a larger impact in a protestant public, large parts of which had moved beyond reformism and were convinced of the necessity of abolitionism by the early nineteenth century.[119] This public, however, had not taken note of Philip Quaque since the 1780s and never learned of Fountaine's allegations.

Conclusion

Over the course of his life, the Anglican missionary Philip Quaque was deeply involved in both the Atlantic slave trade and Gold Coast slavery. Quaque responded and contributed to an eighteenth-century discourse which aimed to integrate protestant mission into the slave system of the early modern Atlantic. Proponents of Christian slavery argued that slave trading and ownership could be reconciled with mission and enslaved people were not empowered in any meaningful way by becoming protestant Christians. Quaque employed his experience as a missionary to put forward the idea that at least the way in which the Atlantic slave trade manifested itself on the Gold Coast was an obstacle to mission because it encouraged unchristian behaviour among the people he sought to convert. This line of thinking lent itself well to arguments made by abolitionists who contacted Quaque several times to profit from his expertise on the supply side of the Atlantic slave trade. While Quaque's statements were vague enough to allow for both a reformist and an abolitionist reading, they did sometimes function as building blocks for abolitionist arguments.

Despite these comments on the manifestations of the Atlantic slave trade in West Africa, Quaque's ideas were rooted in the reformist arguments of missionary organisations like the SPG which left room to articulate criticisms of slavery but were based on the assumption that Christian slave holding was not only acceptable but had a role to play in missionary endeavour. Philip Quaque extended this idea of Christian slave holding to the Gold Coast where he bought, sold, owned and profited from the labour of a moderate number of enslaved people throughout his life. Quaque rarely shared glimpses of his understanding of the forms of ownership of enslaved people he personally engaged in. Nevertheless, the available sources suggest that he conceptualised them as a

118 Minute Book 1798–1806, TNA, T70/148; Minute Book 1807–1813, TNA, T70/149. Fountaine died in 1809 without ever having received an answer from his superiors; Governor and Council of CCC to the Committee of the Company, Jan. 25, 1809, CCC, TNA, T70/35, 136.

119 On the importance of the protestant public for British abolitionism from the 1780s onwards see for example Drescher, *Abolition*, 212–241.

Christian form of slavery in keeping with reformist ideas. These ideas may have combined with a conviction that the relationships of dependence which constituted Gold Coast slavery differed from Atlantic slavery since they were not a monolithic institution and did not turn enslaved persons into chattel.

For most of his life, the positions Philip Quaque took on slavery seem to have been little noticed and hardly controversial. Only in the early nineteenth century, with abolition on the horizon, did one detractor employ Quaque's treatment of enslaved people as an appropriate line of attack, thereby foreshadowing the disputes about slavery which missionaries in West Africa would be engaged in for the rest of the nineteenth century.

Works Cited

Adéẹ̀kọ́, Adélékè (2009). "Writing Africa under the Shadow of Slavery: Quaque, Wheatley, and Crowther." *Research in African Literatures* 40.4, 1–24.

Amponsah, David Kofi (2013). "Christian Slavery, Colonialism, and Violence: The Life and Writings of an African Ex-Slave, 1717–1747." *Journal of Africana Religions* 1.4, 431–457.

Andrews, Edward E. (2009). "Christian Missions and Colonial Empires Reconsidered: A Black Evangelist in West Africa, 1766–1816." *Journal of Church and State* 51.4, 663–691.

Andrews, Edward E. (2013). *Native Apostles. Black and Indian Missionaries in the British Atlantic World.* Cambridge, MA et al.: Harvard University Press.

Andrews, Edward E. (2017). "Tranquebar: Charting the Protestant International in the British Atlantic and Beyond." *William & Mary Quarterly* 74.1. 3–34.

(1766) *A Sermon Preached before the Incorporated Society* [...] *on Friday February 21, 1766.* London: E. Owen and T. Harrison.

(1767) *A Sermon Preached before the Incorporated Society* [...] *on Friday February 20, 1767.* London: E. Owen and T. Harrison.

(1785) *A Sermon Preached before the Incorporated Society* [...] *on Friday February 18, 1785.* London: T. Harrison and S. Brooke.

Bartels, Francis Lodowic (1955). "Philip Quaque, 1741–1816." *Transactions of the Gold Coast & Togoland Historical Society* 1.5, 153–177.

Brown, Christopher Leslie (2006). *Moral Capital. Foundations of British Abolitionism.* Chapel Hill: University of North Carolina Press.

Carretta, Vincent (2005). *Equiano the African. Biography of a Self-Made Man.* Athens, GA: University of Georgia Press.

Casely Hayford, Augustus Lavinus (1992). *A Genealogical History of Cape Coast Stool Families.* PhD diss. The School of Oriental and African Studies.

Christaller, Johann Gottlieb (1881). *A Dictionary of the Asante and Fante Language Called Tshi (Chwee, Tŵi)*. Basel: The Evangelical Missionary Society.

DeCorse, Christopher (2016). "Tools of Empire. Trade, Slaves, and the British Forts of West Africa." Daniel Maudlin and Bernard L. Herman eds. *Building the British Atlantic World: Spaces, Places, and Material Culture, 1600–1850*, Chapel Hill, NC: University of North Carolina Press, 165–187.

Deffontaine, Yann (1999). "Pouvoir monarchique et creation étatique sur la Côte de l'Or au XVIIIe siècle. Brɛmpɔng Kojo et la creation de l'Etat d'Oguaa (Cape Coast)." Valsecchi, Pierluigi and Fabio Viti eds. *Mondes Akan. Identité et pouvour en Afrique occidentale/Akan Worlds. Identity and Power in West Africa*. Paris et al.: L'Harmattan, 188–213.

Drescher, Seymour (2009). *Abolition. A History of Slavery and Antislavery*. Cambridge: Cambridge University Press.

Everts, Natalie (1996). "Cherchez la Femme. Gender-Related Issues in Eighteenth-Century Elmina." *Itinerario* 20.1, 45–57.

Frey, Sylvia R. and Betty Wood (1998). *Come Shouting to Zion. African American Protestantism in the American South and British Caribbean to 1830*. Chapel Hill, NC: University of North Carolina Press.

Füllberg-Stolberg, Claus (2011). "Die Herrnhuter Mission, Sklaverei und Sklavenemanzipation in der Karibik." Elisabeth Herrmann-Otto ed. *Sklaverei und Zwangsarbeit zwischen Akzeptanz und Widerstand*, Hildesheim et al.: Georg Olms Verlag, 254–280.

Gerbner, Katherine (2018). *Christian Slavery. Conversion and Race in the Protestant Atlantic World*, Philadelphia: University of Pennsylvania Press.

Glasson, Travis (2012). *Mastering Christianity. Missionary Anglicanism and Slavery in the Atlantic World*. Oxford et al.: Oxford University Press.

Haenger, Peter (1998). "Reindorf and the Basel Mission in the 1860s. A Young Man Stands Up to Mission Pressure." Paul Jenkins ed. *The Recovery of the West African Past. African Pastors and African History in the Nineteenth Century. C.C. Reindorf & Samuel Johnson*. Basel: Basler Afrika Bibliographien.

Haenger, Peter (2000). *Slaves and Slave Holders on the Gold Coast: Towards an Understanding of Social Bondage in West Africa*. Basel: P. Schlettwein.

Hernæs, Per (2002). "'Fort Slavery' at Christiansborg on the Gold Coast: Wage Labour in the Making?" Per Hernæs and Tore Iversen eds. *Slavery Across Time and Space. Studies in Slavery in Medieval Europe and Africa*. Trondheim: Department of History, NTNU, 197–229.

Holsey, Bayo (2008). *Routes of Remembrance. Refashioning the Slave Trade in Ghana*. Chicago et. al.: The University of Chicago Press.

Hondius, Dienke (2010). "'No Longer Strangers and Foreigners, but Fellow Citizens': The Voice and Dream of Jacobus Eliza Capitein, African Theologist in the Netherlands (1717–47)." *Immigrant & Minorities* 28.2–3, 131–153.

Hopkins, Samuel (1776). *A Dialogue, Concerning the Slavery of the Africans* […] *Dedicated to the Honorable the Continental Congress*. Norwich, CT: Judah P. Spooner.

Hüsgen, Jan (2016). *Mission und Sklaverei. Die Herrnhuter Brüdergemeine und die Sklavenemanzipation in Britisch- und Dänisch-Westindien*. Stuttgart: Franz Steiner.

Kidd, Thomas S. (2007). *The Great Awakening. The Roots of Evangelical Christianity in Colonial America*. New Haven et al.: Yale University Press, 228–232.

Ipsen, Pernille (2015). *Daughters of the Trade. Atlantic Slavers and Interracial Marriage on the Gold Coast*. Philadelphia: University of Pennsylvania Press.

Klingenberg, Frank J. (1939). "Philip Quaque: Pioneer Native Missionary on the Gold Coast, 1765–1816." *The Journal of Negro Education* 8.4 (1939), 656–672.

Konadu, Kwasi (2010). *The Akan Diaspora in the Americas*. Oxford and New York: Oxford University Press.

Law, Robin (1985). "Human Sacrifice in Pre-Colonial West Africa." *African Affairs* 84.334, 53–87.

Law, Robin (2013). "The Government of Fante in the Seventeenth Century." *Journal of African History* 54, 31–51.

Lockley, Tim (2012). "David Margrett: A Black Missionary in the Revolutionary Atlantic." *Journal of American Studies* 46.3, 1–17.

Lovejoy, David S. (1967). "Samuel Hopkins: Religion, Slavery, and the Revolution." *The New England Quarterly* 40.2, 227–243.

Lovejoy, Paul E. (2014). "Pawnship, Debt, and 'Freedom' in Atlantic Africa during the Era of the Slave Trade: A Reassessment." *Journal of African History* 55, 55–78.

Lovejoy, Paul E. (2012). *Transformations in Slavery. A History of Slavery in Africa*. 3rd ed. Cambridge et al.: Cambridge University Press.

Lovejoy, Paul E., Igor Kopytoff and Frederick Cooper (1979). "Indigenous African Slavery [with Commentary]." *Historical Reflections / Réflexions Historiques* 6.1, 19–83.

(1791) *Minutes of the Evidence Taken before the House of Commons* […] *respecting the African Slave Trade*. London: n.p.

(1790) *Minutes, Reported to the House,* […] *on the Part of Petitioners, who have petitioned the House of Commons against the Abolition of the Slave Trade*. London: n.p.

Müller, Karl (1931). *200 Jahre Brüdermission, 1. Band, Das erste Missionsjahrhundert*. Herrnhut: Verlag der Missionsbuchhandlung.

Odijie, Michael Ehis (2024). "Exploring African Abolitionism: Fante Perspectives on Domestic Slavery in the Nineteenth-Century Gold Coast." *Law and History Review* 42.1 (2024), 1–22.

Parker, Grant (2001). *The Agony of Asar: A Thesis on Slavery by the Former Slave*. Princeton, NJ: Markus Wiener.

Parker, John (2021). *In My Time of Dying. A History of Death and the Dead in West Africa*. Princeton et al.: Princeton University Press.

Perbi, Akosua Adoma (2004). *A History of Indigenous Slavery in Ghana. From the 15th to the 19th Century*. Accra: Sub-Saharan Publishers.

Perbi, Akosua Adoma and Yaw Bredwa-Mensah (2007). "Slave Camps in Pre-Colonial Ghana: The Case of Jenini in the Brong Ahafo Region" James Kwesi Anquandah, ed. *The Transatlantic Slave Trade: Landmarks, Legacies, Expectations*. Accra: Sub-Saharan Publishers, 138–147.

Perbi, Akosua Adoma (2002). "Slavery and Ghana's Pre-Colonial Social Structure" Per Hernæs and Tore Iversen eds. *Slavery across Time and Space. Studies in Slavery in Medieval Europe and Africa*. Trondheim: Department of History, NTNU, 159–172.

Perbi, Akosua Adoma (1992). "The Relationship between the Domestic Slave Trade and the External Slave Trade in Pre-Colonial Ghana." *Research Review* 8.1–2, 64–75.

Porter, R. and A. Porter (1968). "An English Family at Cape Coast 1802–1804." *Transactions of the Historical Society of Ghana* 9, 43–64.

Postma, Johannes Menne (1990). *The Dutch in the Atlantic Slave Trade 1600–1815*. Cambridge: Cambridge University Press.

Priestley, Margaret (1967). "Philip Quaque of Cape Coast" Philip D. Curtin ed. *Africa Remembered. Narratives by West Africans from the Era of the Slave Trade*. London: The University of London Press, 99–139.

Priestley, Margaret (1969). *West African Trade and Coast Society. A Family Study*, Oxford et al.: Oxford University Press.

Quaque, Philip (2012). *The Life and Letters of Philip Quaque. The first African Anglican Missionary*. Eds. Vincent Carretta and Ty M. Reese. Athens, GA et al.: University of Georgia Press.

Quarterly, Seth (2004). *Mission Practices on the Gold Coast, 1832–1895. Discourse, Gaze and Gender in the Basel Mission in Pre-Colonial West Africa*. Youngstown, NY: Cambria Press.

Reese, Ty M. (2004a). "Liberty Insolence and Rum. Cape Coast and the American Revolution." *Itinerario* 28.3, 18–37.

Reese, Ty M. (2009). "'Eating' Luxury: Fante Middlemen, British Goods, and Changing Dependencies on the Gold Coast, 1750–1821." *The William and Mary Quarterly* 66.4, 851–872.

Reese, Ty M. (2004b). "'Sheep in the Jaws of So Many Ravenous Wolves': The Slave Trade and Anglican Missionary Activity at Cape Coast Castle, 1752–1816." *Journal of Religion in Africa* 34.3, 348–372.

Reese, Ty M. (2010). "Facilitating the Slave Trade: Company Slaves at Cape Coast Castle, 1750–1807." *Slavery & Abolition* 31.3, 363–377.

(1789) *Report of the Lords of the Committee […] Concerning the present State of the Trade to Africa, and particularly the Trade in Slaves; and concerning the Effects and Consequences of this Trade, as well in Africa and the West Indies, as to the general Commerce of this Kingdom*, London, n.p.

Reynolds, Edward (1974). *Trade and Economic Change on the Gold Coast 1807–1874*. Harlow et al.: Longman.

Rugemer, Edward B (2018). *Slave Law and the Politics of Resistance in the Early Atlantic World*. Cambridge, MA et. al.: Harvard University Press.

Sarbah, John Mensah (1897). *Fanti Customary Laws. A Brief Introduction to the Principles of the Native Laws and Customs of the Fanti and Akan Sections of the Gold Coast*. London: William Clows and Sons.

Sensbach, John (2006). *Rebecca's Revival. Creating Black Christianity in the Atlantic World*. Cambridge, MA et al.: Harvard University Press.

Shumway, Rebecca (2014). "Castle Slaves of the Eighteenth-Century Gold Coast (Ghana)." *Slavery & Abolition* 35.1 (2014), 84–98.

Shumway, Rebecca (2017). "Anti-Slavery in Nineteenth Century Fanteland." Trevor R. Getz and Rebecca Shumway eds. *Slavery and its Legacy in Ghana and the Diaspora*. London et al.: Bloomsbury, 85–104.

Sinha, Manisha (2016). *The Slave's Cause. A History of Abolition*. New Haven et al.: Yale University Press.

Smallwood, Stephanie E. (2007). *Saltwater Slavery. A Middle Passage from Africa to American Diaspora*. Cambridge, MA et al.: Harvard University Press.

Sparks, Randy J. (2013). "Gold Coast Merchant Families, Pawning, and the Eighteenth Century British Slave Trade." *The William and Mary Quarterly* 70.2, 317–340.

Sparks, Randy J. (2014). *Where the Negroes Are Masters. An African Port in the Era of the Slave Trade*. Cambridge, MA et al.: Harvard University Press.

Spricksley, Judith (2013). "Pawns on the Gold Coast: The Rise of Asante and Shifts in Security for Debt." *Journal of African History* 54, 147–75.

St. Clair, William (2007). *The Door of No Return. The History of Cape Coast Castle and the Atlantic Slave Trade*. New York: Blue Bridge.

Strong, Rowan, *Anglicanism and the British Empire c. 1700–1850*. Oxford: Oxford University Press, 2007.

Styles, Ezra and Samuel Hopkins (1776). *Address to the Public. Concerning the Sending of Black Freemen to the Coast of Africa*. Newport, RI: Solomon Southwick.

Thompson, Thomas (1758). *An Account of two Missionary Voyages by the Appointment of the Society for the Propagation of the Gospel in Foreign Parts. The One to New Jersey in North America, the other from America to the Coast of Guiney*. London: Benjamin Dod.

Thompson, Thomas (1772). *The African Trade for Negro Slaves Shewn to be Consistent with the Principles of Humanity, and with the Laws of Revealed Religion*. Canterbury: Simmons and Kirkby.

Titus, Noel (2000). "Concurrence without Compliance: SPG and the Barbadian Plantations, 1710–1834." Daniel O'Connor, *Three Centuries of Mission. The United*

Society for the Propagation of the Gospel 1701–2000, London and New York: Continuum, 249–261.

Vogelsanger, Cornelia (1977). *Pietismus und Afrikanische Kultur an der Goldküste. Die Einstellung der Basler Mission zur Haussklaverei*. Zürich.

Wheatley, Philis (2019). *The Writings of Phillis Wheatley*. Ed. Vincent Carretta. Oxford: Oxford University Press.

Wiecek, William M. (1974). "Somerset: Lord Mansfield and the Legitimacy of Slavery in the Anglo-American World." *The University of Chicago Law Review* 42.1, 86–146.

In the Shadows of War: Early Ottomans and the Controversy of One-Fifth Booty (*Pençik*)

Bahar Bayraktaroğlu

Introduction

> Kara Rüstem: "Why do you let so much state income go to waste?"
> Çandarlı Halil: "What is this income that going to waste?"
> Kara Rüstem: "The income of those war captives, the one-fifth share belongs to the ruler, based on God's will. Why do you not take this share?"[1]

The given passage is extracted from Âşık Paşazâde's *Tevârîh-i Âl-i Osman* (Histories of the Osman Family).[2] It stands as one of the oldest surviving primary sources, providing valuable insights into the early history of the Ottoman Empire. Âşık Paşazâde offers a profound understanding of the origins and architects of the one-fifth (*pençik*) notion, which dates back to the late fourteenth century. Above, Âşık Paşazâde noted that Kara Rüstem was the one who came up with the idea, which seemed to be unfamiliar to many influential Ottoman officials at the time, including Sultan Murad I, the ruler, who was unaware of the one-fifth (*pençik*) right.

Linguistically the word *pençik*, which means one-fifth, is derived from the combination of two Persian words – "penç" meaning "five" and "yek" meaning "one."[3] Given the Ottoman context, the term *pençik* simply refers to the

1 All translations are my own unless indicated otherwise. Chapter 45: "Çandarlı Halil'in kadıasker olduğu zamanda bir gün Karaman ülkesiden Kara Rüstem denen bilgili bir kişi gelip: "Efendi hana verilmesi gereken bu kadar malı neden yok yere harcarsınız?" dedi. Kadıasker bunun üzerine: "O nasıl bir maldır ki boşuna harcanır?" deyince Rüstem: "Bu gazilerin alıp tutup sattıkları esirlerin beşte biri Tanrı emrine göre padişahındır." cevabını verdi. Sonra da "Niçin almıyorsunuz?" dedi. Kadıasker bu sözü işitince gidip Paddişah'a arzetti. Hükümdar bunun üzerine "Eğer Tanrı buyruğu ise öyle yapın dedi" diye söylediler. Kendisi gidip Gelibolu'da oturdu. Her esirden 25 akça aldı. İşte bu şekilde âdet o iki bilgin kişinin tedbiri idi. Bunlardan biri Çandarlı Halil, biri de Karamanlı Kara Rüstem'dir." (Âşık Paşazâde, 98).

2 For the sake of clarity and consistency, all Ottoman Turkish terms and names, mostly *pençik* itself, will be spelled using their Turkish equivalents.

3 Pakalın, *Osmanlı Tarih Deyimleri ve Terimleri Sözlüğü*, I–II, Vol. I, 766–769, Bearman et al., "Pendjik", 293–94, Özcan, "Pençik", 226–228.

 | DOI:10.30965/9783657796328_006

one-fifth share of the sultan from the war spoils. In fact, it is not that simple. Exploring the complexities of the term *pençik* uncovers a multifaceted idea that surpasses temporal and spatial boundaries. That is one of the aims o this paper to show that the term pençik has more nuanced history in itself. Although the concept of *pençik* is often linked to the early Ottoman period, first and foremost, it is not only a brief episode in a certain epoch. Upon being introduced and implemented, the *pençik* as a concept gained several different meanings and adaptations to new circumstances throughout time. Hence, considering it as an antique practise would be an obvious error.

The significance of *pençik* lies in its transformation into a recognized component of the empire. As the empire expanded, imperial officials attempted to structure practising *pençik* in accordance with imperial regulations. This occurred when Ottoman empire underwent increased organization and establishment of its institutions. *Pençik* evolved from a mere concept and right into an established levy – in-kind or monetary, and an emblem for enslaved individuals, verifying their legal standing. What the term *pençik* refers to indeed depends on one's perspective—distinct periods and locations attribute diverse significances to it. In order to have a comprehensive understanding of *pençik*, it is necessary to closely examine its complex details and trace its evolution from a suggested idea in the fourteenth century to its diverse manifestations within the social, economic, military and political dynamics of Ottoman empire.

As early as the 1950s, the early discussions on *pençik* is largely conducted by scholars who have been actively engaged in the historiographical debates surrounding the origins of the Ottoman empire.[4] A wealth of research has examined the *pençik* system within the broader contexts of military, economic, administrative,[5] and slavery institutions of the Ottoman empire.[6] Notable contributions to the extensive body of *pençik* literature have been made by scholars who conducted comprehensive explorations of child levy (*devşirme*) and its enduring connection to the Janissaries (Sultan's Private Troops).[7]

---

4 Cahen, "Note sur l'esclavage musulman et le devshirrme Ottoman, à propos de travaux récents", 211–218, Palmer, "The Origin of the Jannisarries", 448–81, Wittek, "Devshirme and Sharī'a", 271–278, Repp, "A Further Note on the Devshirme", 137–9, Vryonis, "Isidore Glabas and the Turkish Devshirme", 433–443, Ménage, "Devshirme", 210–213.

5 Uzunçarşılı, *Kapıkulu Ocakları*. Halaçoğlu, *XIV–XVII. Yüzyıllarda Osmanlılarda Devlet Teşkilâtı Ve Sosyal Yapı*. Akgündüz, *Osmanli Kanunnâmeleri ve Hukuki Tahlilleri*.

6 Toledano, *The Ottoman Slave Trade and Its Suppression 1840–90*, 69–71. Erdem, *Slavery in the Ottoman Empire and Its Demise 1800–1909*, 19f. Erdem, *KARAR Newspaper*, "Pençiğin Sadaka Olduğu Zamanlar" 21.04.2018.

7 Yılmaz, "The Devshirme System and the Levied Children of Bursa in 1603–4", 901–930, Dec. 2015. Öz and Özel, *Söğüt'ten İstanbul'a - Osmanli Devletinin Kuruluşu Üzerine Tartişmalar*, 555–557.

Building upon the present secondary literature, the present article seeks to conduct a scholarly analysis of initial execution of the *pençik*, based on some certain early Ottoman chronicles. The chosen texts provide fragments that offer insight into an earlier period, wherein the legitimacy of *pençik* existence is called into doubt. Did the early Ottomans in fact assert the rights of taking one-fifth share of the war spoils? The present article analyses the claim that the *pençik* was a divine decree as some early Ottoman histories reveal, when it was first established, investigating its legal basis and considering the viewpoints of the Sunnī schools of Islamic jurisprudence, namely Ḥanafī, Mālikī, Ḥanbalī, and Shāfiʿī. It reveals to the perspectives of some certain distinguished Ottoman scholars in Anatolia from fourteenth and fifteenth century to have a better understanding of their opinion on introduction of the one-fifth right. Based on some selected Ḥanafī teachings, this study, in a broader frame, questions to what extend the early Ottomans were Ḥanafī and argues that the early Ottomans lacked the rightful power to exercise the *pençik* according to some Ḥanafī perspectives of the time.

The Genesis of *Pençik*

Some early Ottoman chronicles provide critical insights into the origins, initial applications, subsequent modifications, and evolutionary trajectory of *pençik*. According to Âşık Paşazâde's account, the entire narrative is as follows:

(In the aftermath of the conquest of Edirne during Sultan Murad I's time)

> One day when Çandarlı Halil was a chief judge (*kadıasker*), a wise man named Kara Rüstem who came from Karaman (told him that): "Why do you let so much state income go to waste?" Upon that, the chief judge asked, "What is this income that going to waste? Rüstem replied: "The income of those war captives, the one-fifth share belongs to the ruler, based on God's will." And then (asked) "Why do you not take this share?" Upon hearing that the chief judge went to the sultan and told that. Upon that, the ruler (said): "If this is God's will, then apply it." They called Kara Rüstem and (said): "Our master, if it's God's will then carry it out." He himself came to Gallipoli and governed there, taking 25 *akçe* per captive. It was in this way that tradition initiated by those two wise men. One of them was Çandarlı Halil, the other one was Karamanlı Kara Rüstem. On the other side, Gazi Evrenoz: "Take one out of every prisoner that was captured during the raids. If someone has only four prisoners, take 25 *akçe* per captive." They acted upon this request, and Evrenoz assigned a judge. They recruited plenty of boys, who were later sent to the sultan".[8]

8 Chapter 45: "Çandarlı Halil'in kadıasker olduğu zamanda bir gün Karaman ülkesiden Kara Rüstem denen bilgili bir kişi gelip: "Efendi hana verilmesi gereken bu kadar malı neden yok

It is evident from the preceding passage that the term "pençik" referred to the deliberate selection of one captive out of five, which was specifically accomplished in times of conflict. By virtue of this honour being bestowed upon the sultan by a divine decree, the importance of God in Âşık Paşazâde's story should be stressed. It is probable that the incorporation of God as a pivotal figure expedited the procedure of choosing one of the five people as a captive. It is essential to observe, nevertheless, that this does not mean that objections or complications do not exist. On the contrary, it functioned as a mechanism to justify and rationalize the practice. Along the text, it becomes apparent that the *pençik*, which initially required the selection of one-fifth of the war captives, evolved into a monetary tax.[9] A novel arrangement of twenty-five *akçe* per captive was proposed by Gazi Evrenos. The proposition to exchange *pençik* for cash payment presents thought-provoking implications. The limited availability of funds in the state treasury or the failure of each raider to apprehend a minimum of five captives during their expeditions may account for this outcome.

When considering the aforementioned excerpt, it is important to highlight that Âşık Paşazâde does not express disapproval concerning the implementation of the *pençik*. On the contrary, he views it as a rightful claim of the sovereign to one-fifth of the spoils. On the other hand, he underscores the fact that the origin of this structure was attributed to two intelligent advisors, Kara Rüstem and Kara Halil of Çandar. Kara Rüstem, an individual originally from the influential Anatolian principality of Karaman, is depicted as a crucial figure in the introduction of the *pençik*. In the portrayal of Sultan Murad I by Âşık Paşazâde, he is portrayed as a generous and modest who seemed satisfied with the suggestions and efforts proposed by his advisors. The persuasive inquiry that this depiction prompts is the reason why Sultan Murad I appeared to be devoid of knowledge regarding the divine will. Might this have been the result of his lack of knowledge regarding the manner in which the *pençik* which

yere harcarsınız?" dedi. Kadıasker bunun üzerine: "O nasıl bir maldır ki boşuna harcanır?" deyince Rüstem: "Bu gazilerin alıp tutup sattıkları esirlerin beşte biri Tanrı emrine göre padişahındır." cevabını verdi. Sonra da "Niçin almıyorsunuz?" dedi. Kadıasker bu sözü işitince gidip Paddişah'a arzetti. Hükümdar bunun üzerine "Eğer Tanrı buyruğu ise öyle yapın dedi" diye söylediler. Kendisi gidip Gelibolu'da oturdu. Her esirden 25 akça aldı. İşte bu şekilde âdet o iki bilgin kişinin tedbiri idi. Bunlardan biri Çandarlı Halil, biri de Karamanlı Kara Rüstem'dir." in Âşık Paşazâde, *Tevârîh-i Âl-i Osmân*, 98.

9 Erdem, *Slavery in the Ottoman Empire and Its Demise 1800–1909*, 19.

required the seizure of one-fifth of the spoils, was executed in opposition to the early Ottomans' beliefs?[10]

Furthermore, beside the initial quote by Âşık Paşazâde, historian Mehmed Neşrî from the fifteenth century provides similar accounts, although with noticeable differences and exclusions. Neşrî offers crucial information regarding the *pençik* that is lacking in Âşık Paşazâde's narrative.

> But they used to take this tax as one-fifth (*h̲ums*) at that time. Now, after taking one-fifth in the raiding ground, they take the tax named *âlem-berî* per captive as a transit fee. (Because) it was known to take tax per captive at the pier, (they) did not bring their captives to the pier and hid (them) in some places.[11]

A bit of text above emphasizes a significant observation. Neşrî employs the term "h̲ums" instead of "pençik." In Arabic, the term "h̲ums" precisely denotes the one-fifth piece that is taken from the spoils, which will be discussed below. This language divergence presents a thought-provoking aspect that warrants additional investigation. It seems that the raiders tried various ways to avoid paying this transit fee and hid their captives. Due to the topic's exceeding the limits of this study, I shall conclude this debate at this point.

Legal Grounds of *Pençik*

The legal foundations of a particular practice can be identified in a multitude of Islamic sources, in addition to the Qurʾān, which is the preeminent and definitive authority of any Islam-based teaching and community. A critical examination of the claimed "God's will" regarding *pençik* becomes essential in light of the references mentioned in the above-mentioned early Ottoman histories. Through an in-depth analysis of these sources, our objective is to critically examine the religious rationales and understandings linked to *pençik*, thereby illuminating its divine validity or absence thereof.

---

10 Although there are raids and the act of taking people into captivity in this story, Hakan Erdem suggests that we cannot get the impression from this narrative that the raiders paid the *pencik* tax with cash or gave one-fifth of their loot. There is even no sign that the prisoners shared the other acquired spoils among all the raiders adequately. Erdem, *KARAR Newspaper*, "Âşıkpaşazâde Haramilikte," 5.5.2018.

11 "Amma bu akçayı ol vakit hums deyü alurlardı. Şimdi humsı esir alunduğu yirde alduktan sonra yine her esirden geçit akçası deyü *âlem-beri* akça alurlar ve iskelede esir içün akça aldukların bilicek iskeleye esir getirmeyüb her biri bir tarafda gizler oldılar." The emphasis on "âlem-beri" is on the original text. Neşrî, *Kitâb-ı Cihannümâ*, 199.

After conducting an extensive examination of related verses from the Qurʾān and Islamic teachings (*ʿilm-i ḥāls*)[12] that are intended to instruct Muslims of all faiths, it becomes evident that the discussion pertaining to *ẖums* originates in the Qurʾān. The chapter entitled "Al-Anfal" (The Plunder of War) of the Qurʾān contains detailed instructions concerning the proper allocation of plunder obtained during battle. These instructions illuminate the intended recipients and outline the prescribed procedure for distributing the spoils. It is worth mentioning that the historical precedent for the practice of appropriating one-fifth of the spoils can be found in the actions of the Prophet Muhammad.

> Know that whatever spoils you take, one-fifth (*ẖums*) is for Allah and the Messenger, his close relatives, orphans, the poor, and (needy) travellers, if you (truly) believe in Allah and what we revealed to our servant on that decisive day when the two armies met (at Badr). And Allah is most capable of everything.[13]

Serving as a significant historical source, the Qurʾānic verses that delineate the distribution of one-fifth of the spoils provide an elaborate depiction of the intended recipients. This includes, God, His messenger, and His relatives, migrants as well as orphans and the destitute. An intriguing aspect is the lack of reference to the actual combatants sharing the spoils; this omission suggests a more altruistic and charitable intention.

The one-fifth share appeared to have been designed with the intention of supporting those in need, bearing resemblance to the principle of almsgiving. By distributing the spoils among different groups, an individual demonstrates a commitment to assisting those less privileged and a broader sense of societal responsibility.

On the contrary, some historical records ascribe Prophet Muhammad sole responsibility for the custom of *ẖums*, which entails appropriating one-fifth of the spoils.[14] The aforementioned action caused Islamic scholars to experience disarray in the aftermath of his demise, as they pondered the consequences and interpretation of this custom.

12 *ʿilm-i ḥāl* was a term that possessed two distinct connotations: firstly, it denoted the fundamental understanding of the Islamic faith that was mandatory for every Muslim; and secondly, it was a tool intended to impart that understanding. For a few scholarships on the *ʿilm-i ḥāl*, see Tekin, "XIV. Yüzyıla Ait Bir Ilm-i Hâl: Risâletü'l-islâm" [An ʻilm-i Hal from the Fourteenth Century: The Treatise on Islam]; Aynaci, *Osmanli Kuruluç Dönemi Türkçe İlmihal Eserleri Çerçevesinde ilmihallerin Fikhî Yönden Değerlendirilmesi* [An Analysis of the Turkish ʻIlm-i Hal Works of the Early Ottoman Period from the Point of View of Islamic Jurisprudence].

13 Qurʾān *Al-Anfal*, 8:41. https://quran.com/8?startingVerse=41.

14 Apaydın, "Humus", 365.

Subsequent sections explore the varied viewpoints of Islamic schools concerning the appropriateness of a fifth portion of the spoils. This study aims to estimate the extent to which the early Ottomans followed Sunnī-minded teachings through an examination of *pençik*. Its contribution to the historiographical discourse on the overarching process of sunnitization/confessionalisation will be moderate.

The diversity of religious principle interpretations and applications that have shaped the cultural and historical landscape is a fascinating phenomenon.

Views from Early Islamic Jurisprudence

The concept of *ẖums*, which refers to the one-fifth part of the war spoils, is significant in the framework of Islamic jurisprudence. The *ẖums*, often associated with Muslims giving a tax to Prophet Muhammad and his family, is actually a multifaceted term that can be interpreted in different ways. A key issue centres on the circumstances surrounding its revelation, its interpretation, and its relevance following the Prophet's decease. Moreover, there is uncertainty over the exact timing of the initial deployment of *ẖums*, whether it took place prior to the Battle of Badr, during the conflict itself, or in later conquests and triumphs.

Diverse branches and sects of Islam hold distinct interpretations. Sects or denominations, schools of Islamic jurisprudence, and schools of Islamic theology are among the numerous in number. Divergences can arise even among Islamic organizations themselves. For instance, Sufism encompasses various orders, while Sunnī Islam is comprised of distinct schools of theology Atharī, Ashʿarī, Māturīdī and jurisprudence Ḥanafī, Mālikī, Shāfiʿī, and Ḥanbalī. The aforementioned schools of thought derive their respective names from their founders Mālik ibn Anas, Abū Ḥanīfa al-Nuʿmān, Muḥammad ibn Idrīs al-Shāfiʿī, and Aḥmad ibn Ḥanbal, respectively.

The question of *ẖums* has been the subject of intense debate among Islamic jurists, leading to the development of shifting beliefs over time. The Ḥanafī, Mālikī, Ḥanbalī, and Shāfiʿī schools of Islam differed in their teachings about the acceptance of *ẖums*. To put it briefly, Abū Bayḍawī (d. 1316) stated that Abū Ḥanīfa (d.768) considered that the parts attributed to the Prophet and his family lost their validity after his decease. Furthermore, the portion designated for the Prophet should be distributed among the military forces and armaments.[15] Al-Shaybânī (d. 802) states that Abū Ḥanīfa (d.768) proposed categorizing hums into three distinct groups: the destitute, the orphaned, and the travellers. The

15 Sachedina, "Al-Khums: The Fifth in the Imāmī Shīʿī Legal System", 278.

difference of perspectives within a single school about the allocation of *ẖums* results in substantial perplexity.[16] On the same page, Abdulaziz Sachedina suggests that the substantial growth of the Islamic empire might have played a role in causing this state of inconsistency.

According to Mālikī beliefs, the authority to collect *ẖums* is passed on to the *imāms* after the Prophet's decease, granting them the power to distribute it based on the welfare and need of the Muslim community. Mālik ibn Anas (d. 795) asserted that the *imām* has the authority to bestow hums upon the Prophet's family as well.[17]

The instruction of Shāfiʿī was to distribute the *ẖums* into five proportional sections, following the guidance of the Qurʾān. One share was allocated to God, and another share was allocated to the Prophet. Upon Prophet Muhammed's decease, the allocation designated for him was intended to be utilized for the collective welfare of the Muslim community or for the sustenance of the Muslim military forces.[18] The Ḥanbalī school concurs with the Shāfiʿī school in terms of the allocation of *ẖums*. The Ḥanbalī school posits that God serves as a precursor to other components, implying that all in existence ultimately belongs to Him and should not be quantified.[19]

After the decease of the Prophet, the Ḥanbalīs, similar to the Shāfiʿīs, uphold the acknowledgment of these five portions. The distribution encompasses the Prophet's portion, which currently addresses the requirements of the Muslim community, together with the portions allocated for close relatives, orphans, destitute, and travellers. In general, the Ḥanbalī, Shāfiʿī, and Mālikī schools of Islam hold a common viewpoint, stating that the caliphs inherited one-fifth of the Prophet's share at his death.

Having discussed the ways in which early Islamic jurisprudence perceived *ẖums* or one-fifth share of the war spoils, to better comprehend and contextualize the choices that early Ottomans might have made, the present article switches its focus to some selected concise manuals (*ʿilm-i ḥāls*) of Ḥanafī school. This is because the Ottoman Empire's reputation as a Sunnī empire.[20] Nevertheless, this ideology had not been formally adhered to since

16 Sachedina, "Al-Khums: The Fifth in the Imāmī Shīʿī Legal System", 279.

17 Sachedina, "Al-Khums: The Fifth in the Imāmī Shīʿī Legal System", 279. The term "imam" refers to a leadership position of the Islamic community after the Prophet Muhammed.

18 Sachedina, "Al-Khums: The Fifth in the Imāmī Shīʿī Legal System", 279.

19 Sachedina, "Al-Khums: The Fifth in the Imāmī Shīʿī Legal System", 279.

20 While acknowledging that traditional Islam did incorporate elements of the Turks' pre-Islamic beliefs, they make the assumption that the Seljuk and Ottoman authorities consistently sanctioned Sunni Islam. Köprülü, *Anadolu'da İslamiyet*; Ocak, *Babailer isyanı: Aleviliğin tarihsel altyapısı yahut Anadolu*.

the inception of the Ottoman empire. Scholars who are interested in religious politics and the diverse Islamic discourses of the early modern Ottoman empire have adopted the term "sunnitization" (also known as "confession building" and "confessionalization") to refer to an increasing preoccupation with establishing and enforcing Sunnī orthodoxy and orthopraxy within the Muslim communities of the "Lands of Rum."[21] This preoccupation began in the early sixteenth century and persisted until the seventeenth century. Diverse Ottomanists have placed emphasis on distinct rationales as pivotal to this progression. Numerous scholars have cited the theological and political challenge that the rise of the Shi'a Safavid empire posed to the legitimacy of the Ottoman dynasty as a significant factor in the increasing focus on delineating and regulating the limits of Sunnī Ḥanafī orthodoxy in the early 1500s.[22] Cemal Kafadar introduced the notion of "metadoxy" and asserted that discussing orthodoxy among Anatolian and Balkan Muslims between the eleventh and fifteenth centuries was virtually impossible.[23] In this vein, this paper joins the previous scholarship and argues that early Ottomans might not fully follow a single school of the Sunnī branch, let it be arguing that following the early practices of *pençik* stands as a historical instance for that.

Pençik in *Hanafī* Literature of Anatolia

Our investigation has recognized the integration of the *pençik* into the social and economic activities of the early Ottomans, namely during the reign of Sultan Murad I, as previously established. The claim that the sultan was entitled to one-fifth of the war profits can be traced back to the standpoint of that time, potentially supported by a scholar named "Kara Rüstem." Examining the account offered in Ottoman historiography by Âşık Paşazâde and Neşrî raises the question of why Sultan Murad I swiftly embraced Kara Rüstem's suggestion and how come he was unaware of it. Did the concise manuals originating from Anatolia, inspired by the Hanafî school of Islam, record any

21 Krstić, *Contested Conversions to Islam*; Terzioğlu, "Sufis in the Age of State-Building and Confessionalization"; Terzioğlu, "How to Conceptualize Ottoman Sunnitization: A Historiographical Discussion"; Burak, "Faith, law and empire in the Ottoman 'age of confessionalization', 1–23.

22 Terzioğlu, "Where 'İlm-i Ḥāl Meets Catechism", 85.

23 Cemal Kafadar defines the term metadoxy as "a state of being beyond doxies, a combination of being doxy-naive and not being doxyminded, as well as the absence of a state that was interested in rigorously defining and strictly enforcing an orthodoxy" in Kafadar, *Between Two Worlds: The Construction of the Ottoman State*, 76.

disagreement as the Ottomans of that time started to adopt a one-fifth portion of war spoils? In order to find out how these manuals were received, we will now focus on a specific group and examine the scholarly approaches of the time.[24] Mehemmed b. Feramurz b. 'Alî, commonly known as Mollâ Hüsrev authored *Dürerü'l-Ḥükkâm fi Şerḥî Ġureri'l-Aḥkâm* in the fifteenth century.[25] Mollâ Hüsrev's work encompasses the "Bâb-ı Ġanime ve Ḳısmetihâ" chapter, which delves into the discussion of war spoils and their allocation. Another noteworthy source is *Kitâbü'l-Ġunya*, penned at the end of the fourteenth century in Anatolia and subsequently published by Muzaffer Akkuş.[26] Next is a translation of *Vikâyetü'r-Rivaye* by Devletoğlu Yusuf of Balıkesir, completed in 1424–25, presents valuable insights on distribution of war profits. Lastly, anonymous *Risâletü'l-Islam,* written in Old Anatolian Turkish and titled "Gazilik Tarikası," serves as a final source to be considered.[27] The selection of these sources was based on the fact that they are pertinent to the *pençik* and that they offer significant insights within that context. Through making use of these sources, one can obtain entry to an extensive array of viewpoints concerning the subject being examined, thereby facilitating a thorough analysis of the *pençik* in the context of early Ottoman history as a whole. In light of the extensive array of sources at hand, it is necessary to recognize that conducting an entire examination of each one exceeds the boundaries of this chapter. Hence, with respect to the subject matter, this research predominantly concentrates on only a handful of sources that significantly contribute to the understanding of the topic at hand.

As a brief manual, *Gazilik Tarikası* clarifies the rules of holy war (*ġazā*), the conditions of being a raider (*ghāzī*), the exchange of war captives, and the fair

---

24 For some other sources on this topic, see Tekin, "XIV. Yüzyılda Yazılmış Gazilik Tarikası 'Gâziliğin Yolları' Adlı Bir Eski Anadolu Türkçesi Metni ve Gazâ/Cihâd Kavramları Hakkında". Şinasi Tekin provides us with an Arabic work of the tenth century by Ebû'l-Leys-i Semerkandî, titled Tenbîhü'l-Ġâfilîn, which also exists in an Old Anatolian Turkish translation known as "Usanları Alerter", 139.

25 Tekin, "XIV. Yüzyılda Yazılmış Gazilik Tarikası 'Gâziliğin Yolları' Adlı Bir Eski Anadolu Türkçesi Metni ve Gazâ/Cihâd Kavramları Hakkında", 139. Erdem, "Gazi Dediğin Nasıl Olmalı?" *KARAR Newspaper*, 14.4.2018.

26 Tekin, "XIV. Yüzyılda Yazılmış Gazilik Tarikası 'Gâziliğin Yolları' Adlı Bir Eski Anadolu Türkçesi Metni ve Gazâ/Cihâd Kavramları Hakkında", 140. Erdem, "Gazi Dediğin Nasıl Olmalı?" *KARAR Newspaper*, 14.4.2018.

27 There are more sources to consult. For instance, Sedîde'd-dîn b. Muḥammad's twelfth-century work Şir'atü'l-Islâm constitutes another valuable source. Additionally, an anonymous Persian text known as Baḥrü'l-Fevâ'id, written in the mid-twelfth century, contributes to our understanding of the subject. See Erdem, "Gazi Dediğin Nasıl Olmalı?" *KARAR Newspaper*, 14.14.2018.

and detailed distribution of war spoils (*g̲hanīma*). Concerning the allocation of spoils, *Gazilik Tarikası* clearly states that (1) whatever captured should not be shared in the battleground and it should not be sold before sharing. (2) The beg who commanded the raid should know how much cavalry and infantry will attend to military action since the portions for the spoil must be calculated accordingly.[28] (3) The raid commander should not take slaves and non-adults out of the spoil; he should provide "something" for non-adult slaves who put themselves for sale. (4) Suppose the women took care of the raiders and treated those who got hurt during the raid; in that case, the raid commander should not disregard these women from the spoils and give "something" to them. (5) If the non-Muslims who paid their poll tax (*d̲jizya*) participated in the raid show, the commander of the Muslim raiders in the areas where non-Muslims hid their precious fabrics should provide "something" for them as well. (6) Finally, the commander should distribute the spoil into five portions. The commander should share four portions amongst his raiders who took a role in that particular raid. The remaining one portion is *pençik*, which means one-fifth. This one portion, *pençik,* should be distributed amongst three people: orphans, paupers, and needy wayfarers (*ibnü's-sebil*). *Gazilik Tarikası* does not mention any particular portion for the above-mentioned "something."[29]

In *Gazilik Tarikası*, one-fifth of the share belonged to Prophet Muhammad when he was alive. In Islam, no more prophets came after the Prophet Muhammed and his death outlawed the right of *pençik* from the rulers; the ones who came after Prophet Muhammad do not have the right to enjoy one-fifth share.[30] As mentioned in *Gazilik Tarikası*, the one-fifth portion called *pençik* refers to alms to be given to three categories of people, and nothing more. It should be underlined that there is no particular portion clearly allocated for the raid of commander or the state.

In the early Ottoman chronicles discussed above, Kara Rüstem introduced the idea of taking one-fifth from the war spoils to the Ottoman commanders in the aftermath of Edirne's conquest during the reign of Sultan Murad I. Let us assume that the early Ottoman chronicles are unreliable and that they did not learn from Kara Rüstem to take *pençik*. However, it is known that they

28 The term "beg", alternatively rendered *Baig, Bayg, Beigh, Beig, Bek, Baeg*, or *Bey*, denotes a chieftain in Turkic and was historically bestowed with honorific status upon individuals who originated from the rulers or chieftains of diversely sized territories within the plethora of Turkic empires, emirates, kingdoms, and sultanates.

29 Tekin, "XIV. Yüzyılda Yazılmış Gazilik Tarikası 'Gâziliğin Yolları' Adlı Bir Eski Anadolu Türkçesi Metni ve Gazâ/Cihâd Kavramları Hakkında", 145.

30 Tekin, "XIV. Yüzyılda Yazılmış Gazilik Tarikası 'Gâziliğin Yolları' Adlı Bir Eski Anadolu Türkçesi Metni ve Gazâ/Cihâd Kavramları Hakkında", 145.

seized one-fifth of the spoils of war and later institutionalized this practice. Considering that the *Gazilik Tarikası* was composed in the fourteenth century, what is the probability that Sultan Murad I either read the text or was aware of its contents?

In reality, *Gazilik Tarikası* is not the sole manual from that era advocating against the Ottomans taking one-fifth of the spoils of war, and asserting that this practice contradicts Hanafī principles. From this point of view, how safe is it to assume that the early Ottomans embraced Imam Shāfiʿī or Hanbalî's perception on the *pençik*? How reliable are the early chronicles about the beginning of the *pençik*? Was the *pençik* a complete unknown to the early Ottomans and if so, were they not aware of God's order? *Gazilik Tarikası* provides a lot of theoretical information that does not comply with what the early Ottomans exercised.[31] As it is noted in *Gazilik Tarikası*, the representative of the Shāfiʿī school of Islam, Imam Shāfiʿī believes that the Prophet's right had been transmitted to the caliphs.[32] In contrast, the Hanafī school thinks that the current rulers do not have the right to take the spoils and enjoy it. Presumably, even though the Prophet's death abolished the right to take one-fifth of the share, some Islamic states continued to take that share from the spoils. Therefore, the anonymous author of *Gazilik Tarikası* might want to provide a reminder on the subject matter again.

Devletoğlu Yusuf was one of the poets and writers who expressed his opinion on several topics, including writing in Turkish of the time. Sultan Murad II was one of the Ottoman sultans who supported writing in Turkish; it was during the time that Sultan Murad II was on his throne in 1424–1425 that Devletoğlu Yusuf translated the *Vikâyetü'r-Rivaye*, one of the most fundamental texts of the Hanafī jurisprudence, into Turkish and gifted it to Sultan Murad II.[33] Devletoğlu Yusuf's translation was penned many years after the *pençik* was imposed in the Ottoman realm.[34]

In "Bâbü'l Ġanâyimi ve Ḳısmetihâ" chapter of the translation, Devletoğlu Yusuf mentions war spoils and its distribution. Apart from some linguistic differences in indications, for instance the one-fifth share (*pençik*) has been referred to as *ẖums*, it can be said that *Gazilik Tarikası* is entirely parallel to the translation of *Vikâyetü'r-Rivaye*.

---

31 Erdem, *KARAR Newspaper*, "Pençiğin Sadaka Olduğu Zamanlar" 21.04.2018.

32 Tekin, "XIV. Yüzyılda Yazılmış Gazilik Tarikası 'Gâziliğin Yolları' Adlı Bir Eski Anadolu Türkçesi Metni ve Gazâ/Cihâd Kavramları Hakkında", 145.

33 Erdem, *KARAR Newspaper*, "Devletoğlu Yusuf", 18.02.2018.

34 Erdem, *KARAR Newspaper*, "Gazi dediğin Nasıl Olmalı?", 14.04.2018.

Hem ġanîmet ḳısmet etmekte imam	Imam distributes the spoil
Humsın anuñ çıḳarsa evvel tamâm	First, he takes the one-fifth.
Bâḳî ahmâsını beyne'l-ġanimîn	Others share the spoils.
Ḳısmet itmeklik gerekdür pes hemin	Needs to be distributed right away
Atluya vire iki sehmin imam	Give two shares to cavalry
Pes yayaya vire bir sehmin tamâm	Give one share to infantry
....	....
Humsı hem üç sehm idüp ḳısmet ide	Divide the one-fifth share into three portions
Her birin bir dürlü ṣınıfa iy dede	Give each portion to a different group.
Vire bir sehmin yetîmlere imam	One to orphans, one to migrants,
Dahı miskinlere bir sehmin tamâm	one to needy wayfarers,
Birisin dahi li-ebnâi's-sebil	Know to share it like this.
Böyle ḳısmet idiserdür eyle bil.[35]	

According to this excerpt above, it can be grasped that the right to share the spoils is of the commander. First, one-fifth of the share is taken out of all of the spoils, then the distribution starts. The remaining four shares are to be distributed as two shares for cavalry and one share for infantry. Then, the commander splits the remaining one part in thirds and distributes it to the orphans, the poor, and the needy wayfarers (*ibnü's-sebil*) just as it is noted in *Gazilik Tarikası*. More significantly, there is no mention of any share for the sultan as granted by God, as we observe in early Ottoman chronicles such as those written by Âşık Paşazâde and Neşrî.

Considering Devletoğlu Yusuf's translation work, presented to Sultan Murad II, it may be deduced that Devletoğlu might have wished sultan Murad II knew that he did not have the right to take one-fifth of the spoils of war. Perhaps, Devletoğlu Yusuf was unaware that the Ottoman empire took *pençik* from the prisoners captured during the raids. It is not certain what happened after, especially whether Sultan Murad II read Devletoğlu Yusuf's translation work.[36]

Kitâbü'l-Ġunye manuscript[37] is highly significant as it represents the views of the Ḥanafī school of Islam, providing essential information on the ways in which raiders, raiding culture, war spoils, and especially war captives.[38] With

35 Aktan, "Devletoğlu Yusuf'un Vikaye Tercümesi", 358.

36 Erdem, *KARAR Newspaper*, "Pençiğin Sadaka Olduğu Zamanlar", 21.4. 2018.

37 Tekin, "Bursa ve Manisa İl-Halk Kütüphaneterindeki bazı Türkçe Yazmalar üzerine", 121–148. Tekin, "XIV. Yüzyılda Yazılmış Gazilik Tarikası 'Gâziliğin Yolları' Adlı Bir Eski Anadolu Türkçesi Metni ve Gazâ/Cihâd Kavramları Hakkında", 145.

38 There has been an academic debate on who was the author of *Kitâbü'l- Ġunye*. Semih Tezcan put forward that it was translated from Harzem Turkish to Anatolian Turkish and that the author was a Hanifa jurist named Fahraddin bin Mansur al-Uzcandî al-Farganî

regard to the distribution of spoils, the "Babü'l- 'Izzi ve'l-Cihâdı" titled chapter of the *Kitâbü'l- Ġunye* notes that:

> When a war took place and things were taken as booty, they should not share the spoils in the battleground. In the Shafi'î school, it is proper to do that. And it is not proper to take any share before the distribution of the spoils. When the commander (*imām*) who participated in the battle makes the allocation, he gives two portions to the cavalry and one portion to infantry. In the eyes of Ebû Yûsuf and Muḥammed and Shafi'î, they give three portions to the cavalry and one for the infantry.[39]

In the eyes of Ebû Yûsuf and Muḥammed and Shafi'î, they give three portions to the cavalry and one for the infantry.[40] It is underscored that taking a share from the spoil before the allocation is inappropriate. When the commander (*imām*) is to share the spoils, that commander should give two shares to the cavalry and one share to the infantry. So far, *Kitâbü'l- Ġunye* is in harmony with *Gazilik Tarikası* and translation of *Vikâyetü'r-Rivaye* concerning certain principles to follow such as not to touch the spoils before distributing them, not to distribute it in the battleground, and that the commander (*imām*) has to do it. All three sources underline that one-fifth was to be shared amongst orphans, migrants, and needy wayfarers.

In the chapter titled "Bâbü'l Mağnem ve Ḳısmetüh" (Spoil and its Distribution) in an Arabic work *Dürerü'l- Hükkam fi Şerhi Gureri'l- Ahkam* written by the fifteenth-century Ottoman scholar Mehemmed b. Feramurz b. Ali (d. 1480) who is also known as *Molla Hüsrev*. Molla Hüsrev starts by declaring that:

> one-fifth share (*h̲ums*) is for orphans, paupers, and needy wayfarers (*ibnü's-sebil*). It is distributed among the poor relatives; the wealthy will not be distributed among them. One-fifth of the Prophet's share is gone after his death because no prophet came after the Prophet Muhammad. Nevertheless, Shāfiʿī writes that 'Prophet Muhammad is a property that separates it from booty and does the work of Muslims with it' for the right of the Prophet Muhammad.[41]

Kazîhân who lived in the twelfth century. Tezcan, "Kitabü'l-Gunya'nın Yazarı", 15. Erdem, "Gazi dediğin Nasıl Olmalı?", *KARAR Newspaper*, 14.04.2018.

39 "… ve savaş ḳılup ne bulun kim alsalar savaşdan fariġ olıcaḳ kâfir ilinde üleşmeyeler ve Şâfi'î ḳavlinde üleşmek dahı revâ olur. Ve dahı ol bulundan nesne almaḳ revâ olmaz tâ üleşince … ve ḳaçan imâm ḳısmet ḳılsa, atlulara iki bahş vireler ve yayalara bir bahş vireler Ebû Yûsuf ve Muḥammed ve Şâfi'î ḳavlinde atlulara üç bahş vireler ve yayalara bir bahş vireler …" *Kitâb-ı Gunya*, 378.

40 *Kitâb-ı Gunya*, 378.

41 "Humus; yetîm, miskin ve ibn-i sebîl içindir. Zevi'l-kurbânın fakirleri onlar üzerine takdim olunur. Zevi'l-kurbâ'nın zengini onlar üzerine takdim edilmez. Hz. Pegamber (S.A.V.)'in

Molla Hüsrev continues: "The imām has the right (*tenfil*) to motivate the soldiers. *Tenfîl* stands for the right to give more than a share of the spoils to encourage soldiers to fight in wartime."[42]

The author provides examples from verses of the Qur'ān or companions of the prophet: "For example, imam can say that 'if a person kills an infidel, his belongings belong to its killer.' Allah would be ordered this for the imām. 'O Prophet! Encourage the believers to war.' This purpose only takes place by giving something special to some of the soldiers. In this regard, the cavalry has superiority over the infantry."[43]

Regarding the four Islamic manuals the translation of *Vikaye, Kitâbü'l- Ġunye, Dürerü'l- Hükkam*, and *Gazilik Tarikası*, it is clear that there was an intellectual discussion on how to distribute the spoil, the right to take one-fifth (*h̲ums*) share from it, and how to spend it. They all suggest that a one-fifth share of the spoils must be distributed to the orphans, the penniless, and needy wayfarers (*ibnü's-sebil*).[44] Hence, one can join Y. Hakan Erdem and assume that the one-fifth share was initially a kind of alms, or a sort of charity to be given to people in need.[45]

Given the *pençik*, it is crucial to note that the Ottomans' authority to claim portions belonging to the Prophet and his family became null and void upon his demise, as stipulated in carefully selected concise manuals of Islamic jurisprudence pertaining to the Ḥanafī school. However, when we examine the perspectives of the Ḥanbalī, Shâfi'ī, and Mâlikī schools of Islam, it can be argued that the Ottomans possessed the right to claim these portions, as the Prophet's share of one-fifth was believed to have passed on to the caliphs after his passing.

hissesi vefatından sonra düşmüştür. Çünkü Neb-i Ekrem (S.A.V.) o hisseye risâlet ile müstehakdı. Hz. Muhammed (S.A.V.)'dan sonra ise artık resul yoktur. Nitekim Şafi'iin düştüğü gibi: Resûlüllah (S.A.V.)'in kendisi için ganimetten ayırıp, onunla Müslümanların işlerini gördüğü maldır." *Gurer ve Durer Tercümesi.*

42 "İmâmın tenfîl hakkı vardır. Tenfîl; savaş vaktinde askeri harbe teşvik için ganimet hissesinden daha fazla şey vermektir." *Gurer ve Durer Tercümesi*, "Ganimet Ve Paylaştırılması" chapter.

43 Meselâ imâm; bir kimse bir kâfir öldürürse selebi öldürenindir, der. Bu teşvik, imâm için mendûbdur. Çünkü Allah Teâlâ (C.C.): "Ey Peygamber! Müminleri savaşa teşvik et." buyurmuştur ... Tenfîlden maksûd, Müslümanları savaşa teşvîkdir. Bu ise ancak bazısına husûsî bir şey vermekle hâsıl olur.. Umûmîleştirmekte ise, atlı olanım yayan olan üzere tafdîlin iptali vardır." Erkan, *Gurer ve Durer Tercümesi*, "Ganimet Ve Paylaştırılması" chapter.

44 Tekin, "XIV. Yüzyılda Yazılmış Gazilik Tarikası 'Gâziliğin Yolları' Adlı Bir Eski Anadolu Türkçesi Metni ve Gazâ/Cihâd Kavramları Hakkında". Aktan, *Devletoğlu Yusuf'un Vikaye Tercümesi*, 355. *Kitâb-ı Gunya*, 378. *Gurer ve Durer Tercümesi*, "Ganimet ve Paylaştırılması" chapter.

45 Erdem, *Karar Newspaper*, "Penciğin Sadaka Olduğu Zamanlar" 21.4. 2018.

Nevertheless, it is imperative to consider that this one-fifth share was intended to be allocated among three distinct groups: the orphans, the indigent, and the travellers. Consequently, we must explore the nature of the Ottomans' claim, the divine authority granted according to Ottoman chronicles, and the specific beneficiaries entitled to this share.

Charting the Transformation of *Pençik*

Following an examination of the legal foundation of the *pençik* system and acknowledging the presence of divergent views expressed in early Ottoman concise manuals aligned with the Ḥanafī school, which suggest that the Ottomans did not possess the entitlement to one-fifth of the spoils of war, it is now pertinent to address the series of inquiries posed at the outset of this discourse.

The term "pençik" originally referred to a tax imposed in the form of goods or money, as evidenced in early Ottoman chronicles such as those authored by Âşık Paşazâde and Neşrî. Initially, *pençik* was extracted as one-fifth of the spoils obtained during military raids. In the case of goods-based *pençik*, raiders were required to surrender one out of every five prisoners captured as payment for the tax. However, if the number of captives did not precisely amount to five, raiders had to compensate with an in-cash *pençik* tax of 25 *akçe* per captive. Y. Hakan Erdem suggests the term "monetary pençik" to describe this variant, which typically amounted to less than one-fifth of a slave's market value, leading raiders to often opt for this payment method.[46]

To streamline the practice of *pençik*, the Ottoman central government introduced imperial laws aiming to improve the efficiency of the practice. Two surviving law codes from the reign of Sultan Bayezid II shed light on the *pençik*.[47] Two surviving law codes from the reign of Sultan Bayezid II shed light on the *pençik*. The first code, dating back to 1493, focuses primarily on the contemporary period without referencing earlier practices. It mandates cooperation between the "pençik officer" (*pençikçi*) and the raid commander (*akıncı beyi*) for the collection of *pençik* boys and the *pençik* tax as required by law. Additionally, this code provides a clear definition of "raiding" in relation to

46 Erdem, *Slavery in the Ottoman Empire and Its Demise 1800–1909*, 19.

47 Uzunçarşılı, *Kapıkulu Ocakları*, 86. Akgündüz, *Osmanli Kanunnâmeleri ve Hukuki* Tahlilleri, 128–131.

other military activities.[48] In contrast, the second law code from 1510 differs significantly in content. Erdem refers to it as the "pençik tax law," as it specifies the amount of *pençik* tax to be collected based on the age, gender, and physical appearance of captives. This code resembles a tariff structure for the *pençik* tax, with rates varying according to these factors.[49]

As Ferit Devellioğlu states, the term "pençik" carries two distinct meanings: firstly, it refers to a document issued by customs to slave owners upon payment of a specific tax, serving as legal proof of ownership. Secondly, it denotes a document attached to the neck of slaves, certifying their legal status as slaves and facilitating their sale without legal obstacles.[50] Devellioğlu explains that *pençik* deeds served two functions. Slave merchants (*esirci*) received documents known as "pençik varakası" upon paying the *pençik* tax, originally set at 25 *akçe*. Although some historians have briefly mentioned these documents,[51] a comprehensive exploration is still needed.[52] *Pençik* deeds represent the materialization of the monetary aspect of *pençik*, namely the *pençik* taxation. They provide insights into the functioning of the Ottoman taxation system and bureaucratic practices. Numerous *pençik* deeds from different periods and regions within the Ottoman Empire still remain unexplored in the archives.[53]

The narrative surrounding the *pençik* tax extends beyond the aforementioned circumstances. An important aspect highlighted by Ehud R. Toledano pertains to the eventual integration of the *pençik* tax into the broader tax

---

48 Erdem, *KARAR Newspaper*, "Âşıkpaşazâde Haramilikte," 5.5.2018.

49 The captives in the *pencik* law code were categorized as follows: "shirhor" (lactant; 0–3 years old), "beççe" (3 to 8 year old kid); "gulam" (8 to 12 year old boy); "gulam" (teen), "sakallı" (bearded) and "pir" (old). Women were divided into the sections of "umm'ul- veled" (mother) "duhter" (girl), "fertute" (aged), "bîmare" (ill), "yekdest" (one-armed) and "yekçeşm" (one-eyed) Uzunçarşılı, *Kapıkulu Ocakları*, 90. Akgündüz, *Osmanli Kanunnâmeleri ve Hukuki Tahlilleri*, 131.

50 Devellioğlu, *Osmanlıca-Türkçe Ansiklopedik Lûgat*.

51 Toledano, *Osmanlı Köle Ticareti, 1840–1890*, 58; Erdem, *Slavery in the Ottoman Empire and Its Demise 1800–1909*, 19.

52 Scribes employed several designations for these documents, including "pençik kağıdı," "pençik senedi," "pençik temessüğü," "esir kağıdı," "esir senedi," "pençik tezkiresi," or "pençik makbuzu."

53 Based on my current understanding, I am aware that a portion of the receipts pertaining to the pençik tax has undergone recent digitization within the archive. Specifically, there exists a collection of 13 boxes containing *pençik* receipts from the years 1094 AH (Hijri calendar) or 1682/1683 AD (Gregorian calendar). Regrettably, only a limited selection of 5 boxes is currently accessible for examination, solely within the confines of the research halls. They are identified in the *Bab-ı defteri* catalogue under the heading of "Pençik Resmi."

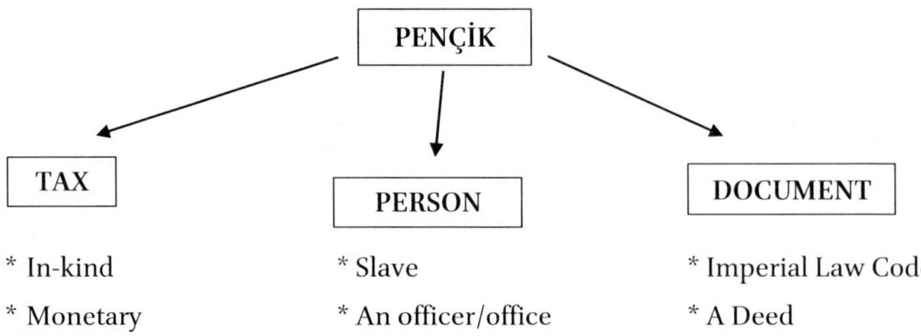

Fig. 5.1

collection system. The privilege of collecting the *pençik* tax was bestowed upon individuals who agreed to make regular cash payments to the state treasury while assuming the responsibility of collecting the tax themselves. Following the abolition of the black slave trade in 1857, the *pençik* tax was eliminated from the tariff, resulting in the forgiveness of refugee debts. The Central Treasury officially declared the cessation of *pençik* tax collection in the Constantinople survey. To ensure compliance with this new prohibition, an Ottoman official known as a "pençikçi" was appointed to monitor adherence to the directive.[54] Ehud R. Toledano speculates that the levying of the *pençik* tax may have persisted for a certain period, as sudden discontinuation was unlikely. The prohibition may have been more effectively enforced in the cities of Constantinople and Smyrna; however, compliance with the *pençik* tax ban related to the 1857 decree might not have unfolded as anticipated. According to accounts provided by local and foreign observers, the *pençik* tax evolved into a form of bribe or hush money.[55]

Conclusion

In the course of this brief debate about *pençik*, a complicated and everlasting concept that transcends both time and space has been uncovered. Something that at first glance could appear to be an archaic practice gradually turns out to be an essential part of the structure of the system of governance. The advancement of *pençik* toward imperial institutionalization reflects the rise of the Ottoman empire as well as the parallel efforts to organize its many components

54 Toledano, *Osmanlı Köle Ticareti, 1840–1890*, 58.
55 Toledano, *Osmanlı Köle Ticareti, 1840–1890*, 59.

through the use of imperial legal codes. As the time passed, *pençik* evolved from an intellectual idea into a reality that can be physically experienced. In addition to that, it has been used as a manifestation of slave dues and as a method of establishing legal status. Nevertheless, the understanding of *pençik* continues to be adaptable, taking into account the fact that its significance and the implications it carries alter depending on the time period and the region.

A primary objective of this research was to determine whether or not the early Ottomans possessed the legal right to engage in *pençik*. The present paper went on an investigation to reveal some traces of the past and shed light on this aspect of the history of the early Ottoman empire. This was accomplished by conducting a detailed examination of some chosen sources. In this article, the legal basis of *pençik* was critically examined, and the perspectives of some early schools of Islamic jurisprudence were taken into consideration. This was accomplished by conducting a review of the narratives that portray *pençik* as a divine decree. Our understanding of the first application of *pençik* has also been improved as a result of the contributions made by some Ottoman scholars who lived in Anatolia during the fourteenth and fifteenth centuries.

We remain at odds with inquiries over the change of a piece of the loot, which was initially designated for orphans, the homeless, and travellers who were living in poverty, into a portion that was awarded to the rulers and imperial treasuries. This study questioned the ways in which the early Ottomans justify the allocation of one-fifth of the revenues to the state treasury while some concise manuals which were written based on Hanafî schools of Islam's perspective did not agree.

Recognizing the extensive nature of the subject matter as well as the inherent limitations of the present investigation is of the utmost importance. The purpose of this study is to create a concentrated academic analysis with the intention of making a contribution to the continuing intellectual discussion regarding *pençik*. By calling into question long-held views and venturing into uncharted territories, this article endeavored to get a deeper comprehension of the complexities that are associated with the Ottomans' relationship with *pençik*, namely with regard to the beginning of the practice and the acquisition of one-fifth of the spoils of war. The findings of this inquiry provide us with insightful perspectives on the socio-economic conditions that prevailed within the Ottoman empire, as well as a deeper understanding of the legal and economic frameworks that existed within that empire.

To provide a brief summary, this brief examination of *pençik* offered a complex storyline of shifting traditions, expanding legal frameworks, and developing interpretations. It aimed to provide a more nuanced understanding of the early Ottomans' relationship with *pençik*.

Works Cited

Primary Sources

Âşık Paşazâde, *Tevârîh-i Âl-i Osmân* (2014). Ed. Kemal Yavuz-Yekta Saraç. İstanbul: Bilimevi Basın.

Gurer ve Durer Tercümesi (1979). Ed. Arif Erkan, vol. II. İstanbul: Eser Neşriyat.

Kitâb-ı Gunya (2018). Ed. Muzaffer Akkuş. Ankara: Türk Dil Kurumu.

Mehmed Neşrî, *Kitâb-ı Cihannümâ* (2014). Ed. Faik Reşit Unat – Mehmed Köymen, vol.1. Ankara: Türk Tarik Kurumu.

Secondary Literature

Akgündüz, Ahmet (1990). *Osmanli Kanunnâmeleri ve Hukuki Tahlilleri*. OSAV, vol. 1.

Aktan, Bilal (2002). *Devletoğlu Yusuf'un Vikaye Tercümesi*. Unpublished Ph.D. Dissertation, Atatürk University.

Apaydın, H. Yunus (1998). "Humus", *TDV DIA İslâm Ansiklopedisi*. İstanbul, T.D.V. Yayınları, vol. 18, 365–369.

Aynaci, Mediha (2009). *Osmanli Kuruluç Dönemi Türkçe İlmihal Eserleri Çerçevesinde ilmihallerin Fikhî Yönden Değerlendirilmesi*. Marmara University: Unpublished Ph.D. Dissertation.

Bearman, P., Th. Bianquis, C.E. Bosworth, E. van Donzel and W.P. Heinrichs "Pendjik" (1995). In *Encyclopédie de l'Islam*. Second Edition, vol 8. Leiden: Brill, 293–94.

Burak, Guy (2013). "Faith, law and empire in the Ottoman 'age of confessionalization' *Mediterranean Historical Review*, vol. 28, 1, 1–23.

Cahen, Claude (1970). "Note sur l'esclavage musulman et le devshirrme Ottoman, à propos de travaux récents", *JESHO*, XIII/2, 211–218.

Devellioğlu, Ferit (2013). *Osmanlıca-Türkçe Ansiklopedik Lûgat*. Ankara: Aydın Kitabevi.

Erdem, Y. Hakan (1996). *Slavery in the Ottoman Empire and Its Demise 1800–1909*. New York: Palgrave Macmillian.

Kafadar, Cemal (1995). *Between Two Worlds: The Construction of the Ottoman State*. Berkeley: University of California Press.

Halaçoğlu, Yusuf (1991). *XIV–XVII. Yüzyıllarda Osmanlılarda Devlet Teşkilâtı Ve Sosyal Yapı*. Ankara: Türk Tarih Kurumu Basımevi.

Köprülü, Fuat (2005). *Anadolu'da İslamiyet*. Ankara: Akçağ Yayınları.

Krstić, Tijana (2011). *Contested Conversions to Islam*. Stanford: Stanford University Press.

Ménage, V. L. (1991). "Devshirme", *Encylopedia of Islam*, vol. II. Brill: Leiden, 210–213.

Ocak, Ahmet Yaşar (1996). *Babailer isyanı: Aleviliğin tarihsel altyapısı yahut Anadolu*. İstanbul: Dergah Yayınları.

Öz, Mehmet, and Oktay Özel (2000). *Söğüt'ten İstanbul'a - Osmanli Devletinin Kuruluşu Üzerine Tartişmalar*. Imge Yayınevi, Ankara.

Özcan, Abdülkadir. "Pençik", *TDV İslâm Ansiklopedisi*, 226–228.

Pakalın, M. Zeki (1971). *Osmanlı Tarih Deyimleri ve Terimleri Sözlüğü*, I–II, vol. I. İstanbul. MEB.

Palmer, J.A.B (1953). "The Origin of the Jannisarries", *Bulletin of the John Rylands Library*, XXXV, 448–81.

Repp, R.C. (1968). "A Further Note on the Devshirme", *BSOAS*, XXXI, 137–9.

Sachedina, Abdulaziz (1980). "Al- Khums: The Fifth in the Imāmī Shīʿī Legal System", *Journal of Near Eastern Studies* 39, no. 4, 275–89.

Tekin, Günay Alpay (1977). "Bursa ve Manisa İl-Halk Kütüphaneterindeki bazı Türkçe Yazmalar üzerine" *TUBA* I, 121–148.

Tekin, Şinasi (1989). "XIV. Yüzyılda Yazılmış Gazilik Tarikası 'Gâziliğin Yolları' Adlı Bir Eski Anadolu Türkçesi Metni ve Gazâ/Cihâd Kavramları Hakkında", *International Journal of Turkish Studies*. IJTS / University of Wisconsin, 139–204.

Tekin, Şinasi (1986). "XIV. Yüzyıla Ait Bir Ilm-i Hâl: Risâletü'l-islâm", *Wiener Zeitschrift für die Kunde des Morgenlandes*, IXXVİ.

Terzioğlu, Derin (2012–2013). "How to Conceptualize Ottoman Sunnitization: A Historiographical Discussion", *Turcica* 44, 301–338.

Terzioğlu, Derin (2012). "Sufis in the Age of State-Building and Confessionalization", in *The Ottoman World*, ed. Christine Woodhead. London: Taylor & Francis.

Tezcan, Semih (1997). "Kitabü'l-Gunya'nın Yazarı" *Türk Dilleri Araştrmaları* 7, 13–18.

Toledano, Ehud R. (1994). *Osmanlı Köle Ticareti, 1840–1890*, Istanbul: Tarih Vakfı Yurt Yayınları.

Toledano, Ehud R. (1982). *The Ottoman Slave Trade and Its Suppression 1840–90*. Princeton: Princeton University Press.

Uzunçarşılı, Ismail Hakkı (1988). *Kapıkulu Ocakları*, vol.1. Ankara: Türk Tarih Kurumu.

Vryonis, Speros (1956). "Isidore Glabas and the Turkish Devshirme", *Speculum*, XXXI, 433–443.

Wittek, Paul (1955). "Devshirme and Sharīʿa", *BSOAS*, XVII, 271–278.

Yılmaz, Gülay (2015). "The Devshirme System and the Levied Children of Bursa in 1603–4", *Belleten*, vol. 79, no. 286, 901–930.

Zysow, A., and R. Gleave. 'Khums'. In *Encyclopaedia of Islam*, Second Edition, edited by P. Bearman, Th. Bianquis, C.E. Bosworth, E. van Donzel, W.P. Heinrichs, P.J. Bearman (Volumes X, XI, XII), Th. Bianquis (Volumes X, XI, XII), et al.

Online Sources

Erdem, Hakan (5.5.2018). "Âşıkpaşazâde Haramîlikte Çocuklar Kadar Şenken" *KARAR Newspaper*, https://www.karar.com/yazarlar/hakan-erdem/asik-pasazade-haramilikte-cocuklar-kadar-senken-6905.

Erdem, Hakan (28.4.2018). "Bir Beyin Oğlu Mihailoğlu Ali Bey" *KARAR Newspaper*, https://www.karar.com/yazarlar/hakan-erdem/bir-beyin-oglu-mihaloglu-ali-bey-6847.

Erdem, Hakan (14.4.2018). "Gazi dediğin Nasıl Olmalı?" *KARAR Newspaper*, https://www.karar.com/yazarlar/hakan-erdem/gazi-dedigin-nasil-olmali-6730.

Erdem, Hakan (16.2.2019). "Kroniklerin Sessizliği", *Karar Newspaper*, https://www.karar.com/yazarlar/hakan-erdem/kroniklerin-sessizligi-9291.

Erdem, Hakan (21.4.2018). "Pençiğin Sadaka Olduğu Zamanlar" *KARAR Newspaper*, https://www.karar.com/yazarlar/hakan-erdem/pencigin-sadaka-oldugu-zamanlar-6789.

Holy Qur'ān, *Al-Anfal*, 8:41. https://quran.com/8/41?translations=131.

Slave Voices Unveiled: Practices of Slavery, Dynamics of Agency and Asymmetrical Dependency in the Early Modern Crimean Khanate

Turkana Allahverdiyeva

> This night at midnight, before the cocks had crowed
> The Tatars flew like the wind into our village
> This night at midnight, an evil came to pass
> When the wild Turkic band plundered all our land.[1]

The practices of Black Sea slavery in the context of the Crimean Khanate during the early eighteenth century remain relatively unexplored. One form of slavery prevalent in the Khanate was household slavery, where numerous non-Muslim slaves were captured, enslaved and settled within the households. However, the voices of these enslaved individuals have often been overlooked. This study aims to uncover the voices of non-Muslim slaves through an analysis of selected *qadiasker* court registers from the early eighteenth century.

By examining court records, this paper considers the extent to which these records document the experiences of non-Muslim slaves and the ways in which their voices can be revealed. The agency displayed by individual slaves who personally approached the *qadi* court to assert their rights, file lawsuits against their slaveholders, and secure their freedom will be analysed to shed light on their experiences.

In a broader context, this study not only contributes to our understanding of the specific practices of household slavery in Crimean Khanate but also highlights the legal aspects of enslavement practices, personal slave experiences, degrees of asymmetrical dependencies and agency of slaves through their indirect voices. By exploring the voices of subalterns within the institution of slavery, it adds valuable insights to the field of Black Sea slavery studies and the broader scholarship on global slavery.

1 Shuvit, *The Ukrainian Cossacks*, 2. See also Subtelny, *Ukraine, A History*, 106.

 | DOI:10.30965/9783657796328_007

Introduction: Can the Slaves be heard? Exploring Subaltern Voices and Slave Narratives

The voices of subalterns have become an illuminating and appealing examination of enslavement practices in the recent historiography. Gayatri Spivak asked "Can the subaltern speak?" many years ago and since then, a lot has been said and written about it.[2] Spivak uses the term subaltern, coined by Antonio Gramsci, to refer to socially, politically, and economically marginalized groups of individuals in colonial and postcolonial period. With hegemonic power structures, these people are frequently denied a voice and agency. In addition, Spivak raises concerns about the possibility of subaltern agency and the difficulties encountered by marginalized individuals both within their own communities and in broader society. She emphasizes the need for nuanced analysis to comprehend the dynamics of power and resistance by highlighting the complexities and contradictions of subaltern agency.

Rosalind Morris, who put together the book with the same name, is a major contributor to the study of subaltern groups.[3] Although since then the field has drawn the attention of social historians all around the world, and a considerable number of studies have been conducted in this regard, subaltern studies, voices of slaves, slave agency, asymmetrical dependency and enslavement practices in the early modern Crimean Khanate have been sorely understudied. J.H. Hagedorn describes agency as "an abstraction of the ability of individuals to influence the world around them and to shape it according to their wishes and desires. It conceptualizes slaves as historical actors rather than as the objects of the actions of others."[4]

When examining the subaltern studies of Gayatri Spivak, one may query the applicability of her arguments to the specific context of non-elite domestic slavery in the Crimean Khanate. Because from the fifteenth to the eighteenth centuries, the Crimean Khanate had its own distinct social, political, and economic dynamics and slave trade was one of the main sources of economic revenue.[5] Individuals from non-Muslim neighbourhoods were kidnapped,

2 Spivak, "Can the Subaltern Speak?" revised edition from the "History" chapter of Critique of Postcolonial Reason, in *Can the Subaltern Speak. Reflections on the History of an Idea*, 21–22.

3 Morris, "Introduction", 1–2.

4 Hagedorn, *Domestic Slavery in Syria and Egypy, 1200–1500*, 20–22.

5 Fisher, "The Sale of Slaves in the Ottoman Empire: Markets and State Taxes on Slave Sales, Some Preliminary Considerations", 150; Fisher, *A Precarious Balance: Conflict, Trade, and Diplomacy on the Russian-Ottoman Frontier*, 8; Smirnov, *Krymskoe xanstvo pod verxovenstvom otomanskoj porty do načala XVIII veka*, reprint edited by Svetlana F. Oreškova. For more

captivated, traded and decreased to slavery.[6] In this regard, Spivak's concept of the subaltern and her analysis of power relations and representation were developed predominantly within the context of postcolonial studies, with an emphasis on the experiences of marginalized groups in colonial and postcolonial contexts. Nevertheless, while her work provides vital insights into the dynamics of power, agency, and voices of the subaltern, its applicability to the unique circumstances of non-elite domestic slavery in the Crimean Khanate must be evaluated critically.[7]

Transitioning into the incorporation of subaltern people into the social and legal history of the Crimean Khanate involves hearing their voices and comprehending their experiences as slaves. By now, the displaced enslaved people, who predominantly came from Eastern Europe and Northern Caucasus and were mostly non-Muslims, were usually ignored and their voices were not heard in the margins of the society. The goal of this study is to give partially those people their voices back, restore their voices, let them be heard, and figure out how enslavement functioned in the legal and social context in the early modern Black Sea Region through their voices by posing the subsequent research questions.

Can the subaltern, specifically slaves, be given voice within the historical context of the early eighteenth-century Crimean Khanate, as elucidated through the examination of *qadi* court registers? To what extent were concepts of bondage, slave ownership, asymmetrical dependency, and diverse forms of agency manifest in this societal framework? How do notions of gendered agency and the interagency dynamics between female and male slaves manifest in the intricacies of daily life and socio-economic interactions?[8] In what ways did enslaved individuals resist and contend against their subjugation? What strategies were employed in the pursuit of freedom and the assertion of their rights within the justice system? Lastly, can discernible evidence be found indicating a reduction in the degree of dependency for these individuals within the context they navigated? In addressing these inquiries, the present study relies upon the examination of *qadiasker* court records originating from the Crimean Khanate spanning the years 1700 to 1720.[9]

---

information on economic and political effects of slave raids on the Crimean Khanate see Yağcı, "Köle Akınlarının Kırım Hanlığı Üzerindeki Siyasi ve Ekonomik Tesirleri".

6 Kizilov, "Slave Trade in the Early Modern Crimea From the Perspective of Christian, Muslim, and Jewish Sources", 11.

7 For more on domestic slavery, see, Hagedorn, *Domestic Slavery in Syria and Egypy, 1200–1500*.

8 Conermann and Şen, "Slavery is not Slavery: On Slaves and Slave Agency in the Ottoman Empire".

9 Turan, "Kırım Hanlığı Kadı Sicilleri Hakkında Notlar", 1.

Opportunities, Challenges and Limitations of the Court Registers

The extensive documentation and meticulous preservation of these records make it simpler to discover the voices of slaves within the court registers of the Crimean Khanate during the early modern period. To genuinely capture and convey the voices, stories, experiences, and suffering of those who were enslaved remains a formidable challenge for historians. Thus, there are both opportunities and constraints when endeavouring to complete this essential task.[10]

One of the prospects is that accomplishing this mission presents a unique opportunity to not only incorporate slaves into the legal and socioeconomic history of the Crimean Khanate, but also to make a contribution to the global study of slavery. By meticulously documenting and analysing the voices of slaves revealed in court registers, we can cast light on their lived experiences, perspectives, and obstacles, thereby enhancing our comprehension of this period in human history.

Moreover, enabling the enslaved to have their voices heard provides a crucial platform for recognizing their agency within a system of slavery. By examining their narratives, we can discern the diverse ways in which slaves navigated and resisted their circumstances, illuminating the intricate relationship between slavery and individual resilience.[11] In addition, investigating the levels of asymmetrical dependency experienced by enslaved can enhance our understanding of power dynamics, social hierarchies, and the broader implications of slavery in the Crimean Khanate and beyond.[12]

Notwithstanding, the limitations are that the court registers are state-centred documents that the litigants' entries are heard by the *qadi* and written down by a scribe after being translated into a bureaucratic and legal language.[13] This implies that the authentic voices of the slaves within the courtroom remain elusive, as we lack direct access to their unfiltered statements or knowledge of the languages they used. While the court registers are documented in Ottoman Turkish with the Arabic alphabet, it would be an assumption to assert that the

10 Zilfi, "Thoughts on Women and Slavery in the Ottoman Era and Historical Sources", 135.

11 Conermann and Şen, "Slavery is not Slavery: On Slaves and Slave Agency in the Ottoman Empire".

12 On asymmetrical dependency, see Winnebeck, Sutter, Hermann, Antweiler and Conermann, *On Asymmetrical Dependency*.

13 Peirce, "'She is Trouble … And I Will Divorce Her': Orality, Honor and Representation in the Ottoman Court of 'Aintab'", 269–300; Özkoray, "From Persecution to (Potential) Emancipation: Female Slaves and Legal Violations in Ottoman Istanbul according to Court Registers (16th and 17th Centuries)", 261.

slaves themselves spoke Ottoman Turkish, given that the prevalent language in Crimea was Crimean Tatar. Considering that household slaves were likely brought to the Crimean Khanate through abduction, it is reasonable to assume that they would have acquired proficiency in the local language over time.

Effectively narrating the voices of the slaves poses an additional challenge, necessitating a profound understanding of the legal framework, the intricacies of Islamic law, and the roles played by local qadi courts within the Ottoman Empire and the Crimean Khanate.[14] Without a comprehensive grasp of how Ottoman courts administered justice, interpreting the voices of slaves may lead to unwarranted assumptions and speculative conclusions.[15]

"Law and Division of Power in the Crimean Khanate (1532–1774)", a seminal book by Natalia Krolikowska, remains indispensable for understanding the legal system and legal complexities of the Crimean Khanate.[16] Krolikowska succinctly outlines the court processes briefly noting that "[...] descriptions of litigants contain indications about their religion. The formulae often reveal their social background, residential affiliation (the names of their villages and sometimes also the names of the judicial districts in which they lived), and occupation as well. The following part of the entries consists of the spoken record. It opens with the plaintiff's statement or accusation, followed by the response of the other party. As oral testimony played a crucial role in the Islamic/Ottoman court procedure, the entries usually contain the "voices" of the parties, edited by court writers."[17]

Boğaç Ergene and Krolikowska caution us to approach the voices captured in court registers with scrutiny, recognizing that these records might not authentically reflect the true voices of the individuals involved. As B. Ergene contends, "the sicil, of course, is nothing but a translation of a particular legal performance into a formal and immensely formulaic language. In the process of this translation, variation is eliminated, and temporal, spatial, and improvisational characteristics of individual performances are left out."[18]

14 Rustamov, "Проблемы в Изучении Крымских Судебных Реестров XVII–XVIII Вв" (Problems of the Study of the Crimean Court Registres of the 17th-18th Centuries), 602–615.

15 Ze'evi, "The Use of Ottoman Sharīʿa Court Records as a Source for Middle Eastern Social History: A Reappraisal", 37.

16 Królikowska-Jedlińska, *Law and Division of Power in the Crimean Khanate (1532–1774)*, 159–169.

17 Ibid, 18.

18 Ergene, *Local Court, Provincial Society, and Justice in the Ottoman Empire: Legal Practice and Dispute Resolution in Çankiri and Kastamonu (1652–1744)*, 130–132.

The pressing question then arises: where and how can we reveal the voices and agency of slaves within the legal system? Direct quotes from litigants and defendants found in court registers are a compelling source to answer these questions. These quotes, employing ego speech such as "I" (Ben), "me" (bana, beni), "my" (benim), create a sense of direct engagement with the individuals involved. According to Ergene, the use of direct quotes indicates the physical presence of these individuals in court, and the *qadi's* inclusion of such quotes serves to establish the legitimacy of the trial.[19] However, Ergene also urges caution in interpreting these direct quotes as the parties' actual words because their voices have been translated and put back together based on the legal language of the registers.[20] Despite the translation, it can be argued that, in many instances, the direct voices of slaves offer valuable details and clues about the events, shedding light on their grievances and demands from the defendants.

To unravel the intricacies of justice within the Ottoman Empire, it becomes imperative to delve into the operational mechanisms of the judicial institutions and understand how the courts operate? Boğaç Ergene's thesis serves as a valuable resource, shedding light on various aspects of the Ottoman courts. This includes insights into the challenges of corruption within these courts, the imposition of court fees, the presence of corrupt *qadis*, the significant role of local customs in decision-making processes, and the sway exerted by the local elite (ayan) over court judgments.[21] The book he co-authored with Metin Coşgel, titled "Economics of Ottoman Justice: Settlement and Trial in the Sharia Courts" aids much in comprehending the voices of the agents in the court records and the process of *qadi* courts.[22]

Ergene's inquiry places a significant spotlight on the pervasive issue of corruption entrenched in the Ottoman justice system. Within the intricate fabric of this judicial framework, bribery, favoritism, and unethical conduct cast a shadow over the pursuit of justice. His exploration delves into the depths of these corrupt practices, unraveling the hurdles faced by individuals in their quest for justice.

---

19 Ibid, 134.

20 Ibid, 134.

21 Ibid, 132–134; For its critic, see Yıldız, "Boğaç A. Ergene'nin Osmanlı Hukuku Eleştirisinin Eleştirisi".

22 Coşgel and Ergene, *The Economics of Ottoman Justice. Settlement and Trial in the Sharia Courts.*

A crucial dimension of Ergene's research centres on the intricate examination of court fees.[23] Through a meticulous analysis, he elucidates the far-reaching consequences of the financial burdens imposed on litigants and their subsequent access to justice. This scrutiny uncovers the economic implications, especially for marginalized groups like slaves, who grappled with additional barriers owing to their social status.

In essence, Ergene's work underscores the intricate interplay of corruption and financial impediments within the Ottoman justice system. Understanding the voices and agency of slaves within this legal milieu demands a nuanced exploration of the contextual intricacies, inherent limitations, and the complexities of translating historical court records.

Onward and Homeward: Where is Vasil's Home?

Analysing the case of Vasil, a non-Muslim slave under the ownership of Şahin Giray Sultan in the Crimean Khanate, provides insights into the complex dynamics of slavery and the agency of enslaved individuals. Vasil's appearance before the court in 1703–1704, where he declares, "I was a run-away slave but I returned to this Land of my own will," raises questions about his motivations and the factors that influenced his decision to come back to Crimea.[24]

Described in the court records as a tall, blonde-haired slave with blue eyes, Vasil's residence in Kerch, a region notorious for slave raids in the Crimean Khanate's Eastern territories, suggests he might have been captured in a raid, either directly by Şahin Giray Sultan or as part of the Girays dynasty's "slave share."

In investigating Vasil's case, we are compelled to consider the distinct perspective and experiences of subjugated individuals, lending weight to their voices, which have frequently been marginalized or eclipsed in historical narratives. Vasil's assertion that he voluntarily returned to Crimea challenges preconceived conceptions about the passive and subservient character commonly associated with slaves. By speaking out and asserting control over his own destinies, Vasil challenges the prevalent narratives of helplessness.

23 Ergene, *Local Court, Provincial Society and Justice in the Ottoman Empire: Legal Practice and Dispute Resolution in Çankırı and Kastamonu (1652–1744)*, 76–77.

24 CCR 37, 65.

The reasons for Vasil's return to Crimea can only be speculated upon. One possibility is that he may have lost his sense of belonging or identity within his previous community. After years of slavery, especially as a slave of the ruling family, he might have struggled to readjust to his former life. It is plausible that his living conditions and level of autonomy within the elite household of Crimea were better than what he would have experienced in his own homeland.

Another possibility is that, after years of enslavement, Vasil may have been unable to locate his close kin or relatives in his hometown. Consequently, he chose to return to a familiar place he knew better than his homeland and where he felt more connected. The experience of enduring slavery for an extended period can create a sense of being caught between two worlds, where one no longer feels a strong connection to their place of birth or the culture they were forcefully assimilated into.

In either case, Vasil's ability to exercise agency is evident in his choice to escape and then willingly return to slavery. His entry in the court record highlights the agency, choices, and mobility that some male slaves possessed. It provides valuable insights into the process of slave raids, the capture of individuals, and their autonomy, decision-making, and mobility.

However, another important nuance in this case is to consider the limitations and constraints imposed on domestic female slaves. The question arises as to whether a female slave would have had the same level of agency and mobility as Vasil. The evidence suggests that female slaves, especially domestic slaves, faced greater restrictions on their mobility and agency compared to their male counterparts. It is unlikely that a female slave would have been able to travel such long distances alone and then return without encountering significant obstacles. Although there may be exceptions, the majority of cases investigated do not demonstrate the same level of mobility for female slaves. It emphasizes the need to consider the varying degrees of dependency experienced by male and female slaves and the constraints imposed on their mobility. On the other side, it is essential to acknowledge that domestic female slaves experienced and enjoyed circulation of knowledge and also possessed agency. In some instances, they were able to decrease their degree of dependency and negotiate their situation, as well.

Overall, the case of Vasil underscores the complexities of slavery in the Crimean Khanate. It highlights the agency and mobility that some male slaves possessed, while also shedding light on the limitations imposed on female slaves. Understanding these dynamics contributes to a broader comprehension of the experiences of enslaved individuals and the power dynamics within the institution of slavery.

Echoes of Freedom: Konasbi's Struggle in the Legal Arena

> [...] Being Beyaz's slave, she had manumitted me from her possessions eight years prior to this record. And now, this Mehmet Monla (Beyaz's husband) claims that I am his property transferred to him by my late owner Temeş ... he has no authority over me. Therefore, I am free from Temeş's ownership after his death, and I am no longer associated with him. Beyaz is the one who possessed the property and rights (and she freed me). In this situation, the mentioned Mehmet bin Monla, attacks me (attempts to re-enslave me), so let him be questioned and let the attack by him on me be banned [...].[25]

This interesting court case of Konasbi(?)[26] bint Abdullah sheds light on the voice and agency of female slaves and their active participation in the Khanate's legal system. The experience of Konasbi narrated by her indirect voice in the year of 1705/1706 as a freed ex-slave enlighten us on the complexities of her journey and the varying degrees of dependency she encountered throughout her life.

According to the record, Konasbi was a *dogma* slave with sheep eyes and short height.[27] Her *dogma* status indicates that Konasbi was born and raised within the Khanate. Her prior origins are unknown, but her name, "bint Abdullah," indicates that she may have been a slave who converted to Islam. She served as a *câriye* (slave woman) for Gazi Kirman for 22 years. Upon his demise, she was handed down and transferred between numerous proprietors. In the end, after the death of her previous owner, she was sold and purchased by a female slave owner named Beyaz, who consequently liberated her eight years before the date of the case 1705/1706.

Konasbi's court appearance was prompted by Beyaz's husband Mehmet Monla ibn Temeş, who claimed ownership over her and sought to re-enslave her. In response, Konasbi introduced witnesses who testified that Beyaz had manumitted her eight years prior. The judge ruled in her favour and ordered Beyaz's spouse to cease his efforts to enslave her. There is a need to examine the agency of a female slave Konasbi through her voice and narrative within this case.

Considering Konasbi's history, it is evident that during her time as a slave she had limited agency. Born into slavery and serving multiple slaveholders for more than 14 years, her autonomy was severely restricted. However, after gaining her independence, her agency became more apparent. She chose to remain in the Khanate, near to the family who formerly possessed her. It is

25 CCR, 38, 45.

26 The name of the slave is not readable. It is either Konasbi, Konambi or Konasil.

27 Özdem, *Kırım Hanlığında Kölelik, 1648–1699*, 29.

possible that she continued to reside with them as a manumitted woman, relishing their protection and support. She could have also married a local man and established her own existence close to the family.

Konasbi's willingness to appear in court with her witnesses, despite the threat of re-enslavement and at the expense of her freedom, demonstrates her determination to assert her autonomy and safeguard her newly-acquired status as a free woman. Although the specifics of her life as a slave remain obscure, her ability to recall the details of her captors and the years she spent under their control exemplifies her tenacity and desire to attain her freedom.

It is essential to acknowledge that the experiences and levels of dependence of female slaves varied considerably. *Dogma* slaves like Konasbi, who were born and raised within the Khanate, experienced a distinct set of circumstances than imported slaves due to their integration into the household and society. This status as a native-born slave implies a degree of familiarity with the local language, culture, religion, and customs. Konasbi's development within the Khanate may have facilitated her integration into the household and society, in contrast to imported captives who may have confronted greater cultural and linguistic barriers. This familiarity with her environment may have helped her navigate the legal system and assert her freedom.

Another crucial point is that the court register does not provide a detailed account of Konasbi's entire existence, nor does it convey the full extent of her agency as a female slave. Nonetheless, it is a valuable historical document that casts light on the experiences of slaves and their participation in the legal system. By examining the case of Konasbi and the larger context of slavery in the Ottoman Empire, we can gain insight into the complexities of slavery, the degrees of dependence experienced by enslaved individuals, and the resilience and voices of female slaves within this system.

A Voice Unheard: Nasta's Courtroom Narrative

> […] My lady Sahibe, when she gave birth to her aforementioned son Cantimur, she linked (made a vow) his riding on a horse to my emancipation, saying that if this son of her grows up and becomes able to ride a horse, then I am emancipated. After one or two years passed, she eventually emancipated me, declaring that I am free. However, when I requested my emancipation certificate, she denied it, intending to keep me as her slave. Furthermore, her son Cantimur is still able to ride his own horse, and he continues to do so. It is clear that I am emancipated. Therefore, I request that my emancipation document (ıtknâme) be delivered to me and my status as a free woman be recognized […].[28]

28 CCR, 36, 50.

The long story of slave Nasta in Bakhchysarai draws attention from many aspects such as resistance, agency, manumission of a non-elite household slave. In 1702, a female slave named Nasta who is described as a Ukrainian-origin (Rus) non-Muslim woman who sues her female owner Sahibe bint Mustafa complaining that when her owner Sahibe gave birth to her son Cantimur, she made a vow clearly stating that when her son Cantimur could mount and dismount a horse without outside aid, she would manumit her slave Nasta. However, when Sahibe's son Cantimur grows up and manages to mount and dismount a horse, Sahibe denies to perform her vow and manumit Nasta. Eventually, Nasta sues her owner in the *qadi* court as she believes she was a free woman even ten years ago. In the court, Sahibe's legal representative denies that vow.

Afterwards, Nasta's Muslim witnesses confirm Nasta's claim. As we understand, Nasta has got four witnesses, overall. They say the fact that they have heard when Sahibe loudly remarked of Nasta's being a free woman ten years ago when she said "I have manumitted Nasta and she is a free woman".

According to the *shariah*, this kind of making a vow is called *Adak* (*Fasl-ı Fi'n-Nezr*). *Adak* is another type of taking an oath and violating it involves paying *kaffarah* (*expiation*).[29] *Kaffarah* of such vow is paid by a manumitting a slave.[30] Necati Demirtaş notes, "*Adak*" or "nadhr" in the lexicon refers to something that an individual has made obligatory (*wâjib*) or promised to do. As a term in Islamic jurisprudence, however, it refers to "a person's promise to perform a mandatory act of worship, even though they are not obligated to do so by Islamic law."[31] A vow is valid when it is said orally or when it is intended. Nasta knows about it and uses this argument against her owner Sahibe to get her freedom.

Oral statement is evaluated as a confession and it has legally binding character and if there are at least two witnesses who have heard that verbal expression, then the case is resolved in the favour of claimer.[32] In this case, *qadi* makes a decision that upon Sahibe's clear expression and the witnesses

29 El-Awa, *The Theory of Punishment in Islamic Law: A Comparative Study*, 79–80.

30 According to verse 5/89 of Surah Al-Maida, the expiation for violating an oath is as follows: 1- To feed ten impoverished people on a scale equivalent to that with which you feed your own families; 2- To clothe them; 3- To set an enslaved person free. "*Allah will not call you to account for your thoughtless oaths, but He will hold you accountable for deliberate oaths. The penalty for a broken oath is to feed ten poor people from what you normally feed your own family, or to clothe them, or to free a bondsperson. But if none of this is affordable, then you must fast three days. This is the penalty for breaking your oaths. So be mindful of your oaths. This is how Allah makes things clear to you, so perhaps you will be grateful.*" Accessed online: https://quran.com/al-maidah/89 (8.6.2023).

31 Efendi, *Açıklamalı Osmanlı Fetvâları: Fetâvâ-yı Ali Efendi (1674–1686) Cild-i Sâni*, 234.

32 Peirce, "She is trouble and I will divorce her: Orality, Honor, and Representation in the Ottoman Court of Aintab", 267–300.

who have heard it, Nasta is free and should be given her freedom certificate 'itkname'.

What does Nasta's case tell us about female slave agency and manumission? Nasta's manoeuvre to get back her freedom demanded a great deal of agency from her to gather the witnesses to speak up against their neighbour Sahibe and through her capability of agency she could get her freedom.

As for the dependency relations between Nasta and her slaveholder Sahibe, we need to ask why Nasta waited for ten years to come to the court for her freedom certificate. Does it mean that Nasta did not want to go to the court or did not need to go to the court or did not want to go to her homeland in those ten years. Was it because of loyalty of Nasta to her owner? Several studies show that in Muslim societies, patronage relationship between a slave and a slaveholder after several years of service became a part of the culture. Especially after so many years, getting adapted to the local culture and learning the language, it might be a terrifying idea for a woman to travel back to homeland into an uncertain future. In this regard, manumitted slaves were in between two worlds, i.e., purgatory. Nasta was aware her rights that *sharia* court heralded her and procedure of the court and had an understanding that how the court functions.

Overall, Nasta's account highlights the complex negotiations and struggles for freedom within the Crimean Khanate. It showcases the agency of enslaved individuals, their ability to leverage personal connections, and their determination to assert their rights and claim emancipation despite potential resistance from slaveholders.

From Conversion to Manumission: The Tale of Slave Hasan bin Abdullah

> [...] My master, El-hac Yusuf bin Abdullah, after the afternoon prayer, when he came to the shop, emancipated me, declaring that I am free and independent ... I request that my emancipation document be written and my freedom be officially recognized [...].[33]

As the last but not least case of interpreting and analysing the voices of subalterns within the context of asymmetrical dependency, slave agency, and resistance, we examine the case of Hasan bin Abdullah, an Albanian convert slave, who applied to the *qadi* court in 1701/1702 to sue his owner el-hac Yusuf bin

33 CCR 36, 96.

Abdullah, offers valuable insights into the agency and manumission practices within the Crimean Khanate during the early eighteenth century. Hasan was characterized by his average height, straight nose, round face, dark eyes, and dark complexion. It is plausible that Hasan bin Abdullah was not his original name.

According to Hasan, after the afternoon prayer when coming back to the shop, his slaveholder Yusuf reportedly announced in front of witnesses that he had emancipated his slave Hasan and that he was now free. Hasan asserted his freedom and asked the court to document his emancipation and recognize his freedom. However, when questioned, Yusuf denied Hasan's claims and stated he had never granted him freedom. This asymmetrical power structure reflects the subaltern position of slaves, who frequently struggled to assert their autonomy and resist their slaveholders.

Hasan presented the testimony of two credible Muslim witnesses to support his case: Can Gâzi bin Hacı Bayram, a grocer, and Mustafa Sûfi ibn Ahmet Atalık, dellal (a trader). Their testimonies supported Hasan's emancipation and freedom in both words and spirit, confirming his narrative. The court accepted the testimony of Can Gâzi and Mustafa Sûfi, recognizing their credibility and their statements' consistency with Hasan's account. Thus, Hasan's freedom was officially recorded and documented. Hasan's agency in navigating the legal system and challenging the power dynamics in the slave society were exemplified by the court's decision, which marked a significant moment of resistance and empowerment.

It appears from the narrative that Hasan was working in Yusuf's shop, which may have functioned as a workshop. Skilled slaves were often costly and typically purchased by artisans to work in their workshops. Thus, Hasan likely served as a skilled slave rather than a household servant, acknowledging that household domestic slaves were also skilled.

Why is this distinction significant? Slaves employed outside of the household generally enjoyed greater agency and less dependency. They had more opportunities for socializing, networking, and acquiring knowledge about legal procedures, such as applying to the court for emancipation. Hasan, familiar with Islamic Sharia law prior to his court appearance, brought two reliable Muslim witnesses with him—Can Gâzi, a grocer, and Mustafa Sûfi, a trader—who shared his owner Yusuf's profession. These witnesses were likely colleagues, working in the same bazaar or market street. Hasan's ability to secure such witnesses against his slave owner Yusuf demonstrates the significant agency he had acquired.

Considering Hasan as a skilled slave in Yusuf's workshop, we can discern a certain level of mutual dependency between them. The question arises as to why Yusuf initially manumitted Hasan immediately after the afternoon prayer in the mosque but subsequently denied it in court. In Islam, granting freedom to a slave is regarded as a virtuous act. Yusuf may have shown compassion towards Hasan, particularly if Hasan converted to Islam during his time in Yusuf's ownership. However, upon their arrival at the shop or workshop, Yusuf likely recognized the extent of his dependency on Hasan in the business realm and retracted his earlier verbal manumission statement. Consequently, Hasan took matters into his own hands, approached the court, fought for his rights, and ultimately gained his freedom.

While the story Hasan presents appears credible, the underlying circumstances remain uncertain. Nonetheless, Hasan's ability to mobilize witnesses and assert his agency in the face of denial and opposition from his erstwhile slaveholder illuminates the subaltern population's potential for resistance and pursuit of freedom.

Conclusion

In conclusion, this study attempted to shed light on the voices of enslaved individuals within the context of the Crimean Khanate, aiming to understand their experiences, agency, and struggle for emancipation. It is evident that the institution of slavery was deeply entrenched in the economic and social fabric of the time, which impacted the access and opportunities available to slaves within the judicial system. While some slaves, like Vasil, Nasta and Konasbi, were able to assert some control over their lives and pursue their freedom, it is crucial to acknowledge that not all slaves had equal access to the *qadi* court or agency. While urban slaves enjoyed more access to the justice system, many rural slaves might have never grasped the chance to reach the court to fight for their rights. The limitations imposed by region, gender, and social structures often prevented many individuals from engaging with the legal system and seeking justice.

Through the available records and glimpses into their lives, we can begin to piece together the narratives of these enslaved individuals and challenge simplistic notions of victimhood. Their stories remind us that despite the severe constraints on their autonomy, some of them grasped a chance to actively navigate their circumstances and seek to shape their own destinies. It is important to recognize the limitations of the available sources and the need for further research and analysis. The sociolinguistic and semantic interpretation of the texts from the *qadi* courts requires ongoing study to fully grasp the nuances of the enslaved individuals' voices and experiences. By amplifying the voices of these subaltern figures, a deeper comprehension of the complexities of slavery in the Crimean Khanate is attained, transcending a one-dimensional portrayal of their lives. Their stories stand as a testament to resilience, agency, and humanity, highlighting their active role in shaping their narratives within a system designed to dehumanize them.

Works Cited

Unpublished Primary Sources

Crimean Court Registers, Fond 917, Otdel Rukopisey Rossiyskoy Natsionalnoy Bibliotek (ORRNB). [CCR]

- A.H. 1013–1118, A.D. 1701–1706, Volume 36.

- A.H. 1114–1116, A.D. 1703–1704, Volume 37.

- A.H. 1116–1117, A.D. 1704–1706, Volume 38.

Published Primary Sources

Çatalcalı Ali Efendi, *Açıklamalı Osmanlı Fetvâları: Fetâvâ-yı Ali Efendi (1674–1686) Cild-i Sâni* (2014). Ed. H. Necâti Demirtaş. Istanbul: Kubbealtı.

Published Sources

Abdalla Selim El-Awa, Mohamed (1972). *The Theory of Punishment in Islamic Law: A Comparative Study*. Phd Dissertation, Univeristy of London.

Conermann, Stephan and Gül Şen (2021). "Slavery is not Slavery: On Slaves and Slave Agency in the Ottoman Empire." Stephan Conermann, Gül Şen ed. *Slaves and Slave Agency in the Ottoman Empire*. Bonn: Bonn University Press, 11–31.

Coşgel Metin and Boğaç Ergene (2016). *The Economics of Ottoman Justice. Settlement and Trial in the Sharia Courts*. Cambridge: Cambridge University Press.

Ergene, Boğaç (2003). *Local Court, Provincial Society, and Justice in the Ottoman Empire: Legal Practice and Dispute Resolution in Çankiri and Kastamonu (1652–1744)*. Boston, Leiden: Brill.

Fisher, W Alan (1999). *A Precarious Balance: Conflict, Trade, and Diplomacy on the Russian-Ottoman Frontier*. The ISIS Press.

Fisher, W. Alan (1978). "The Sale of Slaves in the Ottoman Empire: Markets and State Taxes on Slave Sales, Some Preliminary Considerations." *Boğaziçi University Journal, Humanities*, Vol 6, 149–174.

Hagedorn, Jan Hinrich (2020). *Domestic Slavery in Syria and Egypt, 1200–1500*, published PhD thesis, Bonn: Bonn University Press.

Jedlińska Królikowska, Natalia (2019). *Law and Division of Power in the Crimean Khanate (1532–1774.)* Leiden/Boston, Brill.

Kizilov, Mikhail (2007). "Slave Trade in the Early Modern Crimea From the Perspective of Christian, Muslim, and Jewish Sources", *Journal of Early Modern History* 11, 1–2, 1–31.

Morris, Rosalind (2010). *Introduction*. Ed. Rosalind Morris. *Can the Subaltern Speak. Reflections on the History of an Idea*. New York: Columbia University Press, 1–21.

Özdem, Zeynep (2017). *Kırım Hanlığında Kölelik, 1648–1699*. Unpublished PhD Thesis, Kahramanmaraş Sütçü İmam University.

Özkoray, Hayri Gökşin (2019). "From Persecution to (Potential) Emancipation: Female Slaves and Legal Violations in Ottoman Istanbul according to Court Registers (16th and 17th Centures)." *Journal of Women of The Middle East and the Islamic World*, no. 17. 1–21.

Peirce, Leslie (1998). "She is trouble and I will divorce her: Orality, Honor, and Representation in the Ottoman Court of Aintab," in *Women in the Medieval Islamic World: Power, Patronage, Piety*, ed. Gavin R. G. Hambly (New York: St. Martin's Press): 267–300.

Rustamov, Oleg (2016). "Проблемы в Изучении Крымских Судебных Реестров XVII–XVIII Вв." (Problems of the Study of the Crimean Court Registres of the 17th–18th Centuries), *Золотоордынское Обозрение* Т. 4, No 3, 602–615.

Shuvit, Iryna (2001). *The Ukrainian Cossacks*, Honors Thesis. University of South Florida.

Smirnov V.D. (1887). *Krymskoe xanstvo pod verxovenstvom otomanskoj porty do načala XVIII veka*. St. Petersburg. Reprint ed. Svetlana F. Oreškova (2005). Moscow: Rubeži XXI.

Spivak, Gayatri Chakravorty (2010). "Can the Subaltern Speak?" revised edition from the "History" chapter of Critique of Postcolonial Reason, Morris Rosalind, ed. *Can the Subaltern Speak. Reflections on the History of an Idea*. New York: Columbia University Press, 21–81.

Subtelny, Orest (2009). *Ukraine, A History*. Toronto: University of Toronto Press, Fourth Edition.

Turan, Ahmet Nezihi (2003). "Kırım Hanlığı Kadı Sicilleri Hakkında Notlar." *Türk Kültürü Incelemeleri* 9, 1–16.

Winnebeck, Julia, Ove Sutter, Adrian Hermann, Christoph Antweiler and Stephan Conermann (2021). *On Asymmetrical Dependency*. Concept Paper 01/21. BCDSS, Bonn University, https://www.dependency.uni-bonn.de/images/pdf-files/concept-papers/bcdss_cp_1-_on-asymmetrical-dependency.pdf (10.1.2024).

Yağcı, Zübeyde Güneş (2015). "Köle Akınlarının Kırım Hanlığı Üzerindeki Siyasi ve Ekonomik Tesirleri." Volodimir Melnik, Mehmet Alpargu, Yücel Öztürk and others ed. *Türkiye-Ukrayna İlişkileri, Kazak Dönemi (1500–1800)*. Istanbul: Çamlıca, 393–418.

Yıldız, Kenan (2021). "Boğaç A. Ergene'nin Osmanlı Hukuku Eleştirisinin Eleştirisi." *Journal of Ottoman Studies*, 319–358.

Ze'evi, Dror (1998). "The Use of Ottoman Sharīʿa Court Records as a Source for Middle Eastern Social History: A Reappraisal." *Islamic Law and Society* 5, no. 1, 35–56.

From Slave Violence to the Enchanting Argument. Jesuit Missionary Views of Colonial Paraguay in the *Historia* of Nicolas del Techo

Lionel Mira

> The nobles, the citizens, the plebs, the old men, the women, the Indians, the Blacks and the Spaniards all agreed that after the Jesuits' arrival [in Asunción], the society had changed completely. The city's leaders, judging our usefulness not only from the present benefit but also from the hope of future profit, felt that we should strive to receive this benefit [...]. Consequently, the *regidores* and *oidores* sent letters full of praise for the Society of Jesus to the Catholic King.[1]

Nicolas del Techo S.J. wrote these words in the middle of the seventeenth century, isolated in the heart of Paraguay. He was writing the *Historia Provinciae Paraquariae Societatis Iesu* or, in English, the History of the Paraguayan Province of the Society of Jesus. At that time, del Techo did not know that his book would be published in Liège, the future epicentre of its distribution in Europe. A varied audience, made up of both religious and lay people, would, through his words, discover a piece of land unknown in Europe: Paraguay. According to the provincial entity of the Society of Jesus, Paraguay covered a vast territory over a large part of the Paraná River basin. The *Historia* represents an important source for the historians because it is the first printed history of this region of the world. The *Historia* thus constitutes one of the first "mirrors" of Paraguay in Western Europe. In this book, the author focuses on the first half of the seventeenth century, that is to say the first decades of the evangelising action of the Jesuits settled in the Paraguayan province. Throughout his book, del Techo raises the role played by his religious order in the colonial society in which diverse social groups had already coexisted for many years. The urban society *asunceña*, like that of Paraguay in a more general way, was gradually

---

* I would like to express my warm thanks to Annick Delfosse (ULiège), María Laura Salinas (Universidad Nacional del Nordeste = UNNE) and Josefina Cargnel (UNNE) for the advice they gave me at the very beginning of the research I undertook several years ago in the context of the master thesis.

1 Techo, *Historia Provinciae Paraquariae*, 37: "Denique nobiles, cives, plebei, senes, foeminae, Indi, Aethiopes, Hispani, uno ore fatebantur, post adventum Sociorum plane immutatam Rempublicam. Primores urbis utilitatem non praesenti solum fructu, sed futuri spe emolumenti aestimantes, quoquo modo enitendum censuere, ut bonum [...]. Igitur Magistratus civilis, et Quaestores Regii, ad Regem Catholicum litteras mittunt Societatis laudibus plenas."

 | DOI:10.30965/9783657796328_008

structured by the arrival of flows of populations. In 1537, the conquistadors Juan de Salazar de Espinosa and Gonzalo de Mendoza founded a first fort on the site which became Asunción. This perennial settlement, which occurred early in the conquest of the Río de la Plata – first explored by a European, Juan Díaz de Solis, in 1516 – gave the city the nickname of "mothers of cities". This foundation marked the beginning of a lasting coexistence between the Europeans and the Guaraní, with hundreds of men settling on their lands. Shortly afterwards, the first slaves from Africa were introduced.[2] Their numbers would gradually increase throughout the sixteenth, seventeenth and eighteenth centuries. Several hundred thousand slaves passed through the port of Buenos Aires on their way to the inner part of Latin America. Only several decades later, in 1604, the Society of Jesus founded a province there, having been invited by the colonial authorities. Hernando Arias de Saavedra, governor of the Río de la Plata, promoted the creation of reductions at the boundaries of the Empire at that time, to better mark the border with Portugal. To carry out their project of evangelising the different ethnic groups living in this land, the Jesuits opted for the model of reduction. This corresponds to a kind of "village of converted Indigenous people"[3] or at least one in process of conversion. Several thousand indigenous people were gathered by two Jesuits with the aim of promoting their Christianisation and Europeanisation.[4] At the end of the seventeenth century, the reduction could host up to about 6000 Guaraní souls.[5] African slaves were present in the cities, as del Techo write, but above all in the *estancias*, a kind of ranch belonging to the colleges. Their work allowed the Society of Jesus to develop its economy and thus to finance its actions. The Jesuits quickly took on the role of the mediator between the different groups, being themselves European, but protecting the indigenous people from forced labour and ensuring that the different groups were taught Christianity.

Few works are currently under way to consider the relations between the social groups of modern Paraguay in terms of slavery. More generally, few researchers have examined the relationship between the Society of Jesus and slavery, as Rothman deplores: "The Jesuit entanglement with slavery still does

2 Guillaume Candela recently uncovered an archive document that mentions the presence of an African slave in the port of Buenos Aires with the arrival of Pedro de Mendoza's armada in 1536. This document thus constitutes the oldest trace of the African presence in the Río de la Plata.

3 Duviols, *Indios Guaraníes y Jesuitas*, 13.

4 Each of the thirty reductions founded during the decades of Jesuit presence in Paraguay were led by two fathers. The only exception was Nuestra Señora de la Candelaria, a kind of capital of the reductions. In this village, three Jesuits were permanently present.

5 Jackson, *A population history*, 203.

not always get the attention it deserves"[6]. However, many sources deal directly with this issue, from the relationship between indigenous peoples – whom the Society of Jesus defended from slavery – to the relationships between religious and black slaves. The *Historia* of del Techo, composed of more than 500 chapters, is one of them. Despite its density of information, it has, for now, been paid relatively little attention by historians of the Jesuit missions in Paraguay. In 2005, Bartomeu Melia edited the work of del Techo. But, reproducing the bad Spanish translation of Serrano y Sanz, this text has long remained largely unexploited. It offers the great interest to better understand how the Society of Jesus of Paraguay laid out its action and its relations to slavery in Catholic Europe. In addition, del Techo writes his story from a position on the ground, working in the field, from the missions. Being directly confronted with the slave issue in his daily life, it occupies an important place in his book. Therefore, in this article, we will explore how a Jesuit missionary, Nicolas del Techo, presents slavery in Paraguay and how he situates the Society of Jesus between slave settlers and black and indigenous slaves.

Nicolas del Techo, Writer of the Very First Printed History of Paraguay

The life of Nicolas del Techo begins far from the American continent, while the colonisation and evangelisation by Europe had already begun many decades ago. Del Techo was in fact born in the Spanish Netherlands, in Lille, in 1611, into a family of merchants.[7] Before joining the Society of Jesus, he had studied the humanities, probably at the University of Douai (*Gallia*, he writes).[8] Two years before becoming a monk, he had already turned to Jesuit teaching at the college in Lille. Finally, at the end of 1629, he began to study philosophy under the guidance of Fathers Léonard Robionois and Eustache de la Haye.[9] On 10 January 1630, he entered the Society of Jesus. On the 23rd of the same month, he joined the novitiate in Tournai. During these years he received a solid education: he studied philosophy for three years and theology for four. It was not until about ten years later that del Techo left for Paraguay.[10] He made his way to the port of Dunkirk, in the north of France, to go to Seville,

6 Rothman, "Jesuits and Slavery", 3.
7 Lille, Archives Municipales de Lille [AML], Registre des baptêmes de la paroisse Saint-Étienne (1611–1624), fol. 645.
8 Brussels, Bibliothèque royale de Belgique [KBR], Manuscrits, ms. 3350, fol. 202.
9 Brussels, KBR, Manuscrits, ms. 3350, fol. 202.
10 Brussels, KBR, Manuscrits, ms. 3350, fol. 202.

then Lisbon where he embarked for America. He arrived in the port of Buenos Aires in 1641 and never left the Paraguayan province, where he held various positions, including rector of the college in Asunción and superior of the missions.[11] However, del Techo insisted that he preferred to be in the field, in the missions, among the indigenous people. This attitude led him to doubt his ability to write the history of Paraguay when the Jesuit general wrote to entrust him with this task.[12]

In the midst of the missions, Nicolas del Techo was led to take up his pen to write the history of the first decades of the Jesuit presence in Paraguay, that is, until the middle of the seventeenth century. This source represents a fundamental text for the study of the Society of Jesus, as it is the first printed history of Paraguay. In the seventeenth and eighteenth centuries, this text circulated widely in Europe, as well as in Paraguay. It first crossed the Atlantic in manuscript form, drafted from del Techo's hand. This manuscript version was written in Paraguay in 1658 or shortly afterwards and was examined by the Jesuit censors in Toledo.[13] The text was then printed in Liège in 1673, by Jean Matthias Hovius. From Liège, the printed book spread beyond the borders of the Principality of Liège. The text could be found in Jesuit libraries in Bavaria, France and the Catholic Netherlands.[14] Lay people were also able to obtain the *Historia*. It should also be noted that the printed history was subsequently distributed in Paraguay. Using it as a model, indigenous people copied it, imitating the print.[15] This was the third version of the work. In 1758, the partial translation into Guaraní in the San Carlos reduction constituted the last modern version of the *Historia*. Between these four versions, I have chosen to focus my work on the *Historia* printed in Liège because of the density of the information it contains – over five hundred chapters divided into twelve books – and the diverse audience it reached.

As the preface to his book, Nicolas del Techo told his European brothers that the Society was seeking to recruit new missionaries for Paraguay: "And we hope that this will be a stimulus for the European provinces which have perpetuated the custom of the ancients of sending subsidiaries [...]"[16]. As del Techo had

11 Rome, Archivum Romanum Societatis Iesu [ARSI], Paraquaria 9, Tomas Donvidas, fol. 265 r°-266 r° and Donvidas, ed. 2015, 140.

12 Techo, *Historia Provinciae Paraquariae*, preface.

13 The *Historia* receives the approval of the provincial of Toledo, Diego de Valdes, on December 2nd 1671.

14 This information is obtained from *ex-libris*, that is, handwritten marks of belonging present on the covers of the various copies we have.

15 This book is kept at the Biblioteca Nacional de España (=BNE), in document MSS/5931.

16 Techo, *Historia Provinciae Paraquariae*, preface.

previously gone to evangelise, the primary objective of his *Historia* was precisely to obtain support through the sending of new missionaries. By recounting the events of the Paraguayan past, del Techo hoped to convince the main interested parties, namely the European Jesuits, to apply to work in Paraguay. To do this, he used rhetorical strategies, even if it meant changing the historical reality. He described Paraguay as a land worthy of hell. He emphasised the difficulties encountered, in particular by returning extensively to the struggles that pitted the Jesuits against the Portuguese slavers. The courage and self-sacrifice of the evangelists, which constantly emanate from the *Historia*, led the reader to construct an almost heroic image of the Society of Jesus. Nicolas del Techo's education, especially his four years of theology, and the important positions he held in the Paraguayan province, lead me to believe that he had a solid theoretical knowledge, especially in the field of canon law. Nevertheless, this chapter aims to take the opposite view of a study of the use of law as an anti-slavery weapon in the service of the Society of Jesus. Del Techo positioned himself more as a man of the field, close to the indigenous people and their condition, touched by the horror of a colonial situation unfavourable to religious. He thus chose to act in this way, trying to persuade his readership of the slavery atrocities in his environment and the need for missionary reinforcement.

Horror's Peak: the *mamalucis* Attacks between 1628 and 1641

Within the infernal setting set by Nicolas del Techo in his *Historia*, the struggles between the Jesuits and the Portuguese from São Paulo occupy a prominent place. These conflicts, recounted in several dozen chapters, confronted two positions regarding the slavery of the Natives. The Portuguese, pejoratively referred to as "mamluks" by del Techo, "*bandeirantes*" or more neutrally "Paulists" by historiography, carried out slave raids in the territory of the missions. They left their city, accompanied by indigenous Tupi allies, with the aim of attacking the Jesuit reductions and taking as booty objects from the village and especially hundreds of Guaraní destined to become slaves in Brazil. At the beginning of the seventeenth century, the Luso-Indigenous society based on relationships with shared interests gave way to an organisation whose cornerstone was now the slavery of the Natives.[17] This practice, coupled with disease, quickly led to the decline of the indigenous societies of the Piratininga plateau. The Jesuit reductions in Paraguay were therefore perceived by the Paulists as reservoirs of labour, close to their city – about 500 km away – and vulnerable,

17 Castelnau-L'Estoile, *Un catholicisme colonial*, 177.

as the indigenous peoples were not allowed to use firearms. As soon as the first reductions were established, the Jesuits had to face repeated assaults by slave hunters. These attacks became even more intense between 1628 and 1641, the year in which the Guaraní troops finally managed to gain the upper hand over the Portuguese. Del Techo gives a detailed account of these events, which he describes as tragic for both the indigenous people and the missionaries:

> The *mamluks*, sent by Simón Alvarez, attacked the reduction [of San Antonio], seized it and stole sacred objects and all things they could; killed those they defended themselves against, captured the main Indigenous people, robbed the furniture and clothes of Mola's father.[18]

The theft of objects, the murder and kidnapping of innocent Guaraní and the robbery of the missionary in office, Father Pedro de Mola, all converge to associate the slavery-like action of the assailants with great violence and brutality.

Since their arrival in Paraguay, the Jesuits had been defending another mode of colonisation, rejecting the violent domination of the Natives, embodied by the reduction, "space of freedom and space of conversion"[19]. José de Acosta, in his *De Procuranda Indorum Salute* (Salamanca, 1588), defended the idea that the indigenous people of America were 'complete' human beings, capable of receiving the Gospel, albeit at different levels of development. Acosta divided the American natives' peoples into three categories, according to their degree of idolatry.[20] The first category included those who were farthest from barbarism.[21] It was characterised by "stable regimes of government, public laws, fortified cities, magistrates of notable prestige, prosperous and well-organised trade and, most importantly, the well-recognised use of letter"[22]. The second category included organised indigenous peoples who had complex systems of government when the Spanish started the conquest.[23] However, the monstrosity of some of their customs marred their development.[24] Finally, the third

18 Techo, *Historia Provinciae Paraquariae*, 245: "Altero die Mamalucorum numerosa cohors, Simone Alvaro duce, oppidum aggreditur; diripit, sacra prosanaque miscet, obluctantes obtruncat, in gentis primores vincula injicit, imbellem turbam abigit, Petrum Molam supellectile spoliat".

19 Castelnau-L'Estoile, *Un catholicisme colonial*, 181.

20 Schmidt, "Naissance des polythéismes", 79. For further discussion of Acosta, see the chapter by Stefano Torres in this volume.

21 Thomas, "L'évangélisation des indiens", 13.

22 Acosta, *De Procuranda Indorum Salute*, 63.

23 El Alaoui, *Jésuites, Morisques et Indiens*, 100: This first category does not concern the Native Americans. Indeed, Acosta distinguishes between the Chinese and the Japanese, whom he considered more developed.

24 Acosta, *De Procuranda Indorum Salute*, 65.

category corresponded to that of "wild men, similar to beasts, who hardly have human feelings".[25] According to the Jesuit, these third-class men were only half-humans (*vix homines*).[26] It should be noted that Juan Ginés de Sepúlveda subscribed to this same conception, which he considered valid for all men in America. The indigenous person, however, had the possibility of rising in the human hierarchy imagined by the Jesuits. By converting, the Native came closer to the ideal of humanity as forged by Acosta.

The first Jesuits who worked in Brazil and in the Río de la Plata at the end of the sixteenth century had misinterpreted the Guaraní rituals as devoid of any religiosity. For this reason, the Society had relegated these people to a "sub-human category".[27] They were thus accused on several counts. However, once established in the missions and converted, the Guaraní would prove to be of a particular category: that of the "guaraní misionero".[28] It was a model of its own with original economic, political and social characteristics that constituted, in view of the success of the Jesuit apostolate, a promoted evangelising scheme. Disseminated by the "Jesuit Information Network", it was set up in Paraguay on the basis of the trial previously developed in India.[29] The Paulist attacks undermined this project. It caused thousands of indigenous people to flee, preferring to take shelter in the forests rather than resist willy-nilly in the villages. Del Techo deplored this state of affairs:

> They [the Natives] went through the forests with immense solitude, without provision. Most of them were tormented by hunger or faced uneven obstacles. Remembering the love of their homeland, they retraced their steps [to the forest] dispersing everywhere. The great torment of the fathers was to see their sheep willingly rush into the mouths of the wolves.[30]

The forest was the living environment of the Guaraní before the arrival of the Jesuits and it became again their refuge from the Portuguese attacks. Once they returned to the forest life, in most cases, the indigenous people left the Jesuit fold for good. The choice to flee was well understood by Nicolas del Techo: "It

25 Acosta, *De Procuranda Indorum Salute*, 67.
26 Thomas, "L'évangélisation des indiens", 15.
27 Duviols, *Les jésuites et les Indiens du Paraguay*, 321.
28 Wilde, *Religión y poder*, 113.
29 Clossey, *Salvation and Globalization*, 202.
30 Techo, *Historia Provinciae Paraquariae*, 263: "Ibant omnes per sylvas (sic) et inmensam solitudinem nullo ferme commeatu, et qui plerique aut fame cruciabantur, aut itinerum difficultatibus impares erant, revocanti eos amore patriae, passim ab incoepto itinere redibant; ingenti Sociorum cruciatu oves suas in luporum fauces sponte suam sese praecipitare dolentium".

therefore seems preferable for any of them to flee to a shelter than to expose themselves unarmed to armed and experienced men".[31] That is why protecting them was an absolute necessity for the Society of Jesus. For this reason, in Paraguay, "the most famous Jesuit effort in favour of Indian rights" was carried out.[32]

The missionaries worked on strategies to protect the reductions, each populated by a few thousand Guaraní. The threat from outside turned into a rejection from within: the indigenous converts or those in the process of converting blamed the Jesuits for being complicit in the abductions. They rejected the idea of living together in villages, which they believed was the first act carried out by the religious with a view to handing them over as slaves to the Portuguese.[33] Faced with this, the Society of Jesus opted for defensive strategies, firstly, by encouraging the taking up of arms and defences and, secondly, by fleeing to regions further away from São Paulo. An emblematic figure of the resistance to the Paulist onslaught, Father Diego Alfaro, died at the front. The death of a Jesuit in a war raises a whole host of questions, not least of which is whether he was even allowed to take part. According to del Techo, Alfaro was outside the enclosure, anticipating the advance of the Paulists from the reduction of Caazapá Guazú.[34] At the time of his execution, del Techo writes that the fighting had not yet begun and, as a result, Alfaro could not have taken part in it. He therefore died without engaging in active combat. However, the same account narrated in the *Litterae Annuae* of 1637–1639 offers a different description of the violent end of the superior of the missions. Alfaro had not yet died when "the battle began with great spirit on the part of the Indians".[35] He even took full part in the hostilities: "Then Father Alfaro took charge of the troops, on his horse, in the middle of the battle".[36] Furthermore, "in the heat of the scuffle, one of the enemies hiding in the woods pointed his gun at Father Alfaro and fired a bullet".[37] Alfaro's absence from the battlefield according to del Techo's account contradicts his presence on that very battlefield according to the

31 Techo, *Historia Provinciae Paraquariae*, 256: "Satius itaque videri, quoscumque possent, in tutum fugam retratere quam inermes armatis, expertisque hominibus exponere".

32 McNaspy and Gómez, "Esclavitud negra en América", 1255.

33 Techo, *Historia Provinciae Paraquariae*, 264.

34 Techo, *Historia Provinciae Paraquariae*, 338.

35 Lupercio de Zurbano, *Cartas anuas*, 143: "Comenzó la pelea con mucho brío de parte de los indios".

36 Lupercio de Zurbano, *Cartas anuas*, 144: "Entonces tomó el Padre Alfaro a su cargo la dirección del ejército, metiéndose a caballo en medio de la batalla [...] animándolos en alta voz".

37 Lupercio de Zurbano, *Cartas anuas*, 144: "En el calor de la refriega dirigió uno de los enemigos escondidos en el bosque su arma hacia el Padre Alfaro y le tiró un balazo".

Litterae annuae. Indeed, the intense activity in the writing signed by Francisco de Lupercio Zurbano contrasts with the passivity depicted in the *Historia*. Del Techo adopted a conception of passive martyrdom that he applieed to all the martyrs that appear in the *Historia*. Between the Paraguayan province and the Roman centre of the Society of Jesus, there was considerable correspondence in an attempt to rule on Alfaro's death.[38] Diego de Boroa, who was provincial of Paraguay at the time of the events, defended the thesis of Alfaro's martyrdom in a letter sent to Rome, assuring his readers that he was only encouraging the Guaraní against the Portuguese.[39] As part of this defence, Boroa, as if the Jesuit's passivity had to be supported by his spiritual character, emphasised the need to resist:

> [...] Alfaro's actions were distinctively Jesuit precisely because he was fighting for the just defence of his parishioners. This, as Boroa would argue, was how he put into action the Jesuit obligation to work for the glory of God and the common good. In so doing, he fulfilled his obligations as a Jesuit and a priest and died as a good shepherd defending his flock; as such, Boroa argued, in the manner of his death Alfaro became like Christ.[40]

These elements of martyrdom in the accounts of anti-slavery struggles were highly suitable when it came to attracting new missionaries from the Jesuit colleges in Europe.[41] Del Techo showed how Paraguay was a land of great peril, conducive to martyrdom. From this starting point, he could hope to attract Jesuits from Europe to go to these missions. The Jesuits were thus used to seeing, reading and hearing the martyred image. Del Techo did not innovate by inserting these stories into his *Historia*. On the contrary, he used a well-tested argument that was likely to awaken vocations for Paraguay. The frescoes were already addressed to Jesuits "called to witness to their faith through sacrifice [...] [and who should] nourish a vocation to martyrdom".[42]

---

38 Redden, "The case of Diego de Alfaro", 81–113: In this article, Redden focuses his attention to this arduous question. We regret, however, that he does not consider the trip of procurator Francisco Díaz Taño in his argument. Indeed, during the year 1639, he went to Europe, especially to Rome where he met Urban VIII. The object of his request was to put an end to the Paulist incursions. The death of one of his companions, which is the consequence of it, must certainly have been examined.

39 Redden, "A las buenas personas", 119.

40 Redden, "The case of Diego de Alfaro", 88.

41 See i. a. Bourgaux, "La sporulation du martyre".

42 Dekoninck, *Horreur sacrée et sacrilège*, 33.

In addition to the armed defence of the reductions, the Jesuits worked to move the Natives further west, away from São Paulo, attempting to reduce the danger. This led to the emigration of thousands of people:

> I will tell in a few words how the Jesuit fathers who led so many thousands of neophytes to a space of sixty or seventy *leguas* ... the anguishing solitudes, the lack of the most indispensable. It was common for the missionaries to carry children on their shoulders and deprive themselves of food to care for the children of Christ.[43]

As in this excerpt, del Techo regularly emphasised the suffering experienced by the Jesuit fathers, which was a matter of great self-sacrifice and unfailing courage. He placed the missionaries at the centre of the *Historia*. They represented examples with which friars in Europe were supposed to identify. Their characteristics are clear: they seek to transmit the truth to lost peoples in a context of great threat. This threat, embodied in the slavery-like actions of the Paulists, leads the Jesuits to endure constant suffering.

The "Gentle Evangelisation" in the Mirror of Pro-slavery Brutality

Taken together, the successive narratives of the roundups in the eastern part of the Paraguayan province aim to construct a dualistic conception of the conflict between the Jesuits and the Portuguese of São Paulo. On the one hand, del Techo placed the anti-slavery, God-enlightened Jesuits who tried to announce the Good News at all costs. On the other hand there were the Paulists, slaveholders, led by Satan, who prevented the penetration of the Gospel in these American lands. Each argument, each affront to the attackers, translated, by mimicry, the enhancement of the Society of Jesus. Del Techo actually defined two groups whose value systems were at odds with each other.

The very use of the term 'mamaluci' (*sic*), or 'mamluk', to designate the Portuguese attackers constitutes a strategy of depreciation of the opposing group. As a connotative term, it intends to place the whole group under one banner and to reject both their persons and their actions. In the Mamluk system, children were bought as slaves in different regions, brought back to Cairo

---

43 Techo, *Historia Provinciae Paraquariae*, 332: "Quid porto in itinere sexaginta septuagintave leucarum, per sterilem solitudinem, in deducendis tot mortalibus omnium rerum egentissimis Socii toleravint, quia in omnibus fere patria sunt, sigillatim enartare supersedeo. Passim videre erat Socios ipsos infantibus succollate, qualescumque ciborum cupedias sibi demere, filios, quos in Christo genuerant".

where they were educated and freed once their training was complete. The Mamluks, who were freed slaves, thus bought slaves themselves.[44] There is therefore a slave connotation in the foundation of the Mamluk identity that del Techo attributed to the Portuguese. Moreover, the Mamluk was also a Muslim, considered "infidel" in modern Catholic Europe and whose repulsion was particularly prevalent in post-Reconquista Spain. "The systematic linking of two independent phenomena produces a reasoning by analogy, with the transfer of connotations from the comparator to the compared".[45] In this way, del Techo attributed to the Portuguese a character contrary to the Catholic religion. Under the pen of the Jesuit historian, the Paulists become Mamluks characterised by their brutality and irreligiousness. Del Techo further supported this attack by frequently using the term bandit – *latron, latronis* in Latin – as a synonym for "mamluk"[46]:

> Up until the moment when it has produced, due to the loss of European women, the mixture with Barbarians and the remarkable blood of the Portuguese began to deteriorate. The mixing of races, once several unions had taken place over time, resulted in different sons and corrupt grandsons from the best fathers.[47]

Del Techo justified their criminality by the union of Portuguese with indigenous people. The latter probably belonged to the Guaycurués, who were known for their bellicose character. The two groups collaborated during the slave raids. This probably explains the Jesuit's depreciation of indigenous blood. Here he clearly distinguished the Portuguese who organised the colony from the inhabitants of São Paulo. This can certainly be seen as a preventive attitude on the part of del Techo, or even as an intervention by the censor, who sought to avoid creating a controversy.

Nicolas del Techo, who only occasionally specifies his sources, shows little nuance with regard to the attitude and qualities of the Portuguese in São Paulo, which he decries in the regular way as we have observed in the excerpts quoted above. He is not critical of events that he himself did not experience. For this reason, he reassures the reader that he has met witnesses or that he himself,[48]

---

44 See i. a. Frenkel, "Trade and Education of Slave-Soldiers", 187–212; Mazor, "The Early Experience of the Mamluk", 213–231; Yosef, "Cross-Boundary Hatred", 149–214.

45 Angenot, *La parole pamphlétaire*, 257.

46 E. g. Techo, *Historia Provinciae Paraquariae*, 257, 282, 317.

47 Techo, *Historia Provinciae Paraquariae*, 243: "Donec, ob defectum foeminarum Europearum mixto cum Barbaris genere, insignis ille Lusitanorum sanguis corrumpi coepisset. Quae generis mixtio, ubi interjecto tempore plures corripuit, et optimis patribus successere dissimiles filii, et nepotes vitiosiores".

48 E. g. Techo, *Historia Provinciae Paraquariae*, 316.

decades later, witnessed the consequences of these raids.[49] On the other hand, del Techo tries to convince the reader of the aggressiveness and inhumanity of the Paulists by hammering these events, always told in the same terms, according to the adage of *bis repetita placent*. From this repeated brutality, del Techo wants to detach the actions of the Jesuits from this repeated brutality as much as possible. The more the impetuous harshness of Portuguese behaviour is present in the historical narrative, the more the affability of the Society of Jesus is revealed. During the battle in which the Portuguese seized the reduction of Jesús y María, a bullet pierced the torso of a cacique, named Curuba. In reaction, del Techo writes that Father Simon Mazeta, the village's priest, removed his garment to show his chest and bowed his head. The belligerent himself is said to have confessed that "his ferocity was less than the magnanimity of the Father".[50] Del Techo thus offers an argument *in contra* that tends to nourish the idea that the actions of the Jesuits in Paraguay are a kind of *mundus inversus* in relation to the facts described. In other words, the goodness of the religious was inversely proportional to the wickedness of their enemies.

The brutal slavery practice of the Paulists is in fact portrayed as being a bulwark against the evangelisation of the Natives. At the heart of the *Historia* is in fact the missionary enterprise which, in the author's words, translates into thousands of conversions. Therein lies the real challenge. Repeated incursions have undermined this project. This is all the more damaging because the Guaraní are willing to be Christianised. During the attack on San Pedro and San Pablo:

> When [the mamluks] attracted them [the neophytes], they held a discussion with them without showing any hostile spirit at first; as a result, they brought back [the neophytes], convincing them in a friendly way to want to gather their attention. They arrived at this trickery by abandoning themselves in large groups. The mamluks rushed ferociously at the devotees and chained up the first ones.[51]

The aspiration of indigenous people to receive Christian teaching is such that it is a factor of vulnerability. In the perspective of attracting new recruits to Paraguay, the opening of the Guaraní is a powerful stimulus for the Jesuits of the European colleges to seek to reach America.

49 Techo, *Historia Provinciae Paraquariae*, 317.

50 Techo, *Historia Provinciae Paraquariae*, 246: "[…] minoremque suam ferocitatem Patris magnanimite fassus […]".

51 Techo, *Historia Provinciae Paraquariae*, 282: "Gentis primoribus ad colloquium pellectis edixere, primum non se hostili animo venisse; ergo, reducerent, si operam suam conferre vellent, amice convicturos. Hoc dolo decepti hostilibus se traditum turmatim venere. Sed in deditos Mamaluciērociter involant, primores vinculis onerant".

In addition to this argument of ferocity towards the Portuguese, del Techo shows very clearly that the religious faction moves in the footsteps of God. In Paraguay, in this hellish frontier driven by violence, the Jesuits define themselves as workers of God. Despite the terrible description of the territory and the daily life, they work in an "atmosphere of holiness".[52] Miracles and wonders help them to overcome opponents in order to accomplish their evangelisation tasks. Jesus, Mary and St. Ignatius of Loyola regularly intervene in the *Historia* to encourage conversions, to heal, to advise or to render justice, always in favour of the Society of Jesus. In this way, del Techo frequently evokes the intercession of God or of holy figures who, through various prodigies, support the action of the Jesuits. Through his intervention, "God was not content with restoring a just order, but manifested the truth of the laws and principles of which he was the initiator, in other words, the value attached to a certain number of religious beliefs and practices".[53] God's support was manifested in del Techo's *Historia* by a punitive attitude towards those who stood in the way of Jesuit ambition. The governor of Paraguay, Pedro Lugo de Navarra, was tasked with bringing back to Asunción Portuguese prisoners who, by their actions against the Spanish imperial interest, had engaged the resistance of the colonial authorities. According to the Jesuit historian, his attitude, which was too indulgent towards these criminal captives, caused a ray of sunlight to set his house ablaze and an illness to strike him in the process.[54] In addition to this repressive force, God sends the missionaries preventive signals:

> A singular fact happened in this destroyed reduction [Santa Teresa]. On December 18th, one year ago, a hidden image of the Holy Mary started crying with turned to Brazil. In the same month and day one year later, the inhabitants of Santa Teresa were attacked by les robbers from Brazil. No doubt that these perfect tears of the Virgin were shed from the sufferings linked to these calamities.[55]

Through the intercession of the Virgin Mary, providence made known to the Jesuits the danger that their indigenous flock was in. This prodigy – *prodigia, ostenta, portenta, monstra* – is an extraordinary fact, "included in the vast

52 Deslandres, "Épistémè et missions jésuites", 259.

53 Balzamo, *Les miracles*, 56.

54 Techo, *Historia Provinciae Paraquariae*, 338.

55 Techo, *Historia Provinciae Paraquariae*, 323: "In huius oppidi destructione illud accidit singular, quod superiori anno ibidem decimam-octavam Decembris imago Beatae Virgnis, oculo, quo Brasiliam respiciebat, ubertim fleverit: cumque sequenti año, eodem die et mense recurrente, Theresiani a praedonibus Brasilis oppressi fuerint, nemini dubium fuit, eas lachrymas (*sic*) optimae Matris, fuisse velut compatientis eorum calamitatibus".

group of miracles".[56] It is "experienced collectively, felt by all as a reminder of the divine order or as an announcement of some specific event". These elements clearly lead the reader to believe that the Jesuits are victims of the devil embodied by the Portuguese slavers and that they, on the contrary, are the bearers of good. This Manichean conception of the conflict leaves no room for nuance and different interpretations. Religious people define themselves in opposition to the group they decry and provide an image that is constructed *in contrario* by listing what they are not.

The Place of Afro-American People in the Paraguayan Jesuit Province

While the study of the place of slavery in del Techo's *Historia* inevitably leads us to consider the indigenous people through the numerous accounts of Portuguese raids, the consideration of black slaves is less obvious. This can be explained by the fact that the *Historia* presents Paraguayan society as the meeting of two European and American worlds, while neglecting the continuous arrival of men from Africa. The concealment of the presence of Black people in colonial Paraguay can also be seen in historiography. Indeed, few scholars have devoted themselves to the study of this population and its mixtures in Paraguay during the modern era. In the collective mind, the missions of Paraguay primarily cover the evangelisation of the indigenous peoples by the Jesuits.[57] However, it is a fact that Paraguayan Jesuits were in daily contact with African slaves, above all in the cities, as del Techo affirmed, but also in the countryside, as the order itself participated in the slave trade by buying slaves. As early as 1627, some twenty years after the creation of the Paraguayan province, General Muzio Vitelleschi, from Rome, encouraged the missionaries to acquire slaves: "It is of great importance for the increase in trade that *Rectores* promote the purchase of all the *negros*. It is necessary for cultivating the fields and for taking care of the cattle".[58] The Society of Jesus owned hundreds of black slaves. These were used primarily in the *estancias* belonging to the various colleges in the province.[59] All located in the heart of urban centres,

---

56 Vignaud, "Merveilles", 639.

57 Tardieu, "Ministerios de negros", 141.

58 Morales, *Cartas de los PP. Generales*, 361: "es de grande importançia, para el aumento de las haziendas, que se animen los Rectores a comprar todos los negros, que son menester para labrar las tierras, y guardar el ganado".

59 The Society of Jesus gradually established ten colleges in the Paraguayan province: in Asunción, Buenos Aires, Cordoba, Corrientes, La Rioja, Mendoza, Salta, Santa Fe, Santiago del Estero and Tucumán.

the Jesuit colleges were active in three areas: teaching, pastoral work and economic affairs.[60] The latter led the Jesuits to acquire estates in the countryside. Each college had between two and five *estancias* and *chacras*.[61] For example, the college in Asunción had alone 636 slaves and over 40,000 head of cattle in 1753.[62] These impressive figures highlight the paradox between the close links between black slaves and the Jesuits and the scant information available about them in the studies. In these "ranches", hundreds of slaves lived in near isolation, carrying out the heavy agricultural work that enabled the colleges to grow rich. Jesuits, very few in number compared to the slaves, were present in the *estancias*. The religious of the Society of Jesus quickly attached great importance to the evangelisation of the Blacks, as was the case with the Guaraní. From the very beginning of the organisation of the province of Paraguay, the Christianisation of the Africans who landed at the port of Buenos Aires was given a great deal of attention. To achieve this, learning the language of the slaves, known as the "*lengua de Angola*", was considered virtuous. Mastering the language was a *sine qua non* condition for spreading the Gospel and, by contrast, ensuring that sacrileges were eliminated.[63] For illustrative purposes, del Techo told the story of Blacks baptised in the San Miguel reduction. A Jesuit father asked one of them if he knew what a sacrament meant and this one replied that he did not understand a single word the priest said.[64]

Moreover, the Jesuits showed themselves to be relatively sensitive to the welfare of slaves, even though the Society did not oppose their condition as servants. Several archival documents attest to this sensitivity. At the beginning of the eighteenth century, the Provincial Blas de Silva visited the *estancia* of Santa Catalina, north of Córdoba, and deplored the condition of the slaves:

> The ranches in which the slaves live are in very bad condition and with little or no shelter; some of them are exposed to bad weather and storms and to the slaves become ill; I order that the best possible repairs be made and that new ranches be built in the time that the specific occupations of the estancia will allow.[65]

60 Telesca, "Esclavos y jesuitas", 193.

61 Page, "El espacio arquitectónico", 90f.

62 Telesca, "Esclavos y jesuitas", 194.

63 Tardieu, "Ministerios de negros", 143.

64 Techo, *Historia Provinciae Paraquariae*, 351.

65 Cansanello and Piana, *Memoriales*, 41: "Los ranchos en que viven los esclavos están muy maltratados y con poco o ningún abrigo; algunos de ellos expuestos a las inclemencias y temporales y a que enfermen los esclavos; encargo que se compongan lo mejor que se pudiera y que vayan haciendo otros ranchos nuevos en el tiempo que las ocupaciones precisas de la estancia dieren lugar".

After the suppression of the Society of Jesus in the Spanish Empire in 1767, the slaves in the *estancias* changed owners. The deterioration in their living conditions caused by the sudden departure of the Jesuits led to waves of protests. These culminated in the deportation of the most disobedient slaves.[66]

Nicolas del Techo makes no mention of the existence of *estancias* and gives very little space to the black population in the history of Paraguay. I explain the omission of this social group in del Techo's book by the very issue of its publication. It should be remembered that del Techo's main aim was to attract new missionaries to Paraguay. This is why he presents the reader with a reality from the province's past that is particularly attractive: the establishment of the first reductions, and then the evangelising campaign of the missionaries from the province's early days. In this way, he gives his account of the Jesuit presence in the cities. He speaks of the colleges – which contained the overwhelming majority of the Society's members in this part of America. Secondly, as we read in the excerpt quoted above, the presence of black slaves was intimately linked to the commercial activity of the Society of Jesus. This text, which was to be distributed in Catholic Europe, was not intended to share an image of an enriched religious order, at the risk of giving grist to the mill of anti-Jesuit polemicists. Del Techo therefore focuses more on the indigenous people who also are to be converted than on the Africans who also are to be converted, but who are above all a servile labour force enabling the Society of Jesus to become richer.

The attitude of this religious order is easily seen as ambiguous in the light of the fervent defence of the Natives, for which it was one of the driving forces. The Jesuits, like the Dominican Las Casas, were quick to concern themselves with the rights of the indigenous people; they did not think about what to do with the black people until a later stage. For the Jesuits, "slavery is legitimate if it satisfies five titles or criteria: consented servitude, just war (prisoners), just condemnation (criminals), the sale and purchase of individuals who are sure to be slaves, and birth (children of slaves)".[67] According to them, slavery was not entirely due to a depreciation of the ethnic group in question. In fact, black slaves were bought by the clergy when they already had this status. They did not become slaves under the Jesuit leadership. According to del Techo, the enslavement of the Guaraní was intolerable because it was a matter of taking away the freedom of these men in addition to impeding their conversion. Illustrating the effects of missionary work, the indigenous, once converted,

66 Telesca, "Esclavos y jesuitas", 204–207.

67 Prudhomme, "Esclavage", 647. See also the discussion by Rômulo Ehalt in this volume.

received more consideration by the elevation in the Jesuit conception.[68] For del Techo, the '*barbarus*' then became '*neophytus*'.[69] The historian states: "The rest of this people is caught between so much foolishness and barbarism. Yet they are ideally suited, compared to other American Barbarians, if they cease their culture, to embrace and preserve the Christian faith and become politically organised through mechanical practices".[70] Thus, there was no other nation in America that had such a promising capacity for Christian and cultural instruction.[71] The Guaraní thus achieved a high degree of civilisation in the Jesuit spirit. Del Techo also illustrates several examples of missionary success. Among these is the conversion of the neophyte Piravi. His great piety is raised as an *exemplum*. His faith enabled him to carry out an activity close to that of the missionaries, since he was even responsible for reducing the Indians.[72] In comparison, del Techo uses the term '*Aethiopes*' to refer to slaves from Africa. The people referred to by the *Historia*'s writer should not be associated with inhabitants of the West African continent. The slaves bought by the Jesuits actually came from Southeast Africa. Del Techo specifies that they were '*Angolanos Aethiopies*':[73]

> Throughout the period, the Church made the Christianization of slaves a form of compensation, of consolation for the misfortunes they endured, especially the Jesuits, in their sermon writings, catechisms and treatises. Religion was seen by the authorities as having an integrative role for slaves: a specialized clergy was assigned to them, as well as missions to their attention, brotherhoods and black devotions.[74]

68 Castelnau-L'Estoile, *Les ouvriers d'une Vigne stérile*, 361.

69 Daher, "L'invention capucine du sauvage", 76: At the beginning of the 17th century in Brazil, it was common for Indians to be referred to as "dogs", "pigs", "Negroes" and "Gentiles". Del Techo did not use the first three terms to describe the Natives.

70 Techo, *Historia Provinciae Paraquariae*, 135: "Caeterum gentem hanc inter tantas ineptias, et tantam barbariem, ad Fidem Christianam apessendam retinendamque, necnon ad res machanicas, aliquantulamque politiam, si non desit cultura, prae aliis Americae Barbaris idoneam esse compertum est".

71 Duviols, "Les jésuites et les Indiens du Paraguay", 327: However, the fact that the Natives could not accede to the priesthood indicates an unbridgeable distance established between European and American Christians. The reason given by the Jesuits for inferiorising their Indigenous counterparts was that they were very good imitators but incapable of creating.

72 Techo, *Historia Provinciae Paraquariae*, 158.

73 Techo, *Historia Provinciae Paraquariae*, 304.

74 Castelnau-L'Estoile and Maldavsky, "Religions", 206.

In order to convert these people, the Jesuits were to teach them the catechism. Knowledge of the language was thus essential, as we have already seen. Vocabulary and grammar manuals were published. Black brotherhoods were created in the Spanish colonial area, including Paraguay. But del Techo says little or nothing about them. He does, however, devote an entire chapter to the controversy that arose in 1621 around the question of black baptism. With hundreds of African slaves arriving each year, the Society of Jesus wondered whether it was necessary to baptise them again when they arrived in America. The bishops stationed in Africa granted this sacrament before embarkation. Therefore, the desire to re-baptise these men was frowned upon, as it challenged the work of the pastors in Africa. Del Techo writes that it was the receipt of a letter that allowed them to decide the matter. He transcribes in the *Historia* what is said to be a passage from this letter written by the Jesuit rector of the 'College of Angola':

> In my opinion, the Africans are not baptized and should be renamed under some specific conditions, because they ignore the catechism. The day before they ship them, they are set in droves in front of the Vicar, and asked if they want to be Christian. They give their agreement. Then, they hear a brief sermon, without having to learn the Catholic doctrine. Finally, the priest renames the Africans and baptize them.[75]

This, in addition to leading to the baptism of several thousand blacks, also encouraged the Society of Jesus to work actively, according to del Techo, in teaching Africans. He particularly highlights the role played by Father Diego Torres. He would have succeeded in establishing African parishes in the cities, so that Christian doctrine could be taught. Here again, del Techo uses the miracle as a way of sealing the argument that leads the reader to consider the Society of Jesus useful and even absolutely necessary for the salvation of souls and the spread of Christianity. Indeed, during a boat trip between Panama and Peru, a black man was baptized on the line, dying. When he died, it was decided that his corpse should be thrown overboard. A few hours later, the man's spirit appeared in the air accompanied by birds.

75 Techo, *Historia Provinciae Paraquariae*, 170: "nam mea opinio est, non ese baptizatos, et saltem conditione interjecta rebaptizandos ese, quod nullam ferme praemissam Catechesi Baptismum suscipiant. Pridie enim quam e portu solvant, turmatim sistuntur Vicario, a quo interrogati simul omnes, num Christiani velint fieri, additis pauculis verbis, priusquam qualem Fidem recipiant intelligere possent, acceptis Christianis nominibus (si Superisplacet) baptizantur".

Conclusion

Studying the *Historia* represents the opportunity to open a door to slavery in the seventeenth century. It shows how the Jesuits were opposed to the enslavement of the Natives. At the same time, the silence with regard to the slavery practices perpetrated by the Jesuits towards the Africans reveals all the ambiguity of the position of the Society of Jesus.

Based on what is presented as historical facts taken "on the ground", del Techo uses slavery as a rhetorical argument to convince the European Jesuits to become missionaries in Paraguay. For this purpose, he orientates the narration by focusing his attention on specific elements. In this way, he lends a great deal of importance to accounts filled with violence and brutality. According to del Techo, the struggles against the Portuguese slavers from São Paulo constitutes the major opposition encountered in the first half of the seventeenth century. The repeated attacks hindered the evangelisation project pursued by the Society. At the heart of these dozens of chapters is the desire to pit against two conceptions of the colonial world embodied by the Jesuits and by the slavers. On the one hand, the Jesuits are depicted as the defenders of good, keepers of the Christian religion. Conversely, del Techo describes the Portuguese slavers in the style of the devil. By enslaving the Guaraní, who were in the process of being converted in the reductions, the Portuguese were jeopardising the Jesuit work to evangelise Paraguay, which was not only perceived as terrible by the religious but also by every Catholic reader in Europe. Systematically, del Techo inserts rhetorical arguments that should lead the reader to construct a monolithic vision of the Society of Jesus opponents. Del Techo clearly defines an anti-slavery identity of the religious corps in Paraguay. However, this feature is only true regarding the Natives, because their slavery compromised their Christianisation. When del Techo was writing his *Historia*, thousands of African slaves were already being deported to the Río de la Plata and Paraguay. The Jesuit colleges had several of them at their disposal. The Jesuit historian gives them very little space in his book and does not question the reasons for their enslavement. This omission can be understood as a desire to avoid creating a controversy about the Jesuit increase in wealth. Furthermore, the apostolic work in the reductions and the harshness of the dispute against the Portuguese could do more to awaken the missionary vocation in Europe. Recall that Diego Alfaro, who died in the war against the Paulists, elevated to martyr, was a figure with whom young recruits could easily identify. Thereby, del Techo decides to try to grip his readership through sensitive content. Even if he may have legal knowledge, especially in canon laws, he does not place this argument in the forefront of the *Historia*, instead leaving the laws in the background.

Works Cited

Primary Sources

Acosta, José de (1984). *De Procuranda Indorum Salute*. Gen ed. Pereña, Luciano. Madrid: Consejo Superior de Investigaciones Científicas.

Brussels, Bibliothèque Royale, Manuscrits, *Histoire des jésuites*.

Cansanello, Pablo and Piana, Josefina eds. (2016). *Memoriales de la Provincia Jesuítica del Paraguay (siglos XVII–XVIII)*. Córdoba: Editorial de la Universidad Católica.

Lille, Archives municipales de Lille. *Registre des baptêmes de la paroisse Saint-Étienne (1611–1624)*.

Lupercio de Zurbano, Francisco (1996). *Cartas anuas de la Provincia del Paraguay. 1637–1639*. Ed. Maeder, Ernesto. Buenos Aires: Fundación para la educación, la ciencia y la cultura.

Morales, Martín María ed. (2005). *A mis manos han llegado. Cartas de los PP. Generales a la Antigua Provincia del Paraguay (1608–1639)*. Madrid/Rome: Universidad Pontificia Comillas/Institutum Historicum Societatis Iesu.

Rome, Archivum Romanum Societatis Iesu, *Provincia Paraquariae*.

Techo (del), Nicolas (1673). *Historia Provinciae Paraquariae Societatis Iesu*. Liège: Jean Matthias Hovius.

Secondary Sources

Angenot, Marc (1982). *La parole pamphlétaire. Contribution à la typologie des discours modernes*. Paris: Payot.

Balzamo, Nicolas (2014). *Les miracles dans la France du XVIe siècle. Métamorphoses du surnaturel*. Paris: Les Belles Lettres.

Bourgaux, Aurélien (2021). "La sporulation du martyre. (XVIE–XXIE siècles)." *Radices: Interdisciplinary Journal for the Study of Terrorism and Extremism* 1, 41–53.

Castelnau (de)-L'Estoile, Charlotte & Maldavsky, Aliocha (2021). "Religions." Cécile Vidal, ed. *Une histoire sociale du Nouveau Monde*. Paris: Éditions de l'École des hautes études en sciences sociales, 199–230.

Castelnau (de)-L'Estoile, Charlotte (2000). *Les ouvriers d'une Vigne stérile. Les jésuites et la conversion des Indiens du Brésil. 1580–1620*. Paris/Lisbon: Fundação Calouste Gulbenkian.

Castelnau (de)-L'Estoile, Charlotte (2019). *Un catholicisme colonial. Le mariage des Indiens et des esclaves au Brésil*. Paris: Presses universitaires de France.

Clossey, Luke (2009). *Salvation and Globalization in the Early Jesuit Missions*. Cambridge: Cambridge University Press.

Daher, Andrea (2019). "L'invention capucine du sauvage." Ferrer, Véronique and Millet, Olivier and Tarrête, Alexandre ed. La Renaissance au grand large. Mélanges en l'honneur de Frank Lestringant. Genève: Droz, 73–86.

Dekoninck, Ralph (2018). *Horreur sacrée et sacrilège. Image, violence et religion (XVIe et XXIe siècles)*. Brussels: Académie Royale de Belgique.

Deslandres, Dominique (1999). "'Des ouvriers formidables à l'enfer'. Épistémè et missions jésuites au XVIIe siècle." *Mélanges pour l'École française de Rome* 111.1, 251–276.

Duviols, Jean-Paul (2007). "Les jésuites et les Indiens du Paraguay : 'le joug suave de l'Évangile'." in Molinié, Annie and Merle, Alexandra and Araceli, Guillaume-Alonso eds. *Les jésuites en Espagne et en Amérique*. Paris: Presses universitaires de la Sorbonne, 319–353.

Duviols, Jean-Paul (2018). *Indios Guaraníes y Jesuitas. Misiones de la Compañía de Jesús en el Paraguay (1610–1767)*. Doral: Stockcero.

El Alaoui, Youssef (2006). *Jésuites, Morisques et Indiens. Étude comparative des méthodes d'évangélisation de la Compagnie de Jésus d'après les traités de José de Acosta (1588) et d'Ignacio de las Casas (1605–1607)*. Paris: Honoré Champion.

Frenkel, Yehoshua (2017). "Some Notes Concerning the Trade and Education of Slave-Soldiers during the Mamluk Era." Amitai, Reuven and Cluse, Christoph eds. *Slavery and the Slave Trade in the Eastern Mediterranean (c. 1000–1500 CE)*. Turnhout: Brepols, 187–212.

Jackson, Robert (2019). *A Population History of the Missions of the Jesuit Province of Paraquaria*. Cambridge: Cambridge Scholars Publishing.

Lécrivain Philippe (1991). *Les missions jésuites. Pour une plus grande gloire de Dieu*. Paris: Gallimard.

Mazor, Amir (2017). "The Early Experience of the Mamluk in the First Period of the Mamluk Sultanate (1250–1382 CE)." Amitai, Reuven and Cluse, Christoph eds. *Slavery and the Slave Trade in the Eastern Mediterranean (c. 1000–1500 CE)*. Turnhout: Brepols, 213–231.

McNaspy, Clement and Gómez Fregoso, Jesús. (2001). "Esclavitud negra en América." *Diccionario histórico de la Compañía de Jesús* 2, 1254–1257.

Page, Carlos (2011). "El espacio arquitectónico de negros en las estancias jesuitas del Paraguay: las iglesias." *REDE-A* 1.1, 89–107.

Prudhomme, Claude (2022). "Esclavage." Fabre, Pierre Antoine and Pierre, Benoist ed., *Les jésuites. Histoire et dictionnaire*. Paris: Bouquins, 647–649.

Redden, Andrew (2012). "A las buenas personas no les queda más que le dolor y el gemido: la violencia del martirio y la violencia del mártir en las fronteras de Nueva España y Paraguay." Pescador Osuna, José Ángel ed. *La religión y los jesuitas en el noroeste novohispano*. Culiacán: El colegio de Sinaloa, 101–128.

Redden, Andrew (2016). "Priestly Violence, Martyrdom, and Jesuits: The Case of Diego de Alfaro (Paraguay, 1639)." *Advanced Jesuit Studies* 6, 81–113.

Rotham, Adam (2021). "The Jesuits and Slavery." *Journal of Jesuit Studies* 8, 1–10.

Schmidt, Francis (1985). "Naissance des polythéismes (1624–1757)." *Archives de sciences sociales des religions* 59.1, 77–90.

Tardieu, Jean Pierre (2005). "Los inicios del 'ministerio de negros' en la provincia jesuítica del Paraguay." *Anuario de Estudios Americanos* 62, 141–160.

Telesca, Ignacio (2008). "Esclavos y jesuitas: El colegio de Asunción del Paraguay." *Archivum Historicum Societatis Iesu*, 77, 191–211.

Thomas, Jérôme (2012). "L'évangélisation des indiens selon le jésuite Acosta dans le *De procuranda indorum salute* (1588)." *Cahiers d'études du religieux* 10 https://journals.openedition.org/cerri/942 (1st March 2023).

Vignaud, Laurent-Henri (2002). "Merveilles." Sbalchiero, Patrick ed. *Dictionnaire des miracles et de l'extraordinaire chrétiens*. Paris: Fayard, 522.

Wilde, Guillermo (2019). *Religión y poder en las misiones de guaraníes*. Buenos Aires: SB Editiorial.

Yosef, Koby (2019). "Cross-Boundary Hatred: (Changing) Attitudes towards Mongol and 'Christian' *mamlūks* in the Mamluk Sultanate." Amitai, Reuven and Conermann, Stephan eds. *The Mamluk Sultanate from the Perspective of Regional and World History*. Göttingen: V&R unipress, 149–214.

Historical Freeze Frames on the Infantilisation of Native Americans: Representations of the Relationship between Churchmen and Indigenous People in the Spanish Colonial Context

Stefano R. Torres

Introduction

In an extensive work published in the late 1980s on the colonial missions in southern Chile, historian Jorge Pinto Rodríguez explains that the Franciscans, in despair over the failure of their conversion methods, began to use physical violence ("empleo de la fuer[z]a" to use his own words) against the Native Americans they sought to convert. Seeking an explanation for this violence, the scholar suggested: "It was not that the Franciscans hated the Indians or that they deliberately condemned them. Rather, their love for them and their zeal to save them led them to act in this manner".[1] This explanation for the use of physical violence, assigned to faith and the urge to save souls that would otherwise be sentenced to burn in Hell – that I choose to call from now on the 'soteriological explanation' – actually allows us to understand this phenomenon. But only up to a point. Apart from the necessary philosophical and historical discussion that the application of the word "love" to the situation would deserve, this soteriological explanation frustrates by the superficiality of its content. The same argument is sometimes used to explain the enslavement of Africans, Afro-descendants, and Native Americans carried out by missionaries like the Jesuits.[2] And while it gives us a glimpse into the cosmology of the Catholic churchmen, it provides no further details about the social interaction that were at play between them and the Native Americans: How did the churchmen view the people whom they were forcibly trying to convert? By

* My warmest acknowledgment to Christian Grosse and to Rômulo Ehalt for their precious time and useful comments. Special thanks to Maruša Novak for her support.

1 All translations are my own, unless stated otherwise: "No es que los franciscanos odiaran a los indios o que premeditamente los condenaran. Al contrario, su amor a ellos y su afán de salvarlos, los impulsaba a actuar de esa manera" (Pinto Rodríguez, *Frontera*, 16).

2 According to Jean-Pierre Tardieu, the first reason that led the Jesuits to enslave Africans and Afro-descendants in Iberian-America of the seventeenth and eighteenth centuries was to save their souls: see Tardieu, "La esclavitud", 75–76.

 | DOI:10.30965/9783657796328_009

what conceptual tools were they able to ignore, overcome, or morally justify the violence? Was their meaning of violence even close to a contemporary understanding of it?[3] More broadly, how did they perceive their relationship with Native Americans?

Questioning the use of violence by church agents against indigenous people leads to observing the relationship they sought to have with them. Not denying the relevance of the 'soteriological explanation', this research presents a close examination of it, instead of granting a simplistic "love" to the evangelisers or emphasising its primacy at the expense of other causes (i.e. economic ones). A key element to understand their general behaviour, violent or not, towards Native Americans lay in the representation[4] they had of them, understood as the 'framework' or the 'lens' through which they viewed, comprehend, and described them in their discourse.[5] One barely studied dimension of this representation is mirrored by the missionaries' assignment of infantile characteristics and of children's social status to the Americans. Thus, this paper does not specifically address their enslavement, nor the use of violence against them in its practical aspects. It rather highlights their ascription of an inferior nature and social status as human beings, regardless of their socio-economic status or level of bondage.

Without presenting a complete overview of the subject, this study makes a few freeze frames of the colonial period, from the sixteenth to the beginning of the eighteenth century, through the analysis of normative sources: mainly doctrinal and legislative documents. Two elements unite these sources: firstly, their focus on Native Americans as a whole social group, though basing their

3 The term "violence" in this paper has a broad and contemporary definition. It includes not only physical harm but also other forms of abuse, such as humiliation, harassment, manipulation, blasphemy, destruction of sacred objects, and so on, as well as structural and symbolic violence, as highlighted by the social sciences. Historical research suggests that it is difficult to establish an absolute definition of violence as it heavily depends on the historical context in which it is analysed (Fagan et al. ed., *The Cambridge World*, 3–5). It is therefore essential to understand the perceptions of violence held by actors in the past, which may be very different from the views of the present.

4 About "representing" and understanding the unknown and the unfamiliar in the Colonial American context, see MacCormack, "Limits of Understanding", 79 and 86; Guzinski and Bernand, *De l'idolâtrie*, 6–7. On the construction of otherness in colonial America, see Mason, *Deconstructing America*. For more interdisciplinary studies on the representation of identity/alterity, see Tarantino and Wyss-Giacosa, *Through your Eyes*; Graziani and Spissu, *Il Mito*.

5 As explained by Vivien Burr, "A discourse refers to a set of meanings, metaphors, representations, images, […]. It refers to a particular picture that is painted of an event (or person or class of persons), a particular way of *representing* it or them in a certain light." (My emphasis. Burr, *An Introduction*, 32.)

arguments on the colonial centres, that is New Spain and Peru; secondly, the fact of specifically addressing the complex question of the relationship between settlers and Native Americans using a 'familial' analogy. Special attention will be paid to the Jesuits, as they were among the most active and influential missionaries and scholars in the Americas, and left behind an abundance of written sources. Confronting the institutional foundations and the ideology of the Society of Jesus with the theological and legislative discourse of the sources will enable a better understanding of the relationship with indigenous people that they promoted.

The analogy between Native Americans and children was fully developed during the first half of the sixteenth century in the leading theological school of thought of that time: from one of Salamanca's lecture halls, the Dominican Francisco de Vitoria drew, in 1539, an analogy between the customs and social status of indigenous people and that of children and slaves. It allowed him to oppose war waged against them, and to justify theologically their educational and religious tutelage by the crown until they had fully adopted a Christian way of life. At the end of the century, this perennial analogy found its way into the Jesuit order, whose members learned from the School of Salamanca. One of them was José de Acosta, one of the most influential writers to produce a general description of the 'Indies'. After preaching in Peru and becoming Superior of the Province, Acosta gathered with the Fathers of his jurisdiction to reform the methods of evangelisation of the locals and to mitigate the violent conquests carried out by the seculars. In 1588, Acosta promoted the use of punishments and corrections, including physical ones; a series of measures deemed necessary to gain the obedience of the supposedly child-like natives. Half a century later, Juan de Solórzano y Pereira, a Spanish jurist and former judge in Peru, published an exhaustive jurisprudential synthesis to be applied to the Spanish American colonies, which would be used for over two centuries by the Council of the Indies. Printed in 1647, Solórzano's book restated the inferior and childish social status of the Native American, while emphasising their "miserable" condition, which required special and sometimes protective treatment from the law. The entire body of documents examined so far calls into question the very notion of "child" as it was understood in the Spanish Colonial period and territories. As will be shown, children shared a social status close to that of servants and slaves, submitted to the quasi-omnipotent power of the family father (*paterfamilias*).

The paper finally proposes a closer look at a rarely studied manuscript: Mexican instructions that regulated the operation and organisation of the Jesuit estate (*haciendas*). Written after 1722 and advocating for physical punishments both against slaves and servants, the instructions always reminded the importance for Jesuits to act as if they were benevolent family fathers. Stressing the importance of the workers' obedience and of the paternalistic role to be assumed by the churchmen, the instructions carry an old reminder of the long-lasting attribution of a childlike social status to Native Americans. This particular focus on the 'familial' relationship and on a strongly hierarchical structure governed by obedience is better understood when linked to the rules of the Society of Jesus: the founding documents of the order, namely the *Constitutions* adopted in 1594, established an analogy between the highly hierarchical structure of the order and the paternal-filial obedience that must govern the relationships among its members. The Mexican instructions thus reflect the ideology of the order, in which obedience is of paramount importance, and constitute a key element in understanding the relationship promoted by the Society between its members and the Native Americans.

The Childlike Social Status of Native Americans

Reading the otherness of Native Americans through paternalistic eyes has been a persistent habit of the European scholarlship ever since Columbus commented, in his diary, on the nakedness of the Caribbean inhabitants. This was seen as a sign of their supposed purity, innocence, and proximity to Adam and Eve in the Garden of Eden.[6] Soon after the beginning of the conquest, a specific characteristic was attributed to them: their childishness. One author who particularly developed this idea was Francisco de Vitoria (*c.*1483–1546). The initiator of what would become the most influential theological school of thought of the Renaissance – the School of Salamanca (*Escuela de Salamanca*)[7] – the Dominican theologian developed an ethical reflection on what he called the "affairs of the Indies" (*las cosas de Indias*).[8] After dramatic episodes in the viceroyalty of Peru, in the decade of 1530, the context was that of intensive legal debate about the legitimacy of the Spanish crown's violent colonisation, and the righteousness of enslavement and war waged against the so-called infidels and pagans. The answer to these questions depended on the Native Americans' *dominium* over their own lives, territory, and possessions.[9] At the

6 Greenblatt, *Marvelous Possessions*, 79; Zamora, "Christopher Colombus's", 3–8.

7 Regarding the School of Salamanca, see Pagden, *The Fall*, 59–64; Grice-Hutchinson, "El concepto", 21–26. The existence of such a school of thought has been questioned in the last decade, due to its recent conceptualisation dating from the twentieth century. See Decock, *Theologians*, 49–55.

8 Pagden, *The Fall*, 64–65.

9 Oliveira e Silva, "Francisco de Vitoria", 147.

heart of these debates, therefore, was the discussion of their nature and social status. One of the key arguments in favour of war and enslavement was based on one of Aristotle's ideas: the existence of a species of human beings so inferior that they were naturally destined to be enslaved – in other words, "slaves by nature".[10]

Vitoria's specific *releción* on the Americans – a public lesson given by professors at the end of the academic year – is known as *De indis*. It was delivered in Salamanca in 1539.[11] The theologian addressed the legitimacy of a violent conquest in strictly theological terms discussing its morality, not its legality. Rejecting the servile nature of the Native Americans, or their association with a "third species of animal, between man and monkey" as some of his contemporaries did,[12] the Dominican still had to explain 'unnatural' behaviours in terms of Christian mores.[13] For him, people whose behaviour contradicted 'natural law' (i.e. eating human flesh, or worshipping divinities alien to Christianity) only owned rationality *in potentia*, that is rationality still in the process and waiting to fully develop. Thus, the Native American was like a "fully grown child"; a child who was not yet politically and religiously capable of making reasonable decisions, and who might "one day grow into a free and independent citizen of a true polis".[14] At the same time, drawing on Aristotle's reflections on childhood, Vitoria saw children as sharing the same status and capabilities as slaves. Therefore, Native Americans might be treated like slaves, albeit temporarily. Indeed, considering them as children meant that they were not doomed to be uncivilised and unfaithful people indefinitely: they could be taught the Christian manners and the churchmen were thus justified in taking them under their wing. On the other hand, it also meant that the Spaniards' dominion over them was morally justified, as long as the latter brought them up as parents would raise their offspring.[15]

According to Pagden, Vitoria's association of Native Americans with children was not original. It merely reflected what missionaries and settlers had observed in the field of the conquest. Nonetheless, the Dominican's theological reasoning paved the way for a later evolutionist perspective on humanity.[16]

---

10 Pagden, *The Fall*, 67.

11 Oliveira e Silva, "Francisco de Vitoria", 139–140. *De indis* would later be collected in the *Relectiones theologiae* printed in Lyon, in 1557. For a comprehensive summary of *De indis* and its origins, see Ibid., 141–148.

12 Pagden cites here Bernardino de Minaya (Pagden, *The Fall*, 104).

13 Ibid., 96–97.

14 Ibid., 104.

15 Ibid., 105.

16 Ibid., 106.

The theology developed by the Dominicans of Salamanca also had a significant influence on subsequent theological, economic, and legal thought. One of the scholars who echoed them was the Spanish Jesuit José de Acosta (1540–1600), who spent eight years of his life – from 1559 to 1567 – in Alcalá de Henares, an ideal place to meet the disciples of this school of thought, to follow their teachings and read their works.[17] Acosta's excellence in his philosophical and theological studies soon led his superiors to entrust him with major responsibilities within the order: in 1572, he was sent to the first Jesuit mission in Spanish America, founded in the viceroyalty of Peru in 1568. In response to a severe crisis at that time, the Jesuits in Peru found it necessary to adapt their methods of evangelisation. Their aim was to counter the ongoing violence of a conquest that only seemed to intensify Native Americans' thirst for revenge.[18] In 1576, the Jesuits held the first Provincial Congregation of Peru, called and presided over by Acosta, the newly elected Provincial. During the first session, he noted the problems raised and drafted the essentials of what was to become the *De procuranda indorum salute*. This method carefully addressed every aspect of evangelisation and pastoral work among the Native Americans in order to raise them to Christianity.[19]

Most of the Fathers of the Provincial Congregation sought to distance themselves from the material interests that guided the settlers. It was widely believed that the 'discovery' of America was an act of God that made of Spain the chosen monarchy to spread the message. The crown's providential mission was to help the Americans to liberate themselves from their religious errors and corrupt ways, through the Church's work of education and proselytisation. In that respect, they only perpetuated what Vitoria had already proposed, and the same discourse was proclaimed in *De procuranda*.

This treatise was also based on Acosta's experience. For the past four years, he had been doing missionary work in the ex-territory of Tahuantinsuyo, including Lima, Cuzco, La Plata, Sucre, and La Paz, among other places. He had collected testimonies from the Native Americans, observed their customs

17 The influence of the School of Salamanca on Acosta, as well as on other Jesuit scholars of that time (namely Luis de Molina and Francisco Suárez) has been highlighted by García Mateo, "Ignacio de Loyola", especially from 445 on. See also Höpfl, *Jesuit Political*, 305.

18 Pereña, "Proyecto de sociedad", 18–19. Acosta's presence in Peru coincided with the war waged by the Spaniards against the Chiriguanos, the resistance of the indigenous peoples of Chile, as well as the resistance, from Vilcabamba, of the last Inca descendant, Tupac Amaru, who was sentenced to death by the Spaniards (Ibid., 4).

19 Several parts of *De procuranda* are identical to the final *actas* of the Provincial Congregation. The *actas* constituted a summary of the problems addressed and the solutions proposed at the meeting. The summary was sent to the General of the Order (Ibid., 19).

and behaviour, and above all experienced interaction with this otherness. Although Acosta acknowledged the great diversity of indigenous groups in America, he referred to them as a whole (somethimes calling them "la nación india"[20]), considering those from Peru as a relevant basis for understanding the rest.[21] Acosta had spent only part of the twelve years he would live on the continent, including two in New Spain and the Caribbean, providing him with the material to write his broader landscape on the American inhabitants: the *Historia natural y moral de las Indias*.[22]

While Acosta's first version of the treatise condemned the violent methods of the settlers and their pursuit of greed, he still believed that some degree of physical violence was necessary to the obedience of the Native Americans. Acosta portrayed them as difficult and uncompromising, stating: "Experience has abundantly taught that *the nature of barbarians is completely servile*. In practice, if they are not put in fear and some force is not put upon them *like upon children, they do not enter into obedience*". Acosta emphasised the ability of the "barbarians" to learn Christian customs and dogmas. He asked: "What to do, then? Are only people of free condition and mature judgment to have hope of salvation? *Should not the children also be given an educator in Christ?*" Acosta advocated for the "spiritual" version of the conquest. He promoted the Spaniards' tutelage of the Americans via the presence of the Jesuits at the forefront of colonisation, their educational activities, and a long-term persuasive strategy that included corrections and punishments. Otherwise, those 'children' would only act and live according to their own fantasies: "The Scripture says sticks and reprisals lead to reason, *a spoiled boy* shames his mother."

Carefully enough, Acosta always made it clear that physical violence could only be wielded in the name of God ("It will be necessary to employ a proceeding of greater caution and vigilance; it will be necessary to use the rod at times, but for the love of God."), and with the final goal "to look after themselves [i.e. the Americans] and not after their things".[23] Later on, Acosta

20 Acosta, *De procuranda*, 193.

21 Ibid., 59.

22 Although written in 1576, *De procuranda* was printed for the first time in 1588, introduced in *De Natura Novi Orbis*, which is the Latin and original version of the first two books of Acosta's famous and most reedited work, the *Historia natural y moral de las Indias* (1590) (Mignolo, "Introduction to", XXI). For a now classic and comprehensive study of the *Historia natural y moral*, see O'Gorman, *Cuatro historiadores*, 165–237.

23 My emphasis: "La experiencia ha enseñado abundantemente que *la naturaleza de los bárbaros es completamente servil*. En la práctica, si no se les mete miedo y se les hace alguna fuerza *como a los niños, no entran por la obediencia*. ¿Qué hacer, pues? ¿Sólo la gente de condición libre y de juicio maduro ha de tener esperanza de salvación? *¿No habrá que poner también a los niños un educador en Cristo?* Sin duda alguna. Habrá que emplear un

again addressed the use of punishments as a means of "discipline and correction" for the missionaries to adopt:

> For this reason, the parish priest should not believe that he should neglect this aspect of beneficence which consists in correcting faulty actions. If in some places it is necessary to adopt more severe disciplinary measures, among the Indian peoples this is absolutely necessary, *because they are of a servile condition and of customs that are most of the time childish* [*pueriles*].[24]

Acosta's comparison of Native Americans to children is clear. The characteristics ascribed to them enabled him to emphasise the necessary correction required to bring them into compliance. In practical terms, the Jesuit gave specific examples of "moderate" punishments that a churchman might carefully use – "always with paternal mercy" – towards a faulty American: "A moderate pecuniary fine, a day's shackling, sometimes a few whippings, the cruellest of all a haircut, which the Indians consider the ultimate ignominy".[25]

Acosta is not known for supporting the enslavement of the Native Americans. However, he did associate Americans with "barbarians", whose nature he claimed was "servile". This association was an inheritance from Vitoria's conceptualisation of the nature and social status of Americans as similar to that of slaves. Acosta's definition of "barbarians", which he drew from the "definition of prestigious authors", was made explicit in the preamble of his treatise: "barbarians are those who deviate from right reason and the usual practice

---

procedimiento de mayor cautela y vigilancia; habrá que usar a veces de la vara, pero por amor a Dios; habrá que instalarles a que entren en la cena, pero por amor al Señor. Hay que buscar a ellos mismos y no sus cosas. Dice la Escritura: *Palos y represione meten en razón, muchacho consentido avergüenza a su madre.* Y también: *Sólo con palabras no escarmienta el siervo; aunque entienda lo que dices, rehúsa obedecer.*" (Acosta, *De procuranda*, vol. 1, book 1, chap. 7, 142–143.) There is no significant difference from the published and censored version of the treatise: Acosta, *De Natura*, 163–164.

24 "Por eso tampoco debe creer el párroco en modo alguno que tiene que descuidar este aspecto de la beneficiencia que consiste en la corrección de acciones defectuosas. Si en alguna parte es preciso adoptar medidas disciplinares más severas, entre los pueblos indios es esto absolutamente necesario, porque son de condición servil y de construmbres las más de las veces pueriles. De tal manera se comportan, que si no tienen el estímulo del temor, fácilmente se desvían o se hacen el remolón." (Acosta, *De procuranda*, vol. 2, book 4, chap. 19, 142–145.) Same remarks as the previous footnote: Acosta, *De Natura*, 458.

25 "Finalmente se ha de mirar por que el modo de aplicar el castigo transpire siempre clemencia paternal y propia de un eclesíastico. Una moderada multa pecunaria, echarlo en grillos un día, alguna vez darle unos azotes, el mas cruel de todos un corte de pelo, que los indios consideran la máxima ignominia." (Acosta, *De procuranda*, vol. 2, book. 4, chap. 20, 157.) On the subject of the moderation of punishment, see also Santos and Amezúa Amezúa, "La moderación".

of men".[26] In a nutshell, in the first version of what would later become his renowned classification of humanity, any individual residing outside of Christendom was considered a barbarian.[27] Native Americans were classified into the second and third categories, respectively that of humans that have political institutions and a method for recording collective memory (mainly Incas and Mexicans), and that of humans similar to savage beasts, that barely have human feelings (*Caribes, Chunchos, Chiriguanas, Moxos, Iscaicingas*, those from Brazil, and from Florida).[28]

Acosta also asserted that individuals who resisted Christian conversion should be forcibly brought to Christendom for their own benefit (immediately before emphasising the importance of departing from the violent methods used by the *conquistadores*):

> All these men, or half-men, must be given human instruction, so that they learn to be men, *to be educated like children*. [...] if they stubbornly resist their own regeneration, and rave against their own teachers and doctors, they must be compelled by force, and some suitable pressure must be brought upon them, so that they will not hinder the Gospel, and they must be made to fulfil their obligations; and they must be compelled to move from the jungle to the human convenience of the city.[29]

Acosta was clear and explicit about the necessary use of coercion to convince the recalcitrant, although he always made sure to strongly demarcate it from the abusive and unjustified violence of the settlers. He advocated for physical punishment which he justified by viewing Native Americans as unreasonable children who need to be disciplined in a paternalistic way. It is important to note that the author never labeled this practice as "violent", instead choosing

26 "Según la definición de prestigiosos autores, bárbaros son aquéllos que se apartan de la recta razón y de la práctica habitual de los hombres. Por eso suelen destacar los escritores más ilustres la incapacidad de los bárbaros, su fiereza, incluso sus técnicas y trabajos, significando lo lejos que están de la práctica usual de los demás hombres y lo poco que tienen de sabiduría y actividad racional." (Acosta, *De procuranda*, vol. 1, 61.)

27 For Acosta's classification of humanity, see Imbruglia, "The Invention", 291–311; Pino Díaz, "Contribución del Padre", 13–15; for a discussion of Acosta's classification, see also the chapter by Lionel Mira in this volume.

28 Acosta, *De procuranda*, vol. 1, 65–67.

29 My emphasis: "A todos estos hombres o mediohombres es preciso darles instrucción humana, para que aprendan a ser hombres, *educarlos como a niños*. [...] si se resisten con terquedad a su propia regeneración y desvarían contra sus propios maestros y médicos, hay que obligarles por la fuerza y hacerles alguna conveniente presión para que no pongan obstaculos al Evangelio, y hay que hacerles cumplir sus obligaciones; y convendrá hacerles fuerza para que se trasladen de la selva a la convinencia humana de la ciudad." (Acosta, *De procuranda*, vol. 1, 69.)

to demarcate it as a form of "punishment" or "correction". However, from an analytical perspective, we consider these punishments as a form of violence. Similarly, the Catholic Church's "Spiritual Conquest" project included violent behaviours inflicted upon the indigenous population that are worthy of study, for instance the destruction of their idols and sacred objects[30], forced acculturation of minors, or the strict implementation of penance and punishment.

Acosta's method was in line with the one agreed upon during the Provincial Congregation.[31] It was also enthusiastically approved by the Superior General, despite the manuscript facing significant obstacles before being printed, including a censorship that required the removal of all references to violence committed by the seculars.[32] The *De procuranda* and *Historia natural y moral de la Indias* would have a profound influence on the European and American intellectual scene for the centuries to come, especially among the Jesuits.

Following Acosta's contribution to the theological conceptualisation of the Americans, another significant development can be observed outside of theology: that is, in the setting of the Spanish American legislation (*Derecho Indiano*), which reached its Golden Age during the first half of the seventeenth century. The *Recopilación de Leyes de los Reynos de las Indias*, a watershed in the legislation of Spanish viceroyalties from the 1680 onwards, was preceded by the works of one of its main authors: Juan de Solórzano y Pereira (1575–1655). In 1647, this Spanish jurist gathered and consolidated in *Política Indiana* all the questions and matters related to the government and law of the Indies, which were previously scattered in the thousands of *ordenanzas reales* promulgated since the beginning of the conquest.[33] Solórzano's treatise on jurisdiction and casuistry became the most influential of its kind, and laid the foundation for the law of the Indies. It would remain a leading authority for the Council of the Indies throughout the eighteenth century.[34] After serving as a judge (*oidor*) for the Real Audiencia of Lima in Peru for sixteen years, Solórzano returned to Spain and composed his masterpiece. He drew on a variety of writings, including those of theologians.[35] Divided into five books, this work addressed the

30 Restall, "Legitimised Violence", 415.

31 A similar content was included in the *actas* of the Provincial Congregation (see note 19), including the analogy between the Native and children: see Egaña 1958, doc. 17 ("Acta in Congregatione Provinciali Peru, Limae 1576"), § 25–26, 68–70.

32 The whole process is summarised by Pereña, "Proyecto de", 20–27. Regarding the approval by the General of the methods adopted by the Jesuits from Peru, see Egaña 1958, doc. 72.

33 Tau Anzoátegui, *El Jurista*, 156–157. It was preceded by a Latin and less exhaustive version, *De Indiarum Iure* (1629–1639) in two volumes.

34 Ibid., 17 and 143–144.

35 About Solórzano y Pereira, see Barrios Pintado, "Juan de Solórzano"; García Hernán, *Consejero de ambos*.

most delicate questions about the conquest, such as the legality of the crown's *dominium* over America (known as *Justos Títulos*) and the "liberty, status and condition of the Indians".[36]

In *Política Indiana*, the jurist demarcated the Americans from the rest of society. He categorised them as "miserable people" (*miserables personas*). With this expression, the jurist refers to "all those whom we naturally pity because of their state, quality, or works".[37] Solórzano justified this association by referring to "infinities of authors" and works that preceded him, the preamble of Acosta's *De procuranda* among others.[38] He stated that the status ascribed to the Americans compelled to their protection, as stipulated by another "infinity" of ordinances and royal decrees. These decrees ordered that the authorities (viceroys, *Audiencias*, governors, prelates) must prioritize the protection of the Native Americans, who were to be treated as subjects (*vasallos*) of the Empire.[39] Although severe punishment had to be used when deemed necessary with the same paternalistic "moderation" promoted by Acosta, they had to be protected from any insult, offence, or mistreatment. Any Spaniard who mistreated a Native American would be punished as if the victim were also a Spaniard.[40] In addition to the Native Americans' miserable status, there were other reasons for their protection, that included their recent conversion to the Christian faith, as well as the "rest" of the reasons: "their imbecility, rusticity, poverty, faintheartedness, and continuous works, and services".[41]

According to the jurist, the "miserable" status applied to the Americans was due to the lack of respect and mistreatment they suffered from the Spaniards. The latter tended to attribute less nobility (*nobleza*) to them than to the most worthless and rude Spaniard.[42] However, referring to them them as *miserables* in order to formalise their protective and special treatment also led Solórzano to assess the extent to which they could benefit from the legal favours and privileges (*favores i privilegios*) enjoyed by minors, the poor and the peasants. Their social status and alleged similarity to children gave them the ability to cancel

36 Solórzano y Pereira, *Política Indiana*, book 2, chap. 28, 230.

37 "Miserables personas se reputan, i llaman todas aquellas, de quien naturalmente nos compadecemos por su estado, calidad, ô trabajos" (Ibid., 230).

38 "humilde, servil, i rendida condicion, de la qual dexo ya dicho tanto en los Capitulos pasados, i añaden mas à cada passo infinitos Autores" (Ibid., 230).

39 Ibid., 230.

40 Ibid., 231–232. About tempering punishment, Solórzano refers to Acosta's *De procuranda* (Ibid., 234).

41 "de su imbecilidad, rusticidad, pobreza, pussilanimidad, i continuos trabajos, i servicios" (Ibid., 230).

42 "los mas viles Españoles se tienen, i reputan por mas dignos de honra, i estimacion, que los mas nobles Indios." (Ibid., 233.)

a contract "despite being of full age", particularly after a sale of real estate (*bien raíz*).[43] In some cases, authorities needed to intervene to prevent them from entering into a contract, despite – Solórzano insists – their complete freedom and *dominium* over their possessions. This happened when they planned to sell their estate (*hacienda*) to pay off an unmanageable debt. Because "it seems that they have no free will, and being like they are, exposed to so many tricks [*asechanças*], and hoaxes, and because of their fragility, simplicity, and little constancy". Solórzano then reiterated what other authors had said: these measures were set "like speaking about underage people and women, to whom Indians are compared".[44]

The association established by Solórzano was no novelty: in fact, it dated back to the sixteenth century and the efforts of several bishops, including Bartolomé de Las Casas (1484–1565), who sought to implement a legal protection for the Americans. Caroline Cunill has shown that this legal inheritance from medieval Europe aimed to provide equal protection to the disadvantaged members of society. The category "miserable" was meant to address the imbalance caused by the vulnerable position of a section of the population who faced difficulties in accessing justice due to their social situation or lack of familiarity with the legal system. On the other hand, certain privileges deriving from this special social status, such as the "restitution of goods" studied by Aliocha Maldavsky, helped to maintain the colonists' relationship of domination over the Native Americans, thus doomed to remain "eternal neophytes".[45] In Solórzano's considerations, the brief comparison to children – and in this case, to women as well – appeared as a means of clarification, highlighting the similarities between the rights of the miserable and underaged people.

The sources mentioned above broadly show how comparing Native Americans to children could serve as a tool for the imperial authorities (both religious and secular) to make sense of the American difference. This process involved incorporating indigenous people into the European reality, which appears here in its theological thoughts, its legal instruments, and its

43 "aunque sean mayores de edad, se pueden restituir, i aun dezir de nulidad contra los tales contratos" (Ibid., 236). About other legal privileges that were granted to indigenous peoples: Cunill, "L'Indien, personne misérable", 31.

44 "Todavia, la condicion, i submission tan notable, i rendida de estos miserables, obligô à que se procediesse en sus contratos con este recato: porque no parece que tienen voluntad libre, i estar como estan, expuestos à tantas asechanças, i engaños, i por que su fragilidad, facilidad, i poca constancia, no se convierta, i redunde en daño, i acabamiento de sus haziendas, como hablando de los menores i mugeres, à quienes los Indios se comparan, lo dizen algunos textos, i una celebre Glossa, que pone unos versos de todas las personas que estan prohibidas en enagenar sus haziendas" (Ibid., 237).

45 "La restitución permite construir una dualidad entre el encomendero señor de indios y los indios, eternos neófitos." Maldavsky, "Teología moral", 1145.

social roles. Thus, this assimilation of otherness was not merely an intellectual exercise, for it made it possible to justify and consolidate domination.[46] More precisely, it enabled jurists and theologians to assign an existing social status to Native Americans – that of children – to explain and advocate for similar treatment. This included the necessity to educate and convert them until they were fully grown up and developed reason, as well as the obligation to correct them through penitence and punishment. Additionally, it involved the duty to protect them from, for example, what Acosta denounced as the abusive violence usually used by the *conquistadores*, or from what Solórzano condemned as swindles from the Spaniards. Early commentators on the conquest expressed an equivalent analogy to the whole continent: the French philosopher Michel de Montaigne (1533–1592) stated that the 'New World' was actually *new* in the sense that its people were like children who had barely developed their "arts"; a world "so *new* and so *infant* that we are still teaching it its a, b, c".[47] Montaigne's analogy had an accusatory purpose, as it allowed him to bring out the "infanticide" that the Spanish crown was responsible for.[48]

What exactly was the social status allocated to children? After studying the legal definition of childhood in Colonial Spanish America, associating Native Americans to children, and even to slaves, appears coherent in the reasoning of the time. According to the historian of Indian Law Antonio Dougnac, the Spanish colonial "family" as an institution was still close to the etymological origins of the term, namely the antique concept of *famulus* meaning "slave". The wife and children were legally and socially dependent on the family father, known as *paterfamilias* in Roman law, and subject to his almost absolute power. The father ruled over them like a slave master, possessing the power to punish his children among many other rights (*patria potestad*).[49] At the same time, according to the *Siete Partidas* which partly governed Spanish America until the nineteenth century,[50] servants and slaves were included in the definition of family and therefore considered under the father's *potestad*, although more exactly submitted to the *"dominica" potestas*.[51] Consequently, children had a legal and social status similar to that of slaves, and masters had the authority

46 Gliozzi, *Adam et le Nouveau*, 316–317.

47 "Notre monde vient d'en trouver un autre […] – écrit Montaigne – non moins grand, plein et membru que lui, toutefois si *nouveau* et si *enfant* qu'on lui apprend encore son a, b, c" (Montaigne, "Des Coches", 886, cited by Gliozzi, *Adam et le Nouveau*, 173).

48 Gliozzi, *Adam et le Nouveau*, 173.

49 Dougnac Rodríguez, *Esquema del derecho*, 43.

50 Bravo Lira, "Vigencia de las Partidas", 43–45.

51 "Que por esta palabra familia se entiende el señor de ella y su mujer y todos los que viven bajo él sobre quien ha mandamiento: así como los hijos, y los sirvientes, y los otros criados" (*Partidas* 7,33,6, cited by Dougnac Rodríguez, *Esquema del derecho*, 27–28).

to punish children and were obligated to provide them with food and ensure their religious education.[52]

Although traces of comparisons between Native Americans and children sporadically reappeared here and there over the decades,[53] this analogy lost its relevance as time passed and as the justification for European's *dominium* on America became less topical. However, a 'familial' relationship between the missionaries and the Native Americans took root over time. Regarding punishment, a paternalistic attitude, which was already discretly present in Acosta's instructions, continued to be promoted by the Jesuits. In other words, although the analogy between Native Americans and children almost disappeared, the punishments that were made possible thanks to this analogy remained, and with it the 'moderate' role of the benevolent Fathers.

Regulating Labour in New Spain Jesuit's *haciendas*

The Jesuit *haciendas* of New Spain provided an environment in which a 'familial' relationship between Native Americans and Spaniards found a ground of applicability. These *haciendas* were agricultural and livestock properties that formed the backbone of the Spanish Empire's economic system, primarily based on the trade of sugar and silver. Historiography from the 1950s onwards has demonstrated how the survival of the Society of Jesus in America was bound to the system. Jesuit houses and colleges owned *haciendas* that were intended to provide for the daily needs of their members and pay off their debts through trade.[54] They used various types of workers, to varying degrees dependent on their master including slaves, many of African descent, although indigenous workers were also used in some regions such as Chile. While Potosí was the centre of silver mining in America until the second half of the seventeenth century, New Spain rose to prominence and took the lead from 1700 onwards.[55]

52 Ibid., [318–319 of digital edition]. The situation was similar in Europe: Hall and Malcolm, "Sexual and Family", 275–281.

53 Gliozzi cites an example from 1747: talking about the Natives from Paraguay, the Jesuit José Cardiel blames their childish thinking and inability to take care of themselves (Gliozzi, *Adam et le Nouveau*, 351, n. 31).

54 About Jesuit *haciendas* in New Spain, see Tutino, "Capitalism, Christianity"; Konrad, *A Jesuit Hacienda*.

55 Tutino, "Capitalism, Christianity", 25. On the importance of Potosí in silver trade, see Lane, *Potosí: The Silver*.

The anonymous *Instrucciones a los Hermanos Jesuitas Administradores de Haciendas* were not intended for publication or distribution outside of the order. This document, consisting of ten chapters and forty-nine folios, was edited by the historian François Chevalier in 1950, and was meant to provide internal instructions to the *hacienda* manager. It was usually a coadjutor brother, mainly responsible for applying the rules set by their superiors and supervising religious life and daily work at the *hacienda*.[56] Meant to regulate the *haciendas* of post-1722 New Spain,[57] these instructions dictated how the members and workers were expected to behave, and how to manage the agricultural exploitations and the "cultivation of souls" ("*el cultivo de las almas*"[58]) in the community. The primary aim of soul cultivation was for the Jesuits themselves, but it also extended to the slaves and the other workers, such as the *sirvientes* and *gañanes*, who were mostly Native Americans.[59]

The second chapter of the document provided instructions on the "good education and governance of the servants".[60] It instructed the administrators to "Remember [...] that [they were] family fathers in the [*haciendas*], and therefore [they had] the same very strict obligations as all family fathers with their domestics, and masters and lords with *their servants and slaves*".[61] To clarify, the obligations referred to are the responsibility to look after the "cultivation of souls" and the "good education" of the servants and domestics. The paragraph introduces a series of instructions meant to address the

56 Macera, *Instrucciones para el manejo*, 25.

57 There is ample evidence that this document was produced for the *haciendas* of New Spain: Mexican vernacular terms and expressions; references to works written by authors from New Spain (*Instrucciones a los hermanos*, 12–5); and simply the presence of this document in the Mexican archives. About the date of the manuscript Chevalier stresses the reference to a book printed in 1712 (*Florilegio medizinal*, published in Mexico by the Jesuit Juan Steineffer), as well as the Chalco prosecution ("proceso de Chalco") that happened years later (*Instrucciones a los hermanos*, 11).

58 Ibid., 49, §19.

59 According to Chevalier, the *sirvientes* and *gañanes* chose freely to work in the *haciendas*, although their debt impelled them to do so. Generally, the *gañanes* were Native Americans whereas the *sirvientes* were "mixed-blood" and employed as artisans and for works at a higher hierarchical level (Ibid., 26–27). About the importance of religiosity in the *haciendas*, see Macera, *Instrucciones para el manejo*, 28–30.

60 Chapter 2: "De los que han de guardar los Hermanos Administradores en la buena educación y gobierno de los sirvientes".

61 *Instrucciones a los hermanos*, 50, §20, my emphasis: "Acuérdense, pues, que son padres de familias en las haciendas, y por eso tienen las mismas estrechísimas obligaciones que todos los padres de familias con sus domésticos, y los amos y señores *con sus criados y esclavos*, por eso, para enterarse de estas obligaciones, lean una vez cada año cuando van a ejercicios la Plática 36 del Padre Parra en que recoge y declara la suma de las obligaciones de amos y criados".

pernicious consequences of failing to provide a proper religious education to those under the administrator's control. The master was under threat of provoking "God to the punishment He has threatened against violators of His Law, and more so against the fathers of the family [*padres de familias*] negligent in educating their domestics well, whom St. Paul calls *Apostates of the Faith and worse than infidels*".[62]

When addressing the practice of punishment, the third chapter made the same analogy between the administrator and the fathers of the family. However, unlike the previous chapter, it only focused on the effective governance of "the slaves",[63] and disregarded other categories of workers. Stressing a need of "moderation" and "ease in the punishment of the guilty", the administrator was requested to "*Behave with* [*the slaves*] *as parents*: show that you punish them for not being able to take it anymore, and be easy in admitting suppliants, to temper the punishment because of their intercession; and perhaps also [be easy] to forgive everything".[64] The goal of this "tempered" behaviour was to prevent the slaves from performing their duties unwillingly and poorly, but also to avoid violent responses: "[The administrators] may not want to handle everything rigorously, which will not do anything and [the slaves] will live discontented and serve under duress, and their service will be violent and badly done".[65] The chapter concludes with a final reminder, emphasising again the obligations of the administrators: "*May the administrators remember that they are fathers of the family*, and superiors of a community as important as slavery [*esclavonía*] is [...]. And so may they watch over them, because [in the *hacienda*]

62 Ibid., 49–50, §19: "Si por el contrario fueren omisos y descuidados en esta obligación, y dejaren a los sirvientes que vivan como quisieren, contentándose sólo con que no les falten a su trabajo, provocarán a Dios al castigo que tiene amenazado contra los violadores de su Ley, y más contra los padres de familias negligentes en educar bien a sus domésticos, a los cuales por esto llama San Pablo *Apóstatas de la Fe y peores que infieles*". For a glimpse of the centrality of religiosity, complementary to the productive activity of the *haciendas*, see Tutino, "Capitalism, Christianity", 29–31.

63 Chapter 3: "De lo que han de guardar en el buen gobierno de los esclabos donde los hay".

64 *Instrucciones a los hermanos*, 65, §39, my emphasis: "Pórtense con ellos como padres: muestren que los castigan a más no poder, y sean fáciles en admitir rogadores para templar por su intercesión el castigo, y tal vez también para perdonarlo todo." Part of this quote needs an explanation: in some cases, the administrator was instructed to secretly seek friends or family that could beg for mercy in favour of the punished worker (Ibid., 12–13, and §43).

65 Ibid., 65, §39: "Procuren portarse los Administradores con mucha moderación y reposo en el castigo de los culpados. No quieran llevar lo todo por el rigor, que no harán nada, y ellos [los esclavos] vivirán descontentos y servirán forzados, y su servicio será violento y mal hecho".

they have no other superior who takes care of them".[66] Yet the punishments were not reserved for slaves alone. Another chapter regulating the work in the fields by the administrators[67] explained how they should be treated: "With the Indians who live in the *hacienda*, [the administrators] can use some moderate punishment when needed, acting as fathers of the family".[68]

The *Instrucciones* depict a 'familial' relationship that is more akin to a master-worker dynamic, regardless of the workers' identities, rather than being solely based on a 'childish' trait attributed to the Native Americans. The document does not explicitly mention any childish characteristics unique to any particular group of people, but it implies such inferiority and childishness through the parental role assigned to the administrator. Thus, there is a shift from the label "childlike" that was assigned to Native Americans in legal and theological texts, to the specific role of the Jesuit who is expected to act "like a father" when instructing and disciplining both Native Americans, Africans, and their descendants.

Beyond the normative property of these instructions, which makes it possible to grasp what this study is about – namely the Jesuits' discourse on their relationship with Native Americans – it is currently complex to determine to what extent such a father-son relationship was effectively implemented in the missionary and agricultural field.[69] As noted by historian Pablo Macera in a study on Peruvian *haciendas*, they were theoretically subject to regular control and supervision by the *visitadores*. The "visits" were an institution that developed among both secular and religious authorities. Within the Jesuit community, visits were usually conducted by the order's superiors. In addition to checking the accounting records and inspecting the *haciendas*, the *visitador* would issue orders regarding the functioning of the *hacienda*, including the

66 Ibid., 85, §63, my emphasis: "*Acuérdense los Administradores que son padres de familias*, y superiores de una comunidad tan crecida como es la esclavonía, y por eso han de dar estrecha cuenta a Dios, así de los males que ellos hicieren por su descuido, como de los bienes que omitieren. Y así velen sobre ellos, porque allí no tienen otro superior que los cuide." The term "esclavonía" is here in use, as an obsolete term for "esclavitud". (*Diccionario de Autoridades* (vol. III, 1732). Real Academia Española. < https://apps2.rae.es/DA.html> [30.5.2023].)

67 Chapter 9: "De lo que han de observar los Admnistradores con los sirvientes del campo".

68 *Instrucciones a los hermanos*, 131, §128: "Con los indios que viven en la hacienda podrán usar algún castigo moderado cuando lo necesitan, obrando en esto como padres de familias; [...]".

69 In this respect, I depart from Tutino's account, which summarises the instructions on slaves and bonded workers without discussing their actual implementation. See Tutino, "Capitalism, Christianity", 29–36.

treatment and conduct of the workers.[70] That said, while visits were scheduled to occur annually, some *haciendas*, even those located in areas easily accessible from the college on which they depended, were not visited for several years: over a 50-year period (between 1702 and 1761), the Peruvian *hacienda* of San Juan de la Pampa (also known as El Ingenio de Huaura) was visited only 18 times.[71]

Mexican *haciendas* were also subject to the control of the *visitadores*. However the same sort of instructions as in the Peruvian *haciendas* did not stand the test of time, namely succinct instructions, concentrated on a dozen items, and kept to the essentials without repeating instructions already expressed previously.[72] At the same time, the conciseness of Peruvian instructions limits the information on the relationships that the Jesuits were expected to maintain with the slaves and other workers. Indeed, when considering punishments, they advocate for a form of "moderation" to prevent excesses, cruelty, or lack of charity,[73] without emphasising the need to establish a paternalistic relationship with the slaves. In contrast, the Mexican instructions are notably comprehensive. They deal methodically, and in detail, with most aspects of the *hacienda's* organisation and administration, including the education of the servants, the governance of the slaves,[74] the management of livestock and agricultural products, the accounting and communication with other institutions, the religious behaviour of the residents and religious services provided, and even the policy regarding travellers and beggars.

---

70 Macera, *Instrucciones para el manejo*, 25.

71 Ibidem. Regarding Jesuit *haciendas* in Peru, see Cushner, *Lords of the Land*.

72 The *hacienda* of San Juan de la Pampa accumulated (from 1699 to 1767) the instructions of *visitadores* that, in some cases, decided that no additional instructions from the previous ones were necessary. For example, on the 1st of september 1731, after the visit of Father Alvaro Cabero, the instruction stated that "no le parecio ser necesario poner nuevos ordenes" (Macera, *Instrucciones para el manejo*, 64). Then, on the 1st of november 1734, Father Francisco de Rotalde "juzgo no ser necesario añadir nuevos ordenes sino solo encargo la puntual observancia de los impuestos por sus antecesores" (Ibidem). Something similar was stated in 1747 by Father Francisco de Larreta, who nonetheless judged it necessary to reiterate "la moderación en el castigo de los negros delincuentes". Larreta authorised 25 whippings for minor infractions, 50 for serious ones (Ibid., 65–66).

73 Most Peruvian instructions stated as an appropriate level of punishment 25 to a maximum of 50 whippings, depending on the gravity of the infraction: see the instructions for Pachachaca in 1674 (Ibid., 54), or for El Ingenio de Huaura (also called San Juan de la Pampa) in 1699 (Ibid., 59), in 1747 (Ibid., 65–66), and in 1764 (Ibid., 69), for Tuman in 1742 (Ibid., 78), for Motocache in 1767 (Ibid., 109), or for Santa Beatriz in 1767 (Ibid., 113).

74 Although, as pointed out by Tutino, it did not state anything about "buying, selling, or moving slaves" (Tutino, "Capitalism, Chistianity", 31).

Therefore, the Mexican *Instrucciones* may be the result of a Provincial's desire to compile and summarise all the content of all the previously formulated instructions by the various visitors over the years. The authorship of this document has not been ascertained yet, but it was most certainly the bureaucratic result of several decades of instructions accumulated over time, after the inspection carried out by the *visitadores*.[75] Similar to the legal and theological treatises, this document served as a normative source that depicted how the ideal *hacienda* should operate according to the Society's superiors. The treatment of workers in a paternalistic manner, and consequently the implicit analogy between the bonded workers and children, reflect the norms desired by the hierarchy and the values promoted by the Society. This also legitimised the bonded and slavish work carried out in the *haciendas*.

What is more, this Society's ideal of harmony was to be expected from a religious order that for most of its history had advocated a 'moderate' and 'spiritual' approach to the conquest, focused on the evangelisation of the Native Americans, as illustrated by the Fathers of Peru. Exploiting individuals for agricultural and mining activities had to be justified and handled in an exemplary manner, to avoid reproducing the abuses inflicted by the seculars in similar activities. That being said, the Jesuit conception of the relationship between them and the Native Americans, characterised by a strong hierarchy and by the need of discipline and correction, also makes sense in the ideology and institutional history of the Society, as it highlights the value of obedience.

Children, Servants, Slaves: A Common Bondage to Obedience

Obedience was a crucial concept within the Society of Jesus, to say the least. A closer examination of the concept helps to understand what exactly was at stake in the familial relationship promoted between the Jesuits and the Native Americans.

As much as it was an imperative for behaviour within the Society of Jesus – arguably more important than the vows of poverty and chastity –, it was also a

75 Tutino suggested that the *Instrucciones* was an "evolving guide, first drafted in the era of estate building, then revised over decades to address changing times" (Tutino, "Capitalism, Chistianity", 30). Chevalier, identifying orders dating back to early seventeenth century, suggested that the *Instrucciones* were the result of 150 years of estate experience, summarised in the early eighteenth century (*Instrucciones para los hermanos*, 17). He mentions the reference to seventeenth-century orders from General Claudio Acquaviva (1543–1615) (Ibid., 16–17).

particularly complex one.[76] Since the creation of the Society, Ignatius of Loyola (1491–1556) had required a form of obedience so radical that it had been compared to a dead body being manipulated by the orders of its superior without the slightest hint of physical or mental resistance.[77] The *Constitutions* (*c.* 1556), which are the foundational regulations of the order fixed in 1594, reiterated this idea.[78] In practice, the limits between what was considered obedience and disobedience for Jesuits, and the extent to which they could act according to their own will or discernment, depended largely on the situation or on the person in question. Jesuits were also expected to possess self-reliance and autonomy.[79]

Obedience was considered a capital virtue, not only for its social functions but also for its spiritual benefits. Blindly obeying the orders of a superior was conceived by Loyola as an act of self-relativisation and humiliation, as well as a surrender of one's own person and free will to the will of God through his ministers – the superiors, representatives of God in the temporal world. In this sense, the Jesuits believed that giving up one's own free will to fulfil God's will was the most respectful, virtuous, and pious form of freedom, as it countered the sin of pride (*vana gloria*) that could result from acting according to one's own impulses and egoistic wishes.[80] Hence, the implicit and special significance given to freedom, in a context where slavery and bonded labour were organised by the Jesuits: the absence of temporal subordination to a master was not the first meaning of the term in the Society's ideology.[81]

That being said, elaborating on the virtue and duty of obedience also led the first Jesuits to reflect on the relationship between those who obeyed and those who were obeyed. As Jesuits were expected to view their superiors as the equivalent of God and Jesus Christ, so the relationship of obedience was often likened to that of father and son. This analogy is already present in the chapter on "What pertains to obedience" (part 6, chapter 1) of the *Constitutions* of the Society, approved by the first General Congregation, in 1558:

---

76 Friedrich offers a useful synthesis on the complexity of "obedience" within the Society of Jesus: Friedrich, *The Jesuits*, 94–100. See also the essential work of Mostaccio, *Early Modern Jesuits*; Imbruglia, "Sacrifice and the Missionary".

77 Friedrich, *The Jesuits*, 95.

78 The analogy with the corps appears in the *Constitutions* (part 6, chapter 1, § 547). The idea already existed among the Franciscans – in *Vie de François d'Assise* by Thomas de Celano – as well as among the Desert Fathers from the fifth Century (Loyola, "Constitutions", 528, note g).

79 Friedrich, *The Jesuits*, 98.

80 Ibid., 95; See also the "great letter on obedience" of Loyola: *Monumenta Ignatiana*, 669–81.

81 This aspect was stressed in the works Carlos Zerón and Alcir Pécora on the Jesuit António Vieira and slavery in Brazil: Zerón, "Un filo", 104; Pécora, "Vieira", 432.

> Likewise, it should be strongly recommended to all [Jesuits] that they should have and show great reverence, especially interior reverence, for their superiors, by considering and revering Jesus Christ in them; and from their hearts they should warmly *love their superiors as fathers* in him.[82]

Concluding Remarks

The comparison of Native Americans to children was a common theme in legal-theological treatises of the sixteenth and seventeenth centuries, including among scholarly circles of the Society of Jesus. This comparison was extensively developed by the School of Salamanca to persuade the audience that Native Americans could be raised according to European standards and converted to Christianity. Native Americans were expected to be taught and developed in the same way as children, and were believed to have the ability to learn and fully develop their reason, allegedly still *in potentia*. Therefore, the possibility of conversion justified the presence of missionaries on the front line of the American conquest. Later on, Acosta's reiteration of this comparison served to justify something that Vitoria had only weakly emphasised before him: the need to use punishment and correction as a method of redress for the Native Americans, although it was essential to moderate and apply them in a paternalistic manner. The sources analysed make a clear distinction between violence and punishment. Acosta defined "violence" as the brutal and unjust treatment inflicted by secular settlers on indigenous people for the purpose of exploitation. As in Solórzano's jurisdictional text and comparison of Native Americans to miserable people, infantilising them had the dual objective of protecting them from the abuses of the Spaniards, and controlling them using a form of regulated violence that was deemed legitimate.

This observation brings us back to the concept of violence. As mentioned in the introduction (see note 4), its meaning varies significantly depending on the context. To understand Acosta's view, it is valuable to explore violence as "an act of physical hurt deemed legitimate by the performer and illegitimate by (some) witnesses", if we disregard the exclusively physical aspect of this definition.[83] Matthew Restall argues that a relativist understanding of violence is

---

82 My emphasis: Padberg, *The Constitutions*, 225–226, §551. The same text was approved for the final version of the *Constitutions*, at the fifth General Congregation, in 1594 (Loyola, *Écrits*, 392). For a comprehensive overview of the different versions of the text, see Loyola, *Écrits*, 384–392.

83 Antony, Carroll and Dodds Pennock, "Introduction", 8. The authors adopt the definition proposed by David Riches in 1986 (Riches, David ed. [1986]. *The Anthropology of Violence*. Oxford: Blackwell, 8).

particularly relevant in the context of the Spanish conquests, where certain forms of "controlled" violence were deemed legitimate and even necessary for "civilised" life, as in Acosta's case.[84]

Beyond intellectual circles comes the other face of the analogies to describe otherness. In the field of economic activity (the *haciendas*), the comparison does not represent Native Americans as children, but instead portrays the Jesuit as a father figure (in the sense of *paterfamilias*). The administrator's duty is to provide religious instruction and his power lies in correction and punishment. The use of the father-son analogy aligns with the values promoted by the Society of Jesus such as charity and obedience. It appears to have been employed to justify the authority that the Jesuits had assigned themselves, first to the order itself and then to the outside world. This recurrent analogy circulating within the Society of Jesus took advantage of children's social status, and of social norms regarding the family as an institution.

This paper focused on the Society of Jesus due to the abundance of sources they produced and their significant impact on the religious conquest of America. Additional research on the influential Franciscan friars would be useful, to determine whether they used similar conceptual tools to represent their relationship with the American inhabitants. This study is also limited to an intellectual approach to the representation of Native Americans, whose infantilisation is both a well-known fact and a rarely studied social phenomenon. Examining sources of another typology, such as the internal and abundant correspondence of the Society, would be beneficial to expand beyond the normative and discursive analysis conducted here. Finally, and as previously mentioned, in the Mexican instructions, churchmen were commonly assigned the role of *paterfamilias* in their relationship with slaves and servants, namely Africans and Afro-descendants, as well as Native Americans. It is worth investigating whether the promotion of a 'familial' relationship became a common feature of any relationship involving the dependency of the worker towards the master, regardless of the identity of the former.

84 "Within Spanish culture generally, and specifically within its political and legal culture, there was a relativist understanding of violence. Violence was a valid and acceptable mechanism for exercising authority, communicating political and religious orthodoxy, restoring honour, punishing transfressors and righting wrongs. But there were contexts to when, and rules to how, it could be committed. Violence was never just violence; it had to be *just* violence" (Restall, "Legitimised Violence", 425).

Works Cited

Acosta, José de (1589). *De Natura Novi Orbis Libri duo, et De Promulgatione Evangelii, apud Barbaros, sive De Procuranda Indorum Salute Libri sex*. Salmanticae: apud Guillelmum Foquel.

Acosta, José de (1984–1987). *De procuranda indorum salute*. Bilingual edition dir. by Luciano Pereña. Consejo Superior de Investigaciones Científicas: Madrid, 2 vols (Corpus hispanorum de pace 23–24).

Antony, Robert, Carroll, Stuart, and Dodds Pennock, Caroline (2020). "Introduction to Volume III". Robert Antony, Stuart Carroll, and Caroline Dodds Pennock ed. *The Cambridge World History of Violence*, vol. 3 "1500–1800 CE." Cambridge et al.: Cambridge University Press, 1–14.

Barrios Pintado, Feliciano. "Juan de Solórzano y Pereira." *Real Academia de la Historia, Diccionario Biográfico electrónico* <https://dbe.rah.es/biografias/14530/juan-de-solorzano-y-pereira> (20.6.2023).

Bravo Lira, Bernardino (1985). "Vigencia de las Partidas en Chile." *Revista de Estudios Histórico-Jurídicos* 10, 43–105.

Burr, Vivien (1995). *An Introduction to Social Constructionism*. London; NewYork: Routledge.

Cushner, Nicholas P. (1980). *Lords of the Land: Sugar, Wine, and the Jesuit Estates of Coastal Peru, 1600–1767*. Albany, NY: State University of New York Press.

Cunill, Caroline (2017). "L'Indien, personne misérable. Considérations historiographiques sur le statut des peuples indigènes dans l'empire hispanique." *Revue d'histoire moderne et contemporaine* 64/2, 21–38.

Decock, Wim (2013). *Theologians and Contract Law. The Moral Transformation of the* Ius Commune (ca. 1500–1650). Leiden/Boston: Brill/Nijhoff.

Dougnac Rodríguez, Antonio (2003). *Esquema del derecho de familia indiano*. Santiago: Instituto de Historia del Derecho Juan de Solórzano y Pereyra.

Egaña, Antonio de ed. (1958). *Monumenta Peruana II (1576–1580)*, vol. 2. Rome: Monumenta Historica Societatis Iesu.

Fagan, Garrett G. et al. ed. (2020). *The Cambridge World History of Violence*, vol. 1 "The Prehistoric and Ancient Worlds." Cambridge et al.: Cambridge University Press.

Friedrich, Markus (2022). *The Jesuits: A History*. Translated by John Noël Dillon. Princeton: Princeton University Press.

García Hernán, Enrique (2007). *Consejero de ambos mundos. Vida y obra de Juan de Solórzano Pereira (1575–1655)*. Madrid: Fundación Mapfre-Instituto de Cultura.

García Mateo, Rogelio (2003). "Ignacio de Loyola, la Escuela de Salamanca y América: José de Acosta." *Cuadernos salmantinos de filosofía* 20, 439–48.

Gliozzi, Giuliano (2000 [orig. 1977]). *Adam et le Nouveau Monde. La naissance de l'anthropologie comme idéologie coloniale: des généalogies bibliques aux théories raciales*. Transl. Arlette Estève and Pascal Gabellone. Lecques: Théétète.

Graziani, Irene and Spissu, Maria Vittoria ed. (2019). *Il Mito del Nemico. Identitá, alteritá e loro rappresentazioni*. Bolonia: Minerva.

Greenblatt, Stephen (1991). *Marvelous Possessions. The Wonder of the New World*. Chicago: University of Chicago Press.

Grice-Hutchinson, Marjorie (1989). "El concepto de la Escuela de Salamanca: sus origenes y su desarollo." *Revista de Historia Económica* VII/2, 21–6.

Gruzinski, Serge and Bernand, Carmen (1988). *De l'idolâtrie: une archéologie des sciences religieuses*. Paris: Seuil.

Hall, Dianne, and Malcolm, Elizabeth (2020). "Sexual and Family Violence in Europe." Robert Antony, Stuart Carroll, and Caroline Dodds Pennock ed. *The Cambridge World History of Violence*, vol. 3 "1500–1800 CE." Cambridge: Cambridge University Press, 274–291.

Höpfl, Harro (2004). *Jesuit Political Thought: The Society of Jesus and the State, c. 1540–1630*. Cambridge: Cambridge University Press.

Imbruglia, Girolamo (2014). "The Invention of Savage Society: Amerindian Religion and Society in Acosta's Anthropological Theology." *History of European Ideas* 40, 291–311.

Imbruglia, Girolamo (2022). "Sacrifice and the Missionary." Girolamo Imbruglia, Pierre-Antoine Fabre, and Giovanni Mongini ed. *Cinque secoli di Litterae indipetae: il desiderio delle missioni nella Compagnia di Gesù*. Roma: Institutum historicum societatis Iesu, 429–438.

Instrucciones a los hermanos jesuitas administradores de haciendas (Manuscrito mexicano del siglo XVIII) (1950). Digital edition, prologue and notes François Chevalier. Mexico: Universidad Nacional Autónoma de México, Instituto de Historia <www.historicas.unam.mx/publicaciones/publicadigital/libros/016/instrucciones_jesuitas.html> (25.6.2023).

Konrad, Herman W. (1980). *A Jesuit Hacienda in Colonial Mexico: Santa Lucía, 1576–1767*, Stanford: Stanford University Press.

Lane, Kris (2019). *Potosí: The Silver City that Changed the World*. Oakland: University of California Press.

Loyola, Ignace de (1991). *Écrits*. M. Giuliani dir. Paris: Desclée de Brouwer.

MacCormack, Sabine (1995). "Limits of Understanding. Perceptions of Greco-Roman and Amerindian Paganism in Early Modern Europe." Karen Ordahl Kupperman ed. *America in European Consciousness, 1493–1750*. Chapel Hill; London: University of North Carolina Press, 79–129.

Macera, Pablo (1966). *Instrucciones para el manejo de las haciendas jesuitas del Peru (ss. XVII–XVIII)*. Lima: Universidad Nacional Mayor de San Marcos, Facultad de Letras y Ciencias Humanas, Departamento de Historia.

Maldavsky, Aliocha (2019). "Teología moral, restitución y sociedad colonial en los Andes en el siglo XVI." *Revista Portuguesa de Filosofia* 72/2, 1125–1148.

Mason, Peter (1990). *Deconstructing America: Representations of the Other*. London; New York: Routledge.

Mignolo, Walter D. (2002). "Introduction to José de Acosta's *Historia Natural y Moral de las Indias*." Acosta, José de (2002 [1590]). *Natural and Moral History of the Indias*. Trans. Frances Lopez-Morillas. Durham et al.: Duke University Press, xvii–xxviii.

Montaigne, Michel de (1962 [1588]). "Des Coches". A. Thibaudet ed. *Essais*, III, VI. Paris: la Pléiade.

Monumenta Ignatiana ex Autographis vel ex Antiquioribus Exemplis (1906). *Sancti Ignatii de Loyola Societatis Jesu fundatoris epistolae et instructiones*: vol. 4. Matriti: Typis G. Lopez del Horno.

Mostaccio, Silvia (2014). *Early Modern Jesuits between Obedience and Conscience during the Generalate of Claudio Acquaviva (1581–1615)*. Surrey et al.: Ashgate.

O'Gorman, Edmundo (1972). *Cuatro historiadores de Indias. Siglo XVI*. Mexico: Secretaria de Educacion Publica.

Oliveira e Silva, Paula (2015). "Francisco de Vitoria." Ángel Poncela González ed. *La Escuela de Salamanca. Filosofía y Humanismo ante el mundo moderno*. Madrid: Verbum, 131–62.

Padberg, John W. S.J. ed. (1996). *The Constitutions of the Society of Jesus and Their Complementary Norms: A Complete English Translation of Official Latin Texts*. Sant Louis: The Institute of Jesuit Sources.

Pagden, Anthony (1986). *The Fall of Natural Man: The American Indian and the Origins of Comparative Ethnology*. Cambridge; London etc.: Cambridge University Press.

Pécora, Alcir (1992). "Vieira, o índio e o corpo mistico." Adauto Novaes ed. *Tempo e história*. São Paulo: Companhia das Letras/Secretaria Municipal de Cultura <https://artepensamento.com.br/item/vieira-o-indio-e-o-corpo-mistico/> (25.6.2023).

Pereña, Luciano (1984), "Proyecto de sociedad colonial: pacificación y colonización." Acosta, José de. *De procuranda indorum salute*, vol. 1: "Pacificación y colonización." Bilingual edition dir. by Luciano Pereña. Consejo Superior de Investigaciones Científicas: Madrid (Corpus hispanorum de pace 23–24), 3–46.

Pino Díaz, Fermín del (2019). « Contribución del Padre José de Acosta a la constitutción de la etnología : su evolucionismo. » *Bérose – Encyclopedie internationale des histoires de l'anthropologie*, 1–39.

Pinto Rodríguez, Jorge (2015 [1988]). *Frontera, misiones y misioneros en la Araucanía, 1600–1900*. Temuco: Ediciones Universidad de la Frontera.

Restall, Matthew (2020). "Legitimised Violence in Colonial Spanish America." Robert Antony, Stuart Carroll, and Caroline Dodds Pennock ed. *The Cambridge World History of Violence*, vol. 3 "1500–1800 CE." Cambridge et al.: Cambridge University Press, 408–426.

Rothman, Alan (2021). "The Jesuits and Slavery." *Journal of Jesuit Studies* 8, 1–10.

Solórzano y Pereira, Juan de (1648 [1647]). *Política Indiana*. Madrid: Por Diego Diaz de la Carrera.

Santos, Francisco A. and Amezúa Amezúa, Luis C. (2013). "La moderación de la pena ene le caso de las *personae miserabiles* en el pensamiento jurídico hispano-americano de los siglos XVI y XVII." *Revista de Historia del Derecho* 45, 245–264.

Tarantino, Giovanni and Wyss-Giacosa, Paola ed. (2021). *Through Your Eyes: Religious Alterity and the Early Modern Western Imagination*. Leiden: Brill.

Tardieu, Jean-Pierre (2005). "La esclavitud de los negros y el plan de Dios: la dialéctica de los jesuitas del virreinato del Perú." Sandra Negro and Manuel M. Marzal, ed. *Esclavitud, economía y evangelización: las haciendas jesuitas en la América virreinal*. Lima: Fondo Editorial de la Pontificia Universidad Católica del Perú, 67–81.

Tau Anzoátegui, Victor (2016). *El Jurista en el Nuevo Mundo. Pensamiento. Doctrina. Mentalidad*. Frankfurt am Main: Max Planck Institute for European Legal History.

Tutino, John (2021), "Capitalism, Christianity, and Slavery: Jesuits in New Spain, 1572–1767." *Journal of Jesuit Studies* 8, 11–36.

Zamora, Margarita (1993). "Christopher Columbus's 'Letter to the Sovereigns': Announcing the Discovery." Stephen Greenblatt ed. *New World Encounters*. Berkeley et al.: University of California Press, 1–11.

Zerón, Carlos (2017), "Un filo que no se rompe: la esclavitud en los tiempos modernos y contemporáneos." *Historia y Grafía* 49, 85–115.

Slavery, Law and Protestant Mission in Eighteenth-Century Tranquebar

Christoph Haar

Introduction

The present investigation reflects on the norms of slavery and the slave trade in eighteenth-century Tranquebar. At that time, Tranquebar, in the European orthography of Tharangambadi, the town of waves, belonged to a Danish colonial territory in Southeast India.[1] The territory extended beyond the town to encompass approximately 50 square kilometres and it was further enlarged in the course of the century. Colonial Tranquebar numbered roughly 4000 inhabitants within the Danish territory of about 30.000 inhabitants during the period under discussion.[2] The origin of the trading settlement dated back to 1620, when the ruler of the surrounding kingdom of Thanjavur, Ragunatha Nayak, gave the Danes permission to establish a trading post in exchange for regular tribute payments.[3]

Tranquebar was also the location of the first permanent Protestant Christian mission. In 1706, the first two of what until 1823 would be a total of fifty-four Protestant missionaries arrived on the Coromandel coast. At the time of the mission's founding, the second Danish East India Company, the "Ostindisk Kompagni", was in charge of the colony (1670–1729), following the one that had existed 1616–1650, and it would eventually be replaced by a third, the "Asiatisk Kompagni" or Danish Asiatic Company (1732–1843, private until 1772). The Danes traded in spices and textiles, over time especially in the intra-Indian ocean "country trade" rather than with Europe. All the while their overall

1 Jeyaraj, *Inkulturation in Tranquebar: Der Beitrag der frühen dänisch-halleschen Mission zum Werden einer indisch-einheimischen Kirche (1706–1730)*, 1. All translations in this chapter are my own unless indicated otherwise.

2 For an introduction to the mission, see Neill, *A History of Christianity in India: 1707–1858*, 28–58; see also Liebau, "Die Dänisch-Englisch-Hallesche Mission (Tranquebarmission)".

3 The sources sometimes call the kingdom "Tanjore" or "Tanschaur", and they compare nayak or "Naikker" to the title of a prince. By the early eighteenth century, these rulers called themselves kings, although other powers continued to call them princes. *Malabarische Korrespondenz*, Second Part, letter 6, 234.

 | DOI:10.30965/9783657796328_010

volume of trade, like the one of their British and French equivalents, remained lower by an extremely wide margin to that of the Dutch East India company.[4]

In this situation, the mission would find itself entangled with the interests of the Danish trading company as well as the Europeans and Tamils living on company grounds and in the surrounding kingdom of Thanjavur. The overwhelming majority of the missionaries was German, educated and recruited at the university of Halle under the auspices of the educational and social institution of the local "Glauchasche Anstalten" founded by the Pietist Lutheran spiritual leader August Hermann Francke (1663–1727). By the 1720s, the Anglican mission organisation *Society for Promoting Christian Knowledge* (the equivalent in the Indian Ocean region to the *Society for the Propagation of the Gospel in Foreign Parts* in the Atlantic) expanded what had been its financial and logistic assistance since 1710 to paying missionaries for their work on English company grounds, the first of which was Benjamin Schultze in 1728. The religious background to the mission was thus composed of German Pietist Lutherans who represented the reformed Lutheranism preferred by the Danish royalty and were supported by the Anglican church in England. Throughout the period, Halle remained the European spiritual centre of the mission, supplemented from 1714 by a mission board in Copenhagen which added a line of communication with the trading company leadership as well as the Danish crown.[5]

Research on the Tranquebar mission or Danish-English-Halle Mission, as it has been called in the more recent scholarship, has focused particularly on mission history and social history, or indeed on intellectual history.[6] When it has been mentioned in Tranquebar studies, the topic of slavery has featured in examinations concerning conversion, the mission's position vis-à-vis the Danish colonial authority, and as part of a larger discourse on abolition, possible humanitarian attitudes and European Enlightenment influences in the

4 Krieger, *Kaufleute, Seeräuber und Diplomaten: der dänische Handel auf dem Indischen Ozean (1620–1868)*, passim. Reinhard, *Die Unterwerfung der Welt. Globalgeschichte der europischen Expansion 1415–2015*, 205–233.

5 For the brief time period of 1712–1714, a "Mission Inspectorate" existed in Copenhagen that would be replaced by the mission board.

6 For the coining of the term Danish-English-Halle Mission, see Liebau, "Die Dänisch-Englisch-Hallesche Mission". For the roots of contemporary mission history, see Lehmann, *Es begann in Tranquebar. Die Geschichte der ersten evangelischen Kirche in Indien*. See also Gross, Kumaradoss, Liebau (eds.) *Halle and the beginnings of Protestant Christianity in India*, 3 vols.; for the latest and most comprehensive social-historical treatment, see Liebau, *Die indischen Mitarbeiter*. For a two-volume set of intellectual-historical contributions, see Mann (ed.), *Europäische Aufklärung und protestantische Mission in Indien*, and *Aufgeklärter Geist und evangelische Missionen in Indien*.

eighteenth and nineteenth centuries.[7] It has been a common theme since the early historiography to suggest that the mission treated the question of slavery as analogous to the question of caste in the sense that the mission worked towards the incremental amelioration of the living conditions of the deprived while simultaneously upholding the institution.[8] In the bigger picture of the Indian Ocean World paradigm,[9] Tranquebar has featured as part of the Danish slave trade in the Indian Ocean.[10] Research on slavery has addressed early modern Indian Ocean slavery and the slave trade across vast expanses, including the question to what extent the region could be compared to the Atlantic Ocean area in this regard.[11]

The present investigation seeks to advance the research landscape by placing the institution of slavery in Tranquebar at the centre of the analysis. What was at stake for the (predominantly Hindu and minority Muslim) Tamils and the Europeans when it came to matters of slavery? A variety of sources is available in order to address this research question, in particular the communication between Tranquebar and Europe, centring on the hubs in Halle and Copenhagen as well as the mission's widely distributed journal, in the popularised short name the *Hallesche Berichte* or *Halle Reports* which spread writings about Tranquebar throughout Europe and reached a circulation of 4800 copies by 1771.[12] The source material moreover offers the opportunity to retrieve indigenous voices in the historical records. It bears mentioning that the present

7 For the three research contexts, see, respectively, Liebau, *Die indischen Mitarbeiter*; Nørgaard, *Mission und Obrigkeit: die Dänisch-hallische Mission in Tranquebar 1706–1845*; Kaarsholm, "From abolition of the slave trade to protection of immigrants: Danish colonialism, German missionaries, and the development of ideas of humanitarian governance from the early eighteenth to the nineteenth century", 348–74. The theme of abolition is prevalent in the research on the British East India company in the late eighteenth as well as the nineteenth centuries, cf. Allen, *European Slave Trading*, 188f, and, critically assessing the British role, Major, *Slavery, Abolitionism and Empire in India, 1772–1843*, 59 and 234.

8 Germann, *Ziegenbalg und Plütschau*, vol. 1, 290. Nørgaard, *Mission und Obrigkeit*, 37.

9 The scholarly theme of tracing interactions and movements across vast regions – methodologically in light of globalisation, thus reaching beyond national borders and area studies – has grown since the beginning of the twenty-first century. See, for example, Pearson, *The Indian Ocean*, 9, and, for the early modern period, 159–89.

10 Krieger, "Der dänische Sklavenhandel auf dem Indischen Ozean im 17. und 18. Jahrhundert".

11 A selection: Chatterjee and Eaton (eds.), *Slavery & South Asian History*; Campbell (ed.), *The structure of slavery in Indian Ocean Africa and Asia*; Allen, *European Slave Trading in the Indian Ocean, 1500–1850*; Mann, *Sahibs, Sklaven und Soldaten: Geschichte des Menschenhandels rund um den Indischen Ozean*; Zeuske, *Handbuch Geschichte der Sklaverei: Eine Globalgeschichte von den Anfängen bis zur Gegenwart*.

12 *Der Königl. Dänischen Missionarien aus Ost-Indien eingesandter Ausführlichen Berichten*, 9 vols., 108 "Continuationen" or issues (1710–1772). The journal was then continued as

investigation does not extend to a discussion of caste in South India, that is, the regional social order based on a set of conventions assigning individual and group rank.[13] This would require the analysis of a separate set of source material and a line of enquiry different from the dynamics of enslavement and the slave trade covered here.

The two focal points of this examination lie in the discourses and the practices of slavery, including abduction and the trade in human beings. It proceeds through three sections: the first deals with the ways in which slavery was portrayed as legal in the archival material. This involves an analysis of what slavery meant in Tranquebar and how it was distinguished from other kinds of dependency, such as servitude and contractual labour. Section one thus relates to the "question of definition" that has received much treatment in the scholarship on early modern slavery.[14] Departing from the question of generally applicable definitions, the present piece enquires into what was particular to Tranquebar and thus advances the scholarship concerned with the location of slavery in discursive and practical settings.[15] In the case of the Tranquebar mission, it will be argued that how to deal with enslavement and the slave trade – beyond perhaps the basic assumption of treating humans as private property – represented a contested matter of debate rather than an issue of uncontested legal categories or reliance on Pietist Lutheran spiritual or theological convictions (although such convictions featured in the separate, but related subject of "serving body and soul"). Neither the discursive terminology nor the legal components of slavery remained consistent over time in the eyes of the mission, the trading company and the local inhabitants. Instead, specific practices of slavery motivated the search for legal precedents and principles particularly in the mission environment. One pertinent case was that of marriage and sexual relations. In all of this, it will be seen that the missionaries' interventions as regards slavery did not contradict the core agenda of the Halle Pietist corporate self-identity that stood behind the Tranquebar mission.

---

the *Neuere Geschichte der evangelischen Missionsanstalten zur Bekehrung der Heiden in Ost-Indien*, 8 vols., 95 "Stück" or issues (1770–1848).

13 On the divisions of caste in Tranquebar, see Brimnes, *Constructing the Colonial Encounter. Right and Left Hand Castes in Early Colonial South India*, 39–42 and 106. For a general account of caste in India during the eighteenth century, see Bayly, *Caste, Society and Politics in India from the Eighteenth Century to the Modern Age*, 64–96.

14 Miers, "Slavery: A question of definition". See also Eaton, "Introduction", 2f, and the "Introduction: Slavery, Law and Religion in the Early Modern Period" by Christoph Haar in the present volume.

15 For the "location" of slavery in historical narratives, see the chapter by Rômulo Ehalt in the present volume.

The second section inspects practices considered illegal in the sources, specifically kidnapping and the purchase and sale of kidnapped human beings in the slave trade. One common illegal practice in the colonial period consisted of luring and abducting individuals in order to enslave them. The present analysis demonstrates that colonial Tranquebar was infamous as a destination of such abductions and in general operated as a hub for the trade in human beings. Inhabitants in the countryside feared Tranquebar as what they called the "slave town", where kidnapped human beings were deported on ships as part of the Indian ocean slave trade, while the mission believed it was in its own interest to improve the reputation of Tranquebar in South India by combating abduction and the slave trade. These dispositions produced novel strategies of action.

The third and final part examines the prohibition of the slave trade in Tranquebar. It uncovers the dynamics of normative change produced through law and reputation in colonial Tranquebar. The proclamation of the prohibition in 1745, repeated observations during the following decades concerning the maintenance of the ban and comparisons with other political entities in the region attest to the fact that the reputation of the colonial town and the mission motivated developments in the law regarding slavery and the slave trade. Consideration of every group involved offers a means to locate agency in the legal, economic and socio-political spheres in eighteenth-century Tranquebar.

The Location of Slavery

The matter of slave purchase and sale emerged shortly after the first two missionaries, Bartholomäus Ziegenbalg and Heinrich Plütschau, arrived in Tranquebar.[16] It became an object of consideration when they pondered how to get the mission started: should the mission gain members by purchasing children? Multiple letters sent to the mission centre in Halle demonstrate the serious thought the two missionaries gave this idea.[17] In the end, they decided

16 For biographical details on the missionaries and other individuals connected to the Tranquebar mission and cited in this chapter, see the bio-bibliographical register of the Francke Foundations: https://digital.francke-halle.de/fsbio?lang=en (21.8.2023).

17 AB (letter Ziegenbalg and Plütschau to "all God-loving friends", 18.9.1706), 36: "Es ist höchst nöthig, daß wir vor allen Dingen eine Schule aufrichten, darinnen 18–20 Knaben von den Heiden erkaufet [...] würden."; AB (letter Ziegenbalg to unknown, 25.9.1706), 41: "Wir haben auch in Vorschlag, eine Schule anzurichten, darinnen 12, 18 bis 20 malabarische zu eigen erkaufte Knaben [...] unterrichtet und nachmals wo nicht von uns doch von unsern Nachkommen an diesem Werke mit Nutzen gebraucht werden könnten,

against it, not least because they desired to emphasise that theirs was a project of conversion, not purchase of Christians.[18] While the mission did not purchase slaves, many of its first members, however, were in fact enslaved humans in the local European households.[19]

Following this initial engagement with slavery in the immediate mission environment, the discourse in the subsequent decades incorporated the Tranquebar mission's concerns as regards its outward standing, funding, proselytising aims and slavery's facet as a labour relation. Comparison and contrast with other forms of dependency and labour relations represented a means to reflect on slavery and this included drawing on historical narratives and biblical norms. For instance, in a letter associating the biblical world with observations in contemporary Tranquebar in 1729, missionary Christoph Theodosius Walther likened local slavery to the Pauline "yoke of bondage" in that such biblical slavery referred "not to the free servitude that now has been established everywhere in Europe, but to the previously common slavery" which he claimed to see in contemporary Southeast India (notwithstanding his rather unsuitable generalisation regarding the conditions in Europe).[20] According to Walther, slavery represented a matter that "we can understand better here [than in Europe], in that we see how strictly and how harshly such slaves are treated".[21] The intended message of this response letter to a Halle educator's comparison of accounts from South India with the Bible was to confirm that the local experience was beneficial to understanding particular aspects of the biblical world. But it was not merely an intellectual message directed at the immediate recipient of the letter. It was also a motivational message to garner financial support from potential donors who read the *Halle Reports*. On this

aber hierzu gehört ein großes Kapital." AB (letter Ziegenbalg to A.H. Francke, 1.10.1706), 45: "Indessen wünschen wir, daß uns in äußerlichen zulängliche Mittel möchten zugeschickt werden, daß man hierzu nötige Anstalten machen und das Werk mit allem Ernst anfangen könnte. Zum fördersten erkennen wir sehr dienlich zu sein, daß von den malabarischen hierzu mit Geld erkauften Kindern eine Schule angerichtet werde, darinnen solche Subjecta könnten zubereitet werden, welche nachmals wo nicht uns, doch unsern Nachkommen an diesem Werke zu dienen tüchtig sein möchten".

18 See below, n. 35.

19 For a census that quantified the enslaved humans in Indian and European households in Tranquebar in 1790, see Krieger, "Der dänische Sklavenhandel auf dem Indischen Ozean im 17. und 18. Jahrhundert", 23.

20 AFSt/M 1 B 1:26 (letter Walther to Johann Jacob Specht, 11.1.1729): "solches [the "Geist und Joch der Knechtschaft in den Paulinischen Brieffen"] nicht von der ietzo überall in Europa eingeführten freyen Knechtschaft, sondern der vormals üblichen Sclaverey hergenommen ist". Cf. HB, 27. Cont., 226–8. Specht was a pastor and former an instructor at the *Pädagogium* in Halle from 1724–29.

21 AFSt/M 1 B 1:26.

basis, the description of slavery as a labour relation served to construe historical parallels to Europe and the biblical world.

The reference to harsh treatment therefore must not be confused with a fundamental criticism of slavery or any individual right to freedom. Indeed, the letter switches the perspective in the same paragraph by stating that whoever wanted to have domestics ("Gesinde") had to buy humans because salaried labourers on contracts ("Gemiethete") generally did not produce good work, instead they fled as soon as they were pressured into "fulfilling their obligations". Yet, some enslaved humans were "of such evil nature" that they could not be governed "benevolently".[22] Moreover, "uncontrollable slaves", especially if they had escaped before, received an iron ring beaten around a foot to make them identifiable if they ran away.

Portraying slavery as superior to salaried labour and claiming the purported reasonableness of such bondage had the effect of legitimising slavery as based on a notion of humans as private property. The same tenor would persist throughout the century. In one case, the comparison extended to the contemporary transatlantic region when missionary Johann Friedrich König stated in 1773 that "the slave status here in East India, at least on our coast, [is] far more bearable than in West India, where slavery persists among the children's children and [where there is] grievous plantation work, which does not exist here."[23] This piece of evidence illustrates another effect of the practice of drawing parallels, namely, to qualify the brutality of the institution of slavery. To make his point, König drew what he perceived to be a distinction between transatlantic plantation slavery and Indian ocean household slavery.[24]

Among the labour relations existing in Tranquebar, slavery indicated the distinct status of unfreedom and in the mission it was connected to private rather than institutional property. Hence, while the mission as an institution did not claim to own slaves, enslaved humans were certainly members of the congregation and moreover it was deemed tolerable for other members of the congregation as well as missionaries to own humans. The private correspondence of Dorothea Maria Ziegenbalg, missionary Ziegenbalg's wife, illustrates that from the outset of the mission enterprise, there were many types of "servants" in the

---

22 AFSt/M 1 B 1:26: "solch böser Art"; "durch Güte".

23 NHB, Stück 10, 1354–7, here 1356 (10.2.1773): "Aus diesem werden E.H. ersehen, daß der Sclaven-Stand hier in Ostindien, wenigstens auf unserer Küste, weit erträglicher ist als in Westindien, wo die Sclaverey auf Kindeskinder fortdauert und die schwere Plantagen-Arbeit ist, die hier ganz wegfällt."

24 On the scholarship regarding the differences over time and place as well as assumptions about "mild slavery" in India, see Eaton, "Introduction", 10. See also Zeuske, *Handbuch Geschichte der Sklaverei*, 89.

missionaries' households which probably included enslaved individuals.[25] It also seems that the wives of the first two missionaries owned slaves.[26] In fact, the practice of privately owning slaves appears to have continued throughout the century. An example in 1773 demonstrates this, when Johann Balthasar Kohlhoff addressed his colleague Johann Zacharias Kiernander in Cuddalore on this topic. His letter additionally shows that the themes of unease and the preference of slave labour over contractual labour persisted: "I feel ashamed to write this: my wife, who extends her warm greetings, imploringly asks for a small slave girl of eight to twelve years. We have always had free maids, but they were all taken from us through marriages."[27] In a further example in the final decade of the century, a report by Johann Peter Rottler in 1792 mentioned that fellow missionary Christoph Samuel John had owned (at least) one slave.[28]

All these pieces of evidence attest to the fact that there were multiple kinds of labour relation in Tranquebar, among which slavery constituted a distinct arrangement of dependency. The term indicated a person's unfree status in the sense that the individual was deemed to be the property of somebody else. (In another, metaphorical usage, it was deployed in a political sense to suggest a severe dependence on the ruler. Thus, according to Ziegenbalg's observation in 1709, many inhabitants of Tanjore "almost do not own their goods at all, but rather they are slaves to their prince", which entailed the obligation to give the ruler "four out of five pieces".[29])

Beyond its consistent differentiation from free, contractual labour, the terminology surrounding slavery remained fluid. The term slavery ("Sclaverey") was often used interchangeably with bonded servitude ("Leibeigenschaft"). When "Leibeigene" and "Sclaven" were mentioned separately in the same

25 Lehmann, "Alte Indien-Post. Briefe der Maria Dorothea Ziegenbalg geb. Saltzmann", 495B. This is a print of the manuscript AFSt/M 1 C 9:67 (letter Maria Dorothea Ziegenbalg to Maria Saltzmann, 10.10.1716).

26 Germann, *Ziegenbalg und Plütschau*, vol. 1, 290, n. 1.

27 AFSt/M 1 B 63:36 (letter Kohlhoff to Kiernander, 29.7.1773): "Mein theuerster Bruder: ich schäme es mich zu schreiben: Meine Frau, welche hertzlichst grüßen läst, bittet sehr um ein klein[es] Sclaven-Mädgen von 8–12 Jahren. Wir haben stets freie Mädgens gehabt, [die] uns aber durch Heirathen entrißen worden."

28 NHB, Stück 44 (report by missionary Rottler, 1792), 710: "Eine Witwe aus Sidambaram von etlichen 40 Jahren hatte ihre zwey Söhne in der vorigen Theurung an Herrn John verkauft, und dies war die Veranlassung, daß sie mit uns näher bekannt wurde, und nun den Entschluß faßte, selbst auch eine Christin zu werden."

29 AB (letter Ziegenbalg to Weitzmann, 7.10.1709), 117: "Die Länder auf dieser Küste werden regiert fast eben in der Form als wie im Vaterlande, ohne daß weit größere Kontributionen sind, also daß die Einwohner fast keine Possessores ihrer Güter sind, sondern lauter Sklaven ihre Königes, weil sie von 5 Teilen 4 Schoß geben müssen und nur einen Teil für sich behalten."

document, for example in a report on the status of the mission in 1726, it is not clear whether the two words carried separate meanings.[30] Walther's above-mentioned letter of 1729 contrasted both slavery as well as bonded servitude with "free servitude" ("freye Knechtschaft).[31] In July 1734, the mission baptised eight "Leibeigene" belonging to four European households, evidently enslaved individuals, and the same term was used for the baptism of four "Leibeigene" or slaves on 13 August 1738, while, in the same genre of mission diaries, the entry for 24 February 1743 stated that two enslaved females, "Sclavinnen", from European households were baptised.[32] Thirteen individuals were baptised on 20 February 1774, eleven of which were "Sclaven", while two were free, "frey" or a "freye Person".[33]

Competing Interests

From the perspective of the slave-owning European households, the conversion of enslaved individuals and their membership in the congregation constituted an ambivalent development. European slave owners saw the Christian instruction of the enslaved as advantageous in terms of cultural customs in their households, but they worried that catechism might contain a promise of manumission. Because of this perceived threat to the social order in the colony, the matter became a topic of heated discussions between the mission and the trading company, even resulting in a debate in Europe within and between the mission and company hubs. To reassure the trading company, the mission (from the very beginning) as well as the mission board in Copenhagen (from its inception in 1714) were careful to emphasise that freedom was not promised to enslaved humans if they converted.[34] All that was demanded, as missionary Plütschau stated in response to a questionnaire put to him in 1713, was "that one cannot sell a slave again once he has become a Christian", citing the authority of Jacob Lodberg, theology professor and member of the mission board, the "Missions-Collegium".[35]

30 HB, 22. Cont., 899f (report on the status of the mission, 5.10.1726).

31 AFSt/M 1 B 1:26 (letter Walther to Specht, 11.1.1729).

32 HB, 39. Cont., 354 (mission diary for 1734); HB, 48. Cont., 1438 (mission diary for the second half of 1738); HB, 59. Cont., 1608 (mission diary for the first half of 1743). Cf. Liebau, *Die indischen Mitarbeiter*, 125f.

33 NHB, Stück 13, 38f. Cf. Liebau, *Die indischen Mitarbeiter*, 126.

34 Nørgaard, *Mission und Obrigkeit*, 32f and 37.

35 AFSt/M 1 C 5:84 (Plütschau, responses to a questionnaire, 6.2.1713): "daß man einen Sclaven nicht wi[e]der verkauffen könne wenn er ein Christ geworden quod approbata

This demand would, of course, exercise the effect of preserving the congregation because new members would not be lost due to being sold away. Yet, the acknowledgement and enforcement of this norm as a matter of law depended on the political authority on company grounds, the *Ostindisk Kompagni*. Therefore, the mission urged the trading company directors in Copenhagen to recognise the illegality of selling baptised slaves and Plütschau negotiated with the company on this matter when he travelled to Europe.[36] The mission protocol of 1715 reveals that finally an agreement had been achieved: "That a slave, once he had become a Christian, could not be sold, the gentlemen directors acknowledged. [...] As regards the manufactures, so that the newly converted might sustain themselves, the directors did not want to agree to anything, other than if they [the labourers] delivered good work, they would take it [the labour] from one as from another."[37] The insistence on the part of the company directors that they would not distinguish whether they hired Christian or non-Christian workers demonstrates that the company pursued its commercial interests first and foremost and did not seek to collaborate with the mission.

The norm remained in place throughout the eighteenth century, as did the position of the mission on slavery. Christian slaves were not to be sold to non-Christians, however their religious status was integrated into their social and legal status as enslaved individuals. Hence, in 1780, the missionaries submitted a report which included the statement that "the slaves from many different pagan nations who receive the holy baptism in the Portuguese congregation are not manumitted thereafter, but are admonished as Christians to serve their masters all the more faithfully."[38]

---

a Prof. Lodbergio." For an argument pitting the mission against the trading company in this regard, see Nørgaard, *Mission und Obrigkeit*, 37. The questionnaire was authored by the mission board in order to resolve Bövingh's general conflict with his fellow missionaries (including the accusation that conversion in the mission took place based not on faith, but on promises of material welfare), the so-called Bövingh affair. For a summary of the controversy in one of the first histories of the mission, see Fenger, *Geschichte der Tranckebarschen Mission nach den Quellen überarbeitet*, 99–103. For Bövingh's observations on conversion and the economics of slavery in the Cape of Good Hope, see the chapter by Eva Marie Lehner in this volume.

36 Nørgaard, *Mission und Obrigkeit*, 37; Krieger, "Der dänische Sklavenhandel", 19.

37 AFSt/M 1 C 7:27 (minutes of the Mission board meetings, Feb. 1715), fol. 2A-2B: "Daß ein Sclav wenn er ein Christ geworden, nicht könnte verkauffet warden, erkannten die HE Directeurs. An des Command. Stelle werden Sie wol den Vize-Command. Krahe setzen. Von den Manufacturen, damit Neu-bekehrte sich irgends erhalten mögten, wolten sich die Directeurs nicht weiter einlaßen, als wenn sie gute Arbeit machten, würden sie es von dem einen, wie von dem andern nehmen, würden sich aber zu nichts obligiern."

38 This report on the state of the mission went to Batavia: "Der Missionarien Schreiben an die Gesellschaft der Gelehrten zu Batavia", 14.10.1780, reprinted in NHB, Stück 25, 4–11, here 7:

Disparate interests extended beyond the company and the mission to the European owners: despite the exclusion of manumission, owners were now concerned that baptism potentially decreased the economic value of an enslaved human being. It was a persistent theme that Europeans worried about diminishing the value of the exploited humans. Thus, when missionary Nikolaus Dal reported his conversations with slave owners in 1737, he stated that "I once again asked a European whom I had admonished in vain to bring his slaves to Christianity to do so, but he did not let himself be convinced because then he would be unable to sell them to the Mahomedans in Achin, who pay the most."[39] While this confirms that the trading company upheld at least to some extent the prohibition to subject Christian slaves to the slave trade, in this example the sale to Aceh ("Achin"), it shows the European owners' misgivings towards missionary activity because they expected a negative economic impact.

Consequently, the mission repeatedly had to negotiate with the European owners, some of which were members of the mission congregation, about the matter of catechism.[40] In the 1720s, Dal complained that "we can only talk to the male and female slaves in our own houses because their masters forbid us to visit."[41] Entries in a set of supplementary mission reports reveal that attempts to find workarounds became commonplace, such as, in 1725, preaching in the afternoon to those who were forbidden to leave the house on Sunday mornings;[42] alternatively, as the entry for 22 November 1726 shows, "our white mission workers are to be reprimanded firmly that they send their slaves to the regular church service and on Saturdays to the early catechism class."[43] Over time, it appears that these strategies were not always successful.

"Die Sclaven, welche in der Portugiesischen Gemeine aus allerley heidnischen Nationen die heilige Taufe erlangen, werden nachher nicht frey gelassen, sondern angehalten, als Christen ihren Herren desto treuer zu dienen." Cf. Liebau, *Die indischen Mitarbeiter*, 126f.

39 AFSt/M 2 E 46:60 (diary Dal, 4.8.1737), fol. 7: "Einen Europäer, den ich im vorigen Jahr vergeblich anhielt seine Sclaven zum Christenthum zu bringen, ersuchte ich wieder darum, aber er war nicht zu erbitten weil er sie alsdann nicht an die Mahometaner in Achin verkauffen könnte, da doch selbige sie am besten bezahlten."

40 Cf. Nørgaard, *Mission und Obrigkeit*, 159f.

41 AFSt/M 1 H 3:3 (letter Dal to Lange, 19.6.1725), fol. 4. This is a manuscript copy of the original in AFSt/M 2 E 46:2. During the early years of the mission, Christian education took place in the missionaries' houses, including teaching male and female enslaved humans. Cf. HB, 2. Cont., 79f (letter Gründler to Francke, 7.12.1709).

42 RA, Sager fra den tidligere danske Mission i Tranquebar, Protocoll für Special-Conferentz 1725–74, 12.10.1725, fol. 8.

43 RA, Protocoll für Special-Conferentz, 22.11.1726, fol. 24: "Unser blancke Missionsbedienten sind ernstlich dahin anzuhalten, daß sie ihre S[c]laven ordentlich zur Kirche, und des Sonnabends zur Frühcatechisation schicken."

The notes in Dal's diary for the year 1737 maintain that European owners often refused the offer to teach enslaved individuals because "only one maid has to perform all the household duties and therefore had no additional time to study" (24 March), or they attempted to phase out the participation which Dal consequently met by admonishing "a woman not to stall the commenced teaching of her slaves" (16 June).[44]

A few years later, in 1740, missionary Gottfried Wilhelm Obuch noted the same set of circumstances. In this context, he invoked a biblical parallel as Walther had done a decade earlier, and like the latter without demonstrating any intent of criticising slavery in principle: it was difficult to care spiritually for all the enslaved, Obuch stated, since they lived dispersed and "they are plagued by so much work under the Egyptian masters that they only have little time to come together".[45] Obuch's connecting slavery to the Egyptian captivity recounted in Exodus points to the Protestant global communication network as this metaphor was generally employed in the eighteenth century to side with the spiritual needs of the enslaved while at the same time acknowledging the legal status of slavery.[46] By contrast, there was a twofold economic consideration at the forefront of European owners' minds: the impact of catechism on the established labour practices and on the value of a sale (because sales could then occur only to other Christian owners).

Besides the competing aims of mission, trading company and European owners, enslaved individuals took charge of their own interests in the context of Christian instruction. Multiple instances in the source material indicate that enslaved humans deployed the contents of what they studied during catechism to stake out claims for the improvement of their circumstances. In this way, they successfully appropriated theological narratives for social and legal purposes. While it is difficult to gauge the extent to which such actions really occurred (because the extant source material forms part of discursive lines of conflict between trading company, slave owners and the mission), one does not need to assume such accounts were entirely fabricated by Europeans

---

44 AFSt/M 2 E 46:60, diary entries Dal 1736–1737, fol. 3 (24 March: "Er schützte vor daß eine einzige Magd alle Dienste im Hause verrichten müste, und deswegen keine Zeit zum lernen übrig haben könnte") and fol. 6 (16 June: "Ich incouragierte wiederum eine Frau die angefangene information ihrer Sclaven nicht stocken zu lassen"). Cf. Nørgaard, *Mission und Obrigkeit*, 159. Nørgaard emphasises Dal's commitment to the enslaved in the "Portuguese" congregation.

45 AFSt/M 1 B 28:29 (Obuch to Francke, 13.10.1740), fol. 4. Cf. HB, 52. Cont., 698f.

46 On the metaphor of Egyptian captivity and slavery, see the chapter by Maximilian Rose in this volume.

wishing to prevent Christian instruction, seeing that the above examples demonstrated there was no requirement for such a justification.

The agency of the enslaved surfaced already in a trading company report in 1708 that pertained to the governor's polemic against the mission. Governor Hassius protested to the leadership in Copenhagen with the aim to highlight the disturbance the mission brought to Tranquebar, stating that slave owners "complain that they [the enslaved] have since become negligent in their service and are not so willing as before, since they preach and teach them that the slaves are now as good as their masters, and that their masters no longer have power over them to punish or sell them [...] some slaves have become so arrogant and adamant that they hardly consider what their master commands them".[47] There are further indications that the enslaved influenced the circumstances of slavery in colonial Tranquebar. In one instance of Dal's attempts to convince Europeans to send enslaved individuals to catechism, he "asked a woman to bring to Christianity those of her slaves who were still heathen; she categorically denied me this because those among her slaves who were Christian were so obstinate."[48] This episode reinforces the notion that individuals who had participated in catechism creatively appropriated the teaching material in order to reframe their living conditions.

Legal Sources and the Case of Marriage

Having considered the frictions surrounding the slave status, the present section turns to legal practice. The claim pursued here is that matters of practice in Tranquebar motivated theoretical concern with legal precedent and principle. Fortunately, this analysis is able to draw on extant Tamil voices in the source material, albeit as translations by Aleppa, the mission's translator.[49] They exist in the shape of Tamil scholars' response letters to missionaries,

47 The archival company records of the *Asiatisk Kompagni*, Hassius' report to the company leadership, 26.10.1708, 332f, replicated in Nørgaard, *Mission und Obrigkeit*, 256f, with the statement that the originals had been lost to decay by 1988. For partial translations into German, see Nørgaard, *Mission und Obrigkeit*, 33 and 38.

48 AFSt/M 2 E 46:60 (diary Dal 1736–1737, 9.6.1737), fol. 6: "[...] ersuchte ich eine Frau ihre Sclaven die noch Heiden sind zum Christenthum zu befördern; sie schlug mir aber solches rund ab, weil diejenigen, so von ihren Sclaven Christen wären, so arg wären."

49 For an introduction to Aleppa and his personal struggles, see HB, 2. Cont., 82 (letter J.E. Gründler to Francke, 7.12.1709). See also Jeyaraj, "Die Wechselwirkung zwischen Kirche und Kultur in der frühen Tranquebar-Mission", 141. On the outstanding value of this source material for early modern Asian studies in general, see Osterhammel, *Die Entzauberung Asiens*, 79f.

penned between 1712 and 1714 and published in Europe in 1714 and 1717. Most likely, the correspondents (whose names were not recorded by the Tranquebar missionaries for strategic purposes) were well connected Tamils of high social status, including high-ranking teachers and Brahman scholars.[50] While the authenticity of each letter in this "Malabarian Correspondence" remains difficult to ascertain, including the respective authorship, it is notable that the non-Christians usually have the final say in this collection of writings and that the missionaries limited their qualifications and criticisms to annotations in footnotes added to the texts.[51]

The letters conform with three general trends narrated above. Firstly, the repeated mention of norms and practices regarding household slaves indicates that household slavery was the predominant legal form of slavery among the Tamils in the mission's regional setting. Secondly, the correspondence routinely distinguishes between servants and slaves among the relations of dependency in the household. Hence, one letter describing eating habits in the household offers the following division: "When the man and the children have eaten, afterwards the wife eats with the servants ["Dienstvolk"] and slaves ["Sklaven"] in the house."[52] In a further letter, a Tamil respondent listed the general duties of a slave owner towards the enslaved and the obligation of the enslaved in return.[53] Yet another writing offered more precision: household masters were to nourish their domestics and slaves physically as well as spiritually and they should, if the enslaved individuals had served well, allow them to be free and to marry. The enslaved human beings, on their part, were required to be obedient and loyal.[54] Thirdly, enslaved individuals were viewed as private property. Thus, in another piece of writing, a response to a question of inheritance, enslaved humans are listed among the property to be distributed.[55] This stance included, for example, the general acknowledgement of the legality of a sale into slavery. Such a sale was considered legal if the deal fulfilled certain criteria. One of them was the voluntary sale into slavery, motivated not least by climate effects such as droughts and bad harvest which were common

50 K. Liebau, "Einleitung: die 'Malabarische Korrespondenz' als Beispiel indisch-deutschen Dialogs", 16–22.

51 Rajan, "Kontrapunktische Einlagen. Indische Stimmen in den Halleschen Berichten".

52 *Malabarische Korrespondenz*, First Part, letter 14, 149.

53 *Malabarische Korrespondenz*, Second Part, letter 23, 253f.

54 *Malabarische Korrespondenz*, First Part, letter 15, 154.

55 *Malabarische Korrespondenz*, First Part, letter 21, 176: "Gelde, Geschmeide, Sklaven, Kühen und Kälbern".

in Southeast India since at least the sixteenth century.[56] A transaction could involve the sale of one's children.[57]

Hence, several norms relating to slavery existed. But certain social configurations surrounding slavery remained unregulated in Tranquebar and these were heavily debated in the mission throughout the 1720s. A pertinent case was marriage and sexual relations. The mission exercised jurisdiction over the Tamil and European mission members to a large degree in this social domain.[58] In this context, the missionaries time and again argued for laxer moral guidelines, as exemplified in the mission diary of 1728: "at the beginning of the year, we had two slave marriages. We hope that other people will follow this praiseworthy example in the future and in this way, when they provide their slaves with the freedom to marry, help evade the manifold irritation that otherwise arises from the coerced celibate life of the poor slave population".[59] The mention of "irritation" points to the issues of sexual relations and child births out of wedlock which were discussed time and again in the sources. For example, three years prior, in 1725, Dal argued for an increased moral leeway regarding sexual relations before marriage.[60] Dal asked for guidance from Halle and he cited a regulation on adultery in the Danish law code of 1683, *Danske Lov*, to state that he did not believe the mission should apply such a norm.[61] According to that law, repeat adulterers were to be expelled from the territory and if they returned and committed the crime again, they were to be executed.[62] One should not turn to the Danish law to punish female slaves or male adulterers, Dal stated, because the mission would lose some of its co-workers who regularly committed the deed.

56 Krieger, "Der dänische Sklavenhandel", 13 and 16f. Cf. Manickam, *Slavery in the Tamil Country: a historical overview*, passim.

57 See, e.g. HB, 39. Cont. (mission diary, 2.10.1734), 447f.

58 Nørgaard, *Mission und Obrigkeit*, 164–6.

59 AFSt/M 2 D 3:3a (mission diary for 1728): "Bey dem Anfange dieses Jahres haben wir zwo Sclaven-Heyrathen gehabt. Wir hoffen, daß diesem löblichen Exempel auch künftig andere Herrschaften folgen, und auf solche Weise, wenn sie ihren Sclaven Freyheit geben, sich zu verehelichen, das mannigfaltige Aergerniß werden verhüten helfen, so sonst aus dem gezwungenen ehelosen Leben des armen Sclaven-Volcks entstehet." The passage is printed in HB, 26. Cont., 1.

60 AFSt/M 1 H 3:3 (letter Dal to Lange, 19.6.1725). For the claim that the mission should be considered "forward-thinking" ("zukunftsweisend") in this respect, see Nørgaard, *Mission und Obrigkeit*, 161.

61 AFSt/M 1 H 3:3 (letter Dal to Lange, 19.6.1725), fol. 9.

62 For the text of the *Danske Lov* of 1683, see Secher (ed.), *Kong Christian den Femtis Danske Lov*, Book, 6, Chapter 13, Section 24.

The missionaries' doubts about the contemporary practices as well as the Danish codification led them to enquire about historical legal regimes, specifically Greek and Roman law:

> For we would quite like to receive a historical lesson about the erstwhile condition of slave men, women and children among the Greeks, Romans and other nations. Because slavery is entirely common in this region among the Christians, heathen [Hindus] and Mohammedans, and [because] in our congregation there are many slave men, women, and children (born out of wedlock), therefore such a lesson could be useful to us in many respects. In particular, we would like to know whether the slave men or the slave women were officially permitted to marry, or under what prerequisites, and similarly, what legal sources are most known among legal scholars.[63]

This diary entry of 1726 repeated that slavery and slave child births out of wedlock were common in Tranquebar and it underscored the fact that the mission was searching for legal sources in order to frame these customary norms. Matters of practice drove the search for a legal framing of slavery. This theme resurfaced when the missionaries addressed their concern regarding sexual relations to the mission board in Copenhagen in 1740. On this occasion, practice was connected to the biblical norm prohibiting adultery: "The state of the poor slave population in particular must be pitied because they have to live in a forced state of celibacy and are therefore tempted into sins against the sixth commandment. Some are even prevented by their masters from hearing and being admonished by God's word."[64] As they had done nearly three decades prior by referring to the theologian Lodberg on the impermissibility of selling Christians, the Tranquebar mission continued to seek to combine their

63 AFSt/M 1 B 3:18 (Pressier's "special diary" for 1726), fol. 17: "Nämlich wir wollten gern einen historischen Unterricht haben von dem vormaligen Zustande der Sclaven und Sclavinnen und Sclaven Kinder unter den Griechen, Römern und andren nationen. Weil in diesem Lande die Sclaverey gantz gemein ist unter Christen und Heyden und Mahomet[anern], und in unser Gemeine viele Sclaven, Sclavinnen, und (unehlich gezeugte) Sclavinnen Kinder sind: so könte uns solche Ausführung in manchen Stücken zu staten kommen. Insonderheit möchten wir gerne wissen, ob die Sclaven oder Sclavinnen ordentlicher Weise sich haben verheirathen dürffen, oder unter welchen conditionen, und dergleichen, welche materien deren Jureconsultis am besten bekannt sind."

64 RA, Indkomne sager den ostindiske mission vedkommende (1738–1808), Missionskollegiet og Direktionen for Vajsenhuset, F39-1 (mission report addressed to the mission board, 10.10.1740), fol. 22B: "Der Zustand des armen Sclaven-Volcks ist insonderheit zu bedauren, weil sie in coelibatu coacto leben müßen, daher sie zu mancher Sünde wider das sechste Gebot verleitet werden. Manche wurden auch von ihrer Herrschaft abgehalten, daß sie aus Gottes Wort nicht öfters können ermahnet werden."

practical requirements in situ with a legal and moral underpinning through accepted authority.

Breaking the Law: Kidnapping and the Slave Trade

The institution of slavery not only represented an object of legal uncertainty in Tranquebar. It was moreover the arena of illegal activity. The present section illustrates that practices understood as illegal were the object of intense negotiation, especially the abduction and subsequent sale of human beings.

To begin with, it must be noted that abduction in the countryside and the sale of such kidnapped humans in Tranquebar occurred frequently during the first decades of the eighteenth century. A (unidentified) Tamil interlocutor in the "Malabarian correspondence" elaborated on the issue in detail: slave trading was marked by buying and selling "Sclaven" or "Leibeigene" (the two terms in translation appearing synonymously here, too).[65] One way in which slaves were acquired was by persuasion and promises of nice clothes and jewellery in order to get the person to leave secretly at night, provide good food and then sell that person to a slave trader. Another way was to drug individuals, and a third way was if people "foolishly sell either themselves, or their child, or their brother as slaves."[66] The first two means described the tactics of abduction and subsequent slave trading. Anyone who participated in this practice by buying and selling slaves was reprehensible, according to the Tamil interlocutor. Indeed, slave trading represented a great sin.[67] The Tamil correspondent concluded by making a reference quite clearly to the town of Tranquebar: "A city that permits this kind of slave trade cannot find acceptance. This is clear among the Malabarians."[68]

This practice was ongoing although a colonial law prohibiting kidnapping was already in place. As it had been the case with the ban of selling Christian slaves, the missionaries exerted much effort to get the trading company to enforce the prohibition of trafficking abducted individuals – not out of a desire for the rule of law or humanitarian motivations, but, as the missionaries stated, because such a prohibition would further the cause of the mission and,

65 *Malabarische Korrespondenz*, Second Part, letter 21, 250.

66 *Malabarische Korrespondenz*, Second Part, letter 21, 251.

67 For the statement that "it is honorless here in Asia to be a slave trader" (governor P.K. Pank, introduced below), see Mentz, "Handelsstationen Tranquebar 1630–1750", 109.

68 *Malabarische Korrespondenz*, Second Part, letter 21, 251f.

anyhow, it would benefit the Danes themselves because the trade damaged their reputation "here in India".[69]

The colonial law obliged slave owners to obtain a proof of slave status document from the Danish company authority and it was designed to prevent abduction.[70] The mission supported this trading company regulation and supplemented the reasoning with biblical and Roman law concepts. In the piece of writing of 1729 examined above with respect to comparisons between contemporary South India and the biblical world, the matter that received the most extensive treatment was abduction as it was mentioned as a crime in Exodus 21 and 1 Timothy 1:[71]

> When in Europe unsuspecting people read about kidnappers (2. Moses 21, 16, 1. Tim. 1, 10), they may ask, what benefit does a thief obtain from stealing humans? Here [i.e. in Tranquebar], one can see that these kidnappers ["plagiarii"] make promises and drug countryside children or young adults, and sell them into slavery. The authorities [i.e. the trading company] instituted a strict decree because of this: nobody may purchase someone to be enslaved ["mancipandus"] if his or her parents or close relatives do not come with the person and bring witnesses with them.[72]

69 RA, Indkomne sager den ostindiske mission vedkommende (1738–1808), Missionskollegiet og Direktionen for Vajsenhuset, F39-1 (mission to the Mission board, 1744), fol. 73: "Ob vieleicht Eur. Excellentz und sämtl. höchst geehrte Herren gehörigen Orts zur gäntzlichen Abstellung solches höchst ungerechten Sclaven-Handels etwas contribuiren könten. Die Compagnie hat bisher keinen andern Vortheil davon gehabt, als was [für] die Sclaven-Oles [i.e. a proof of slave status document] und an Zoll für ein und ausgesandte Sclaven [...] bezahlet werden muß. Hingegen ist es der gantzen dänischen Nation hier in Indien nicht allein sehr praejudicirlich, sondern auch dem Missions-Werck höchst hinderlich [...]."

70 HB, 39. Cont. (mission diary, 2.10.1734), 448.

71 *Exodus* 21:16: "And he that stealeth a man, and selleth him, or if he be found in his hand, he shall surely be put to death." 1 *Timothy* 1:9f: "knowing this, that the law is not made for a righteous man, but for the lawless and disobedient, [...] for whoremongers, for them that defile themselves with mankind, for menstealers, for liars, for perjured persons, and if there be any other thing that is contrary to sound doctrine". All biblical quotations are taken from the *King James Bible* (*Authorised Version*).

72 AFSt/M 1 B 1:26, fol. 2f: Wenn in Europa Einfältige von Menschen-Dieben lesen (2. Moses XXI 16, 1. Tim. 1.10.) so dencken sie wol, Was ist einem Diebe mit Menschen gedienet? Allein hier sieht man, wie dergleichen plagiarii oft heimlich Kinder oder iunge Leute aus dem Lande betrieglicher Weise herbringen, indem sie ihnen dort allerley süße Versprechungen thun, und ihnen hernach Tollkraut, oder dergleichen etwas anders, eingeben, daß sie nicht recht bey Sinnen seyn, u. sie so zu Sclaven verkauffen. Deswegen die hiesige Obrigkeit eine scharfe Verordnung gemacht, daß niemand einen Sclaven kauffen soll, deßen Eltern oder nächste Anverwandten nicht mitkommen, und Zeugen mitbringen, daß der mancipandus ihnen angehöre."

This exposition of the biblical parallel made use of Latin terms and themes in Roman law.[73] In the Roman legal tradition, *plagiarii* denoted kidnappers, particularly slave dealers who acquired individuals by illegitimate means.[74] The term *mancipandus* with the reference to multiple witnesses points to the Roman legal notion of *res mancipi* or property in question, in this case, the enslaved individual, and the formal exchange of such property, *mancipatio*.[75] A real sale by means of *mancipatio* required, among other things, the immediate transfer of property and the presence of "no less than five witnesses" – alluded to in the conclusion of the above narrative that it was necessary that witnesses accompany that individual, besides parents or relatives.[76] This was what the Danish trading company demanded. The letter's fleeting exposition without further explanation indicates the correspondence partners' and – seeing that this piece of writing was moreover published in the *Halle Reports* – the wider audience's familiarity with Roman law vocabulary. The mission explained the Danish laws regarding slavery in Tranquebar in these terms. Hence, not only the colonial leadership, but also the mission and its wider correspondence network framed the institution of slavery in European legal concepts.

Kidnapping continued to occur frequently despite these regulations. However, local inhabitants were not reduced to having to accept this circumstance, but rather sought ways to make the legal and political institutions work in their favour. In various instances, they were able to recruit the colonial power for their own interests. In one case recorded to have occurred in 1727, a Tamil father whose son had been stolen and subsequently sold in Tranquebar found out in which house he was located, complained to the authorities and eventually received his son back.[77] According to the missionary account, the man was so grateful that he decided to become a Christian and join the mission's countryside parish. In this case, a Tamil inhabitant successfully appropriated the colonial authority and its legal framework to serve his interests.

---

73 For the relevance of Roman law in early modern European legal thought, see Cairns, "The Definition of Slavery in Eighteenth-Century Thinking", 61–66.

74 Sale is one of the four possibilities of enslavement known from Roman law, besides enslavement as a spared war captive, birth from an enslaved woman or punishment for crimes. For the connection of slave dealers in antiquity as "plagiarii" who illegitimately procured slaves (mainly free citizens) rather than legitimate ones (mainly war captives), and an examination of 1 Timothy 1, see Harrill, "The Vice of Slave Dealers in Greco-Roman Society: The Use of a Topos in 1 Timothy 1:10", 101–3.

75 For a concise account, see Capogrossi Colognesi, "Ownership and Power in Roman Law", 524–36. For the relevant passage in Roman law authored by Gaius, see Huschke (ed.), *Gai Institutionum Commentarii Quattuor*, I, 119, at 31.

76 Gaius, *Institutionum Commentarii Quattuor*, I, 119.

77 AFSt/M 1 B 1:26, fol. 3.

Negotiations moreover took place in occurrences of sales that had adhered to the Danish regulations. Thus, in one example a woman from a nearby fishing village approached the mission to sell her child. The missionaries replied that they would not pay her but would agree to take the child into their school with free boarding.[78] In search of remuneration, the woman ended up selling her child to one of the mission's parishioners. When her relatives found out what had happened, they approached the trading company in an attempt to free the child. However, the colonial authorities claimed that the sale had been legal because there was a trading company's proof of purchase document. After their unsuccessful complaint, the relatives approached the missionaries who in turn advised their parishioner to offer to free the child against the promise that it would be taught in the mission school and become Christian (and against the repayment of the incurred expenses).[79] In this particular case, the fishermen refused the offer. But the account reinforces the point that local inhabitants engaged with and sought to exploit the institutions in the colonial territory for their own purposes, in this instance by attempting to liberate a child that had been sold.

In the ways reconstructed in this section, generally agreed legal principles of enslavement in Tranquebar were accompanied by a lack of implementation in the case of illicit kidnapping and a repeated negotiation in the case of legalised sales. The mission addressed these legal and political inconsistencies through contextualisation with biblical norms and Roman law concepts. Moreover, a closer look revealed a space in which Tamils and Europeans exercised agency to influence the respective situations.

Although the trading company leadership instituted a strict requirement for the documentation of slave purchases and sales in the 1720s, the practice of drugging potential victims, one of the three tactics of abduction recounted already in the "Malabarian correspondence" of 1712–1714, remained ongoing when Walther wrote in 1729. In short, the political authority was ineffective – already then, and even more so during the following decade of the 1730s, in fact not least because company members acting as private individuals had found workarounds, as the following section will illustrate.

78 AFSt/M 1 B 5:5 (mission diary for 1727). Cf. HB, 25. Cont., 66.

79 AFSt/M 1 B 5:5. The relatives refused this and the child remained in slavery. The underlying issue concerning the role of religious affiliation goes beyond the scope of this article.

The Slave Trade

As was the case globally in the early modern period, long-distance slave trading was treated separately from the institution of slavery in eighteenth-century South India.[80] In the sources on colonial Tranquebar, considerations of slave trading dealt with the purchase and sale of human beings in combination with their forced displacement, particularly their deportation via merchant ships. The slave trade caused repeated friction in Tranquebar, and it was connected to the issue of kidnapping.

In early November 1743, missionary Kohlhoff articulated his concerns to Friedrich Michael Ziegenhagen, court preacher in London and promoter of the Protestant missionary cause in England. In his letter to England, Kohlhoff compared the accounts of the transatlantic region with Tranquebar, specifically the Protestant Ebenezer colony in Georgia where Halle Pietists were also involved.[81] In the course of his account seeking to discredit the Danish slave trade, he claimed that the Europeans in Tranquebar behaved a lot worse than the Europeans in Ebenezer. The most salient issue he pointed out was the slave trade: kidnappers apprehended countryside inhabitants, Hindus as well as Christians, and the Danish trading company members in Tranquebar knew this. Still, with full intent, company members sold such individuals "to the French or even to Hindu and Muslim, or to other Christian" buyers (presumably the Dutch and the English). In this way, many Christians were deported from the country and nobody knew, neither the mission nor family or friends, whether they had died, had fled, or where they even were.[82] One can easily imagine the Tamils' reproach, the letter stated, and how this practice hindered the work of the mission in Tranquebar.[83]

In this context, it is important to note that the standing of Tranquebar in the region was highly relevant to the operation of the mission because it was common practice among countryside Tamils to go to Tranquebar for a period of time in order to prepare for baptism. This was how they joined the mission community before returning home. Sometimes, the initial impetus came from journeys by European missionaries and Tamil catechists who often

80 For the case of Madras, see Ahuja, "Labour Relations in an Early Colonial Context: Madras, c. 1750–1800", 803–5.

81 AFSt/M 1 B 32:5 (7.11.1743, Kohlhoff to Ziegenhagen). For the transatlantic activities of Halle Pietists, see Roeber, *Palatines, liberty and property: German Lutherans in colonial British America*.

82 AFSt/M 1 B 32:5, fol. 1.

83 AFSt/M 1 B 32:5, fol. 1: "Was hieraus für ein Vorwurf unter den Heiden entstehe u. wie hinderl[ich] solches dem Miss. Wercke sey […]."

travelled together through the countryside to talk about their faith and subsequently extend invitations for further Christian instruction in Tranquebar.[84] In one example representing many, European missionaries Breithaupt from Tranquebar and Kiernander from Cuddalore together with Tamil catechist Ambros travelled to Wandilpaleiam and Trippoplore in September 1747.[85] It was therefore crucial to the functioning of the mission that countryside inhabitants were comfortable travelling to the town. Moreover, their stay should not take too long because they had jobs or were needed to help sustain their families at home. Hence, the Tamil mission catechist Aaron reported on his travels to the countryside congregations in 1732 that the parishioners in Tirupalaturei requested him to communicate to Tranquebar that those members who had gone there to be prepared for baptism may soon be sent back home.[86] Back and forth movement between the countryside and Tranquebar therefore was embedded in the operation of the mission.

Kohlhoff followed up his complaint regarding the Danish colonists and the regime with another bitter accusation two weeks later, still in November 1743, this time to the mission hub in Halle: the Danes had no qualms about buying kidnapped human beings from the countryside, some of them Christians, and selling these individuals to Europeans (Dutch, French, English), Muslims or Hindus.[87] This second letter of complaint placed an emphasis on the fact that the mission leaders immediately went to the company authority and demanded their release whenever they found out about such a circumstance. However, oftentimes they did not hear about such instances before it was too late, i.e. before kidnapped parishioners had been sold and transported away. The narration contains one example of a Christian girl who had been taken to Aceh and was thus gone.

References across various sources make it clear that there was a regular trading ship route between Tranquebar and Aceh serviced by the "Achinsche Schiff", the European merchant ship that travelled back and forth. In 1735, it was already customary that "from here annually many [slaves] are taken

84 It must be noted that European missionaries often were not welcome in the areas outside the company territory, which increased the importance of Tamil catechists in the remote regions. Cf. Liebau, *Die indischen Mitarbeiter*, 85–9.

85 HB, 68. Cont., 1349f. The names of the locations are reproduced from the sources, although in other source material the spelling differs, as does current spelling.

86 HB, 35. Cont., 1172, 13 May 1732. Aaron would become the first ordained Tamil pastor in 1733.

87 AFSt/M 1 B 32:4 (letter Kohlhoff to G.A. Francke, 19.11.1743), fol. 1.

there".[88] Every year, a 1744 report to the mission board stated, between forty and over a hundred enslaved humans were taken to Aceh.[89] In one instance, the European ship on this route was unable to gather the goods it was supposed to transport from Tranquebar and spontaneously decided to take 150 enslaved individuals instead.[90] Among these were numerous Christians and, in this case, the missionaries intervened successfully, so that the Christian slaves were taken offboard and handed over to the mission. It was their testimonies that informed the missionaries of the manner of abduction: Danish company members not only knew about the practice, but in fact instigated and conspired with traffickers ("Sclaven-Diebe"). These thieves then promised countryside Tamils wonderful things and drugged them in order to take them to Tranquebar and hand them over to the Danish traders. The traffickers forbade the abducted to claim they were Christians to the authorities. If they did, the Danish company members – "so-called Christian Danes", Kohlhoff wrote – beat them.[91]

It is significant to realise that merely the Christian enslaved humans were taken off the ship. Evidently, the complaint targeted the prohibition of selling Christians, a preoccupation shared widely among missionaries in Southeast Asia. Correspondence between the Tranquebar mission and a Catholic priest in Aceh in 1732 attests to this observation. The exchange, led by Dal, centred on the religious confession of the deported. Writing to the mission, the Catholic priest confirmed that arriving Christian slaves were converted to become Muslims and remained slaves their entire lives. Consequently, "the worst" he had "ever seen" occurred on his journey to Tranquebar when he witnessed that countryside Christians, adults as well as children, were kidnapped and sold away.[92]

---

88 AFSt/M 2 E 46:41 (diary entry Dal, 10.3.1735), fol. 1: "die auch von hier jährlich in grosser menge dahin geführet warden".

89 RA, Indkomne sager den ostindiske mission vedkommende (1738–1808), Missionskollegiet og Direktionen for Vajsenhuset, F39-1 (mission report addressed to the mission board, 1744), fol. 73A.

90 AFSt/M 1 B 32:4, fol. 2.

91 AFSt/M 1 B 32:4, fol. 2: "und wenn sie selbige herbringen, verbiethen sie selbige zu sagen, daß sie verführet und daß sie Christen seyn: ja die so genannten christl. Dänen schlagen sie wenn sie sagen, sie sind Christen."

92 AFSt/M 2 E 46:41, fol. 1: "Er [the Catholic priest in Aceh] schreibet davon unterm 28 Jan. 1735 also: Was dasjenige betrifft, so Ihr mich gebeten habt euch zu berichten, ob die Mohren nach einen Jahren ihre Sclaven frey geben, so ist die Sache nicht so. Diejenigen, welche Mohren kauffen, werden Mohren und bleiben Sclaven ihr leben lang. Aber der größte Jammer, den ich iemals gesehen habe, ist daß man hero im Lande Christen, die getauft sind, so wol Kinder als erwachsene, zu Sclaven verkaufft. Aber ich weiß wohl, daß ihr deßen nicht Schuld seyd, und gerne sehet, daß solches nicht geschähe."

It is clear, then, that the Tranquebar colony participated in the slave trade and was known for it. Its entrenchment in the town is evident based on the elaborate scheme that had been established over the years (already alluded to above): Danish traffickers hired locals who in turn subcontracted others – because they themselves were known as traffickers in Tanjore and therefore barred from entry – to lure human beings from the kingdom of Tanjore to the Danish colonial territory. Once the local slave traders had acquired their victims, they commanded them what to tell the Danish colonial authorities for an official slave status document to be furnished. They then handed over the enslaved to the European company members who in turn sold them, either regionally to the French colonies in Pondichéry and Karaikal or the Dutch colony in Nagapatnam, or to the merchant ship headed for Aceh.[93]

For these colonists (acting privately), this was about economic benefits. For the colonial regime, the concern was to maintain tranquillity and order in Tranquebar as well as peace with the ruler in neighbouring Tanjore, raja Pratap Singh, who had even threatened the Danes with war because of the excesses of slave trading.[94] For the missionaries, the relevant matter was the corporate self-identity of the mission as well as the competition for souls: "Wickedness!", Kohlhoff exclaimed in a letter of 1743 addressed to the mission hub in Halle, "in Europe money is collected to buy Christians out of slavery in Turkey, while here, in Tranquebar, humans are sold, even Christians, to the Muslims" (in Aceh, in this case).[95] "No other European power in South India" engaged in the slave trade, specifically the practice of selling kidnapped humans, except for the Danish. When the Dutch needed slaves, they bought them from the Danes and they did not worry about the legality of the purchase because, they would say, "we buy the slaves on the Danish conscience."[96] Kohlhoff deployed his vigorous criticism against the Danish trading company in order to motivate

93 RA, Indkomne sager den ostindiske mission vedkommende (1738–1808), Missionskollegiet og Direktionen for Vajsenhuset, F39-1 (mission report addressed to the mission board, 1744), fol. 73A.

94 RA, Indkomne sager den ostindiske mission vedkommende (1738–1808), Missionskollegiet og Direktionen for Vajsenhuset, F39-1 (mission report addressed to the mission board, 1744), fol. 73B. For a summary of the political history of eighteenth-century Tanjore, see Liebau, *Die indischen Mitarbeiter*, 42–47.

95 AFSt/M 1 B 32:4, fol. 2: "Entschl. Bosheit! In Europa colligiert man Gelder, Sclaven aus der Türckey zu lösen, hier verkaufft man, sogar Christen, an Mohren."

96 AFSt/M 1 B 32:4, fol. 2: "Wenn die Holländer, Sclaven zu ihrem Gebrauche nöthig haben, so kauffen sie selbige hier von den Dänen, und bekümmern sich dann weiter nicht, wie und auf was Art die Dänen solche erhandelt haben, sondern sagen, wir kauffen die Sclaven auf den Dänen Gewißen." The reference to the Danish conscience refers to a much-discussed notion during the early modern period, namely, the question to what extent subsequent

the European mission hub to intervene on the Tranquebar mission's behalf. It is significant what normative level he chose to pursue this agenda (irrespective of the factual accuracy regarding his comparison to other political powers in the region). In this conflict between mission and trading company, law played a central role: it was the law that the Danes were said to be ignoring, in contrast to other European powers.

The mission's strategic interest in improving the reputation of Tranquebar by combating these practices of slavery was especially geared towards the Tamil inhabitants living in the countryside who the mission hoped would travel back and forth to Tranquebar for Christian instruction. Because of the slave trade, the Tamils in the broader area of the trading company grounds and the kingdom of Thanjavur feared kidnapping and enslavement. The issue led them to denounce Tranquebar. In this way, Tranquebar became notorious in the countryside: "Tranquebar is called the slave town [Sclaven-Stadt] in the countryside, and if a person wishes something bad on someone else, he says: may he meet the same fate as the one who comes to Tranquebar".[97] This was the state of affairs, says Kohlhoff, never mind further atrocities.[98] In this period, Tranquebar on the whole was not in the best economic shape, so that Christian inhabitants who did not have roots in the immediate area moved away, particularly to the nearby French colony of Karaikal where they successfully found work.[99]

The above events corroborate the continuing practice of slave trading through the end of 1743, including a general perception of how grave the issue of kidnapping was. They are, moreover, revealing as to the role of law because mission members and inhabitants sought to impose their interests by legal means. Tamils deployed the law to navigate the existing power structure while

buyers may be free from having to consider the justice or injustice of the original enslavement under the perspective of morality.

97 AFSt/M 1 B 32:4, fol. 2: "Daher man im Lande sich sehr fürchtet, anhero zu kommen, Tranckenbar heist die Sclaven-Stadt im Lande, wenn jemand einem recht was übels im Lande wünschen will, so spricht er: ihm muß es so gehen, als dem, der nach Tranckenbar kommt."

98 AFSt/M 1 B 32:4, fol. 2: "So gehts hier zu, anderer Gräuel nicht zu gedenken."

99 RA, Indkomne sager den ostindiske mission vedkommende (1738–1808), Missionskollegiet og Direktionen for Vajsenhuset, F39-1 (letter mission to Missions Collegium, 10.10.1740), fol. 22B: "Daß sich manche unserer Christen von hier weg begeben, sonderlich auch nach Careical, so ietzo den Frantzosen zustehet, kömt hauptsächlich her von dem wahrlosen Zustande dieses Orts, sonderlich bey unangeseßenen jungen Leuten, welche dort Arbeit und Dienste finden."

European missionaries sought to enforce the legal norm prohibiting the trade in Christians against the mercantile interests of the traders.

Reputation and the Fear of Enslavement

Given the ongoing practice of slave trading in Tranquebar, it is unsurprising to take note of an exchange between the European centres in Copenhagen and Halle in 1734 which exclaimed that missionary Dal reported "about almost nothing other than the slave trade."[100] Eventually, a climax was reached by 1744. The Tranquebar mission expressed as much to the mission board in Copenhagen in that year:

> Because of this slave trade, or, rather, this kidnapping, our Tranquebar now has a very disreputable reputation among Europeans and Indians in all of East India, and many people in the countryside have a greater fear of Tranquebar than of the devil himself. If one wants to wish somebody the worst misfortune, one says: you should share the same fate with the one who comes to Tranquebar. Some heathen, who otherwise are drawn to Christianity, are scared off at the mere mention of Tranquebar.[101]

This communication with the mission board reiterated the unfavourable designation of Tranquebar as a "slave town" in the communication with Halle a year earlier (cited above). On both occasions, the mission used the same adage – "the one who comes to Tranquebar" – to reinforce its point, once to its spiritual centre in Halle and once to its logistical centre in Copenhagen. Furthermore, the letter to Copenhagen expanded the notion by suggesting that the fear of enslavement produced a corresponding reputation across "all of East India". Certainly, the Pietist Lutherans were held in the same disrepute among Tamils

100 AFSt/M 1 F 3:65 (letter Schröder to Francke, 9.1.1734).

101 RA, Indkomne sager den ostindiske mission vedkommende (1738–1808), Missionskollegiet og Direktionen for Vajsenhuset, F39-1 (mission report addressed to the mission board, 1744), fol. 73A: "Dieses Sclaven-Handels oder viel mehr Menschen-Dieberey wegens, ist nun unser Tranquebar in gantz Ost-Indien bey Europäern und Indianern in sehr übeln Ruff, und viel leute im Land haben vor Tranquebar eine grössere Furcht, als von dem Teufel selbst. Will man im land einen das allergrößte Unglück anwünschen, so heißt es: es müßte dir so gehen, wie dem der nach Tranquebar kommet. Manche Heiden, so sonst eine Neigung zum Christenthum haben, werden, wenn sie nur Tranquebar nennen hören, dadurch abgeschreckt."

living in the English colonial settlement of Madras located 250 kilometres to the north.[102]

The Halle hub also reacted to these reports by seeking Danish royal intervention (via the mission board) in order to persuade the trading company to halt the practice.[103] Their writings confirmed that predominantly company employees acting as private individuals were engaged in the slave trade. It continued to take place despite an attempted change of strategy in the Danish Asiatic Company, newly founded in 1732 and overseen by Paul Kris Panck who served as governor from 1733 to 1741. The plan had been to curb the activity of private trading in favour of company control.[104] Consequently, it must be assumed that Panck's efforts in the 1730s to have the company control the slave trade ultimately failed.

In the end, a resolution was achieved a few years later when the slave trade in Tranquebar was abolished under governor Hans Ernst Bonsack who succeeded his brother, Hans Iver Bonsack (who himself had followed Panck). H.E. Bonsack even had the slave traders arrested and their houses burnt to the ground.[105] The official prohibition was publicised and proclaimed in the town – to the beating of drums[106] – on 20 July 1745. It therefore occurred even before a separate order prohibiting the slave trade arrived from Europe, issued by the trading company leadership in Copenhagen in 1744.[107]

The decree was announced nearly half a decade prior to the Danish abolition of the transatlantic slave trade in 1792 (but taking effect only in 1803), however it must be emphasised that the Tranquebar prohibition did not concern the practice of slave trading as a whole.[108] Its wording made reference to the specific practice of slave traders kidnapping inhabitants in the countryside and bringing them to Tranquebar for sale and deportation: "the honourable

102 Ahuja, *Die Erzeugung kolonialer Staatlichkeit und das Problem der Arbeit: eine Studie zur Sozialgeschichte der Stadt Madras und ihres Hinterlandes zwischen 1750 und 1800*, 204.

103 AFSt/M 1 B 32:38 (letter G.A. Francke to Kohlhoff, 23.12.1744). AFSt/M 1 F 6:70 (letter G.A. Francke to Finckenhagen, 22.12.1744). Note that the mission derived its authority directly from the Danish king, not from the colonial trading authorities.

104 For Panck's plan, see Mentz, "Handelsstationen Tranquebar", 109. Mentz offers 1753 as the year that the leadership prohibited the company slave trade, discussed as erroneous in Kaarsholm, "From abolition of the slave trade to protection of immigrants", 354.

105 AFSt/M 1 B 36:3 (letter Kohlhoff to G.A. Francke, 19.9.1746): "[...] indem er sogar der Sclaven-Händler Häuser im Rauch aufgehen und die Menschen-Diebe ins Sclaven-Haus setzen ließ."

106 Larsen, "Danmark og Sklavehandelens Ophævelse", 107. Krieger, "Der dänische Sklavenhandel", 21.

107 AFSt/M 1 B 36:3, fol. 1f: "noch ehe die Ordre aus Europa kam, [...]."

108 Kaarsholm, "From abolition of the slave trade to protection of immigrants", 353f.

Directors of the Royal Danish Asiatic Company in Copenhagen have come to realise how unjust and sinful the dealings have been […] with the slaves brought here from the countryside in order to be traded", lured or stolen by slave traders, "in contradiction with the law of nature and of nations."[109] The nod to natural law and the law of nations, rather than Danish norms, makes it clear that the company leadership deemed its decree relevant to all European trading centres in South India and applicable to Christians and non-Christians alike. Indeed, the Tamil Hindu authors of the "Malabarian correspondence" cited above had condemned the practice of abducting and trafficking humans in a similar way.

By exclusively addressing this practice, the limited scope of the announcement explains why slavery would persist in Tranquebar in the subsequent decades. The decree ended by highlighting very clearly what remained permissible, namely, the sale of "slaves who either of their own free will and intent sell themselves or are offered for sale by their true parents."[110] Even the governor responsible for proclaiming the prohibition of the slave trade, H.E. Bonsack, kept his own slaves. When he left Tranquebar in 1754 after ten years of governorship, he manumitted the enslaved humans in his household, had a house built for them and left 600 Reichsthaler with a European inhabitant for him to pay out an annual interest to the former slaves.[111] The entry in the supplementary mission reports of 1755 adds that Bonsack also made a contribution to the mission (200 Reichsthaler) and asked the missionaries to watch over the provisions he had made for the freed individuals. Close to twenty years later, in 1773, the *New Halle Reports* narrated this episode and mentioned additional details. The individuals in question were a couple that had married while enslaved in the Bonsack household and had in the meantime grown into a family with multiple children. Their annual payout was 50 Reichsthaler.[112]

While the new legal setting seems to have led at most to a slight reduction of the slave population in Tranquebar, there are indications that major change took place to the slave trade. Several pieces of evidence demonstrate that the prohibition was effective over at least the next decade. In one example

109 RA, Asiatisk Kompagni, Afdelingen i Trankebar: Trankebarsk rapportbog, 1695–1778, no. 1283, fols. 332–334. P.P. Kramer (secretary of the Secreth-Rath), "on behalf of the entire Government" (i.e. H.E. Bonsack, P.H. Meyer C.F. Høyer, J.C. Saetmann and Kramer), Castell Dansborg 20.7.1745. Cf. Larsen, "Danmark og Sklavehandelens Ophævelse", 108.

110 RA, Asiatisk Kompagni, Afdelingen i Trankebar: Trankebarsk rapportbog, 1695–1778, no. 1283, fols. 333–334.

111 RA, Protocoll für Special-Conferentz, 8.8.1755, fol. 109A.

112 NHB, 10 (letter König to Freylinghausen, 1773), 1356.

of 1751,[113] missionary Oluf Maderup informed the spiritual centre in Halle that the "Portuguese" congregation, which convened separately from the Tamil-speaking "Malabarian" congregation, had not grown much in recent years because catechetical education in preparation for baptism had become rare.[114] The reason he gave was that "the number of slaves in the European households, on which the growth of the Portuguese congregation depends almost entirely, has not increased since the current mister governor [H.E.] Bonsack completely abolished the ill-fated slave trade and up to now has scrutinised meticulously that nobody may be sold here, except if one sells oneself by free will, which rarely occurs."[115]

In the background to all of this, from the perspective of the mission, there stood the matter of reputation. Maderup did not complain about the slowing growth of the Portuguese-speaking congregation. Instead, he emphasised the mission's standing in the region: "As regards the aims of the mission, this is a great relief. For in this way, the bad reputation that Tranquebar previously held among the heathens in the countryside, and the accusations as well as the suspicion that our co-workers, countryside preachers etc. might be slave traders, has steadily declined and now disappeared entirely."[116] Furthermore, the Halle hub wrote to the mission in 1747,[117] and again in 1751,[118] that they were very pleased to

113 AFSt/M 1 B 40:17 (letter Maderup to G.A. Francke, 15.1.1751). There is an excerpt in HB, 74. Cont., 259. As regards the mention of the "Portuguese" congregation consisting to a large part of enslaved humans, cf. AFSt/M 1 B 61:15 (letter König to Knapp).

114 HB., 24. Cont., 999–1002, here 1000 (report by Dal to the mission board, 1726): many members of the "Portuguese" congregation were male and female enslaved humans in Portuguese-speaking European households. The jurist employed in the mission administration in Halle, J.L. Niekamp, wrote a synoptic account of the mission in 1740, where he summarises that the "Portuguese congregation" was recruited mostly from the "Indian Portuguese", who differed from other "Indians" in clothing and language. *Kurtzgefaßte Mißions-Geschichte oder Historischer Auszug der Evangelischen Mißions-Berichte aus Ost-Indien, Theil 1*, chap. 5, §VI, 50.

115 HB, 74. Cont. (letter Maderup to G.A. Francke, 15.1.1751; AFSt/M 1 B 40:17), 259: "[…] indem die Zahl der Sclaven in den Europäischen Häusern, davon der Zuwachs der Portugiesischen Gemeine beynahe gäntzlich dependiret, nun sich nicht vermehret, seit dem der ietzige Herr Gouverneur Bonsack den unseligen Sclavenhandel gäntzlich abgeschaffet, und bis dato sehr scharf darüber gehalten, daß kein anderer hier gekaufet werden darf, als der sich selbst willig verkaufet, welches sehr selten geschiehet. Dieses ist in Absicht der Mission eine gantz besondere Wohlthat. Denn dadurch fällt der übele Name, so Tranckenbar vorher im Lande unter den Heyden getragen, und die Beschuldigung und Verdacht, als wenn unsere Gehülfen, Landprediger etc. Sclavenhändler wären, nach und nach nun gäntzlich hinweg."

116 HB, 74. Cont. (letter Maderup to G.A. Francke, 15.1.1751; AFSt/M 1 B 40:17), 259.

117 AFSt/M 1 B 36:44 (letter G.A. Francke to Kohlhoff, 27.10.1747).

118 AFSt/M 1 C 19:26 (letter G.A. Francke to Maderup, 22.12.1751).

know that the governor strictly implemented the prohibition of the slave trade. For the present enquiry it is crucial to note the reason the Halle centre offered in December 1751 in response, and indeed in confirmation, to the news received from Maderup: this development was to be commended because Christianity in general and the mission in particular were freed from a severe accusation.[119]

Indeed, there are indications that the abolition of the slave trade took effect rapidly. Two Tamil co-workers of the mission, catechist Rayanayakkan and ordained preacher Diogo, reported in 1745 how they had not been welcomed but instead decried as slave traders because of the reputation Tranquebar had developed in the countryside as a slaving town, but that this experience occurred in a region that had not yet received the information that the slave trade had been prohibited:

> Now the heathens hold Tranquebar in better esteem. But it is not yet known everywhere, and Tranquebarians once in a while must bear being called slave traders in the countryside. Our catechist Rayanayakkan, and the countryside preacher Diogo on his journey to Tanjore, were called that as well, and they were chased away.[120]

This incident serves as yet one further indication how strongly the slave trade had influenced the reputation of Tranquebar and led to the desire to reshape the legal norms.

Perhaps it may have been the case that the Tranquebar mission believed that the legal developments favoured the expansion of the mission community. On the one hand, there was limited growth to the "Portuguese" congregation based on its reliance for membership on the slave population in European households, which in turn seems to have consisted to some extent of those otherwise destined for the long-distance slave trade. On the other hand, there was an expectation that the Tamil congregation would grow because of Tranquebar's improved reputation. With the limited number of European households – no more than two hundred at any given time – it would appear obvious that the growth potential among the Tamil congregation was much more promising.

119 AFSt/M 1 C 19:26 (letter G.A. Francke to Maderup, 22.12.1751): "[…] ist allerdings keine geringe Wohlthat für die Mission, da dadurch das Christenthum von einem großen Anstoß und die Mission von einem nicht geringen Vorwurff befreyet wird."

120 AFSt/M 1 B 36:3: "Nunmehro urtheilen die Heiden von Tranckenbar etwas beßer. Doch ist es noch nicht allenthalben bekannt und müßen die Tranckenbarischen auch im Lande hin und wieder Sclaven-Händler heißen. Wie auch unser Catechet Rajanniken, und der Landprediger Diogo auf seiner nämlichen Reise nach Tanschaur, daselbst also tituliert und verfolget worden sind." This letter was written in 1746, after the slave trade had been abolished, but this fact was not yet known in Tanjore, outside of the city of Tranquebar.

However, the crucial aspect lies in the observation that by acting in the way it did, the mission sought to advance the Tranquebar's reputation as well as its own, in the sense that the mission was preoccupied more with its own standing than with maximising its outreach.

Over the longer term, the decree seems to have resulted in the firm decline of the slave trade, but not in its complete disappearance. Hence, in 1754, a missionary report stated that "it has been ten years since the complete prohibition of the regular slave trade" and while there were isolated instances of law breaking, such as illegally dealing an enslaved human being – who could otherwise be legally sold (e.g. after the death of the owner) – to a non-Protestant, but it was not the case anymore that entire ships were loaded with human beings enslaved by the trading company or by private individuals.[121]

Thirty years later, the French purchased many enslaved humans on other parts of the South Indian coast during a high-inflation period to take them to their recently acquired fort Trincomalee on the island of Ceylon in 1784.[122] In one instance when a ship lost its course, 75 people aboard died of starvation, "most of them slaves".[123] The lesser role of Tranquebar regarding enslavement and the slave trade in the region was testified in this account, too: "The local government published a decree against the kidnapping and shipping of slaves from here, except in the case that the owners could prove they were indeed their slaves by showing a legally valid proof of purchase. The overseers on the beach similarly received the order to search every boat thoroughly that rowed from the shore to the ships. Whereas what was not permitted to happen in Tranquebar, occurred all the more frequently in places outside of Danish control."[124]

---

121 AFSt/M 1 B 44:4 (letter mission to G.A. Francke, 5.10.1754): "Es ist nun 10 Jahre seit dem der ordinaire Sclavenhandel hier gäntzlich verboten worden, welches Verbot sowohl die Compagnie selbst, als auch andere particulaire Persohnen anging Bisweilen geschiehet es auch wohl, daß ein oder andern von Christlichen Sclaven heimlich an Catolische Leute verkauft werden, wie in diesem Jahre ein Römischer Capitain auf einem Chinesischen Schiffe heimlich eine junge Sclavin von der Portug. Gemeine bey einer gewissen Herrschaft zu Kauf bekommen, und mit sich entführete solches wir aber nicht hindern können, in ihm wir es nicht leicht eher zu wissen bekommen, als bis es schon geschehen ist."

122 AFSt/M 2 E 12:1, joint diary for 1784, here 11 April.

123 AFSt/M 2 E 12:1, joint diary for 1784.

124 AFSt/M 2 E 12:1, joint diary for 1784: "Das Gouvernement alhier gab indessen eine Ordre aus, daß keine Sclaven von hier sollten eingeschifft und verführet werden, außer im Fall daß die Eigenthümer durch Vorzeigung eines Gerichtlichen Kaufbriefes beweisen könnten, daß es wirklich ihre Sclaven seyn. Die Aufseher am See Strande bekamen auch Befehl alle Boote die vom Lande an die Schiffe fuhren, wohl zu visitieren. Was indessen in

Still, later admonitions to stop the practice point to the continuous recurrence of incidents also in Tranquebar. Thus, missionary Christian Pohle described in his diary how, on 21 June 1783, "on the order of the governor [P.H. Abbestee] it was announced publicly that under penalty no slave was to be deported, neither by sea nor by land. For on occasion children had been stolen and deported by means of this trade. (I wish such a prohibition existed in Tiruchirapalli, where likewise not few children are stolen by the Moors. In this way, one of our Christians, a widow, lost one of her children.)"[125] Pohle was in the position to make this comparison because he worked for the Tranquebar Mission from 1777–8 and was thereafter employed until his death in 1818 as a missionary by the Anglican Society for Promoting Christian Knowledge in Tiruchirapalli, 150 kilometres removed from the town of Tranquebar and beyond company grounds as well as the kingdom of Thanjavur.

Moreover, it remained the case that the slave population in Tranquebar and the Tranquebar mission remained significant throughout this period and it included individuals who came from far-away places. This indicates that the country trade persisted to some extent. For instance, missionary König detailed in 1771 that "a large part of it [the Portuguese congregation] are slaves who are made up of a collection" of individuals from Bengal ("Bengalitern"), Madurai ("Maravern"), Southeast Africa ("Caffern") and the region around the Malay peninsula, particularly Achin and Bago or Pegu ("Maleyern").[126] In 1773, according to König, the members of the "Portuguese" congregation were mainly enslaved humans, "all, except for a few, foreigners who came here from other coasts and regions of India", including the western "Malabar" coast.[127]

Trankenbar nicht geschehen durfte, geschah desto häufiger an anderen Orten außer den dänischen Gebieten."

125 NHB, Stück 29 (diary Pohle, 27.1783), 533: "Sonst wurde den 21sten Jun. zu Trankenbar, auf Befehl des Gouvernements, ausgedrummelt, daß bey Strafe keine Sclaven, weder zur See noch zu Lande, ausgeführet werden sollten. Denn es sind bey Gelegenheit dieses Handels Kinder gestohlen und weggeschafft worden. (Ein solches Verbot wünschte ich auch zu Tirutschinapalli, wo auch nicht wenig Kinder von den Mohren gestohlen werden. Wie denn auch eine unserer Christinnen, eine Witwe, eins ihrer Kinder auf diese Art verloren hat.)" Cf. Liebau, *Die indischen Mitarbeiter*, 127.

126 AFSt/M 1 B 61:15 (letter König to Knapp, 12.10.1771), fol. 3f. For examples of the historical usage of these terms and etymological explanations, the research literature regularly cites the historical dictionary *Hobson-Jobson*, particularly the second edition of 1903, which itself has to be treated critically as a historical source text. For the terms cited here, see Yule and Burnell, *Hobson-Jobson. a glossary of colloquial Anglo-Indian words and phrases, and of kindred terms, etymological, historical, geographical and discursive*, 86, 140–2, 534f and 545f.

127 AFSt/M 1 B 62:14 (letter König to Freylinghausen, 10.2.1773). Cf. NHB, Stück 10, 1354–7.

These pieces of evidence validate that the matter of slave trading persisted in and beyond Tranquebar in the later decades of the century. Yet, the descriptions of the supposed contrast between Tranquebar and Tiruchirapalli as well as that between Danish and other colonial territories attest to the fact that the reputation of Tranquebar had shifted. This development was marked by a notable turnaround in the mission's view of the Danes: in 1744, the mission had polemicised against the trading company by claiming the trade in kidnapped humans was conducted exclusively by the Danes. In 1784, it was everyone but the Danes. According to the narrative presented in this piece, this transformation is remarkable because it shows an underlying consistency. Irrespective of quantitative accuracy or legal agenda concerning the slave trade, the mission was preoccupied throughout with improving Tranquebar's as well as its own reputation.

Conclusion

Slavery was consistently present in eighteenth-century Tranquebar and the newly founded mission did not question the legitimacy of the institution. Comparison and contrast with other relations of dependency demonstrated a basic premise: to be enslaved meant to be unfree and to be considered the property of another. This did not set the situation in Tranquebar apart from other places discussed in this volume. Beyond this, the major groups implicated in slavery in the colonial town, i.e. the trading company, the mission and the local population, repeatedly renegotiated the semantic terms as well as the legal status of slavery. Specific practices, such as marriage and sexual relations, set in motion the search for legal precedents as well as legal principles.

Moreover, accounts of abduction and the slave trade illustrated that Tranquebar gained notoriety as a place of purchase and sale. The *Asiatisk Kompagni* as the political authority dealt with slavery and the slave trade in terms of economic principles and the maintenance of the colonial social order. Based on these governing ideas, it sought, and failed, to restrict private slave trading in favour of a company-controlled trade in the 1730s.

Tamil inhabitants especially in the countryside rejected Tranquebar as the infamous "slave town" participating in the Indian ocean slave trade. While the mission took slavery for granted, it expressed major reservations concerning the slave trade. Mission leaders pursued a change in the law of the slave trade based on two motivating factors: they sought to prevent their members from being sold away and to change Tranquebar's reputation as part of their effort to protect their corporate identity and, derivatively, their proselytising interests. Rejection on the part of countryside Tamils and concern for reputation on the part of the mission produced novel strategies of action and the law served as a tool in these endeavours. When the matter came to a head, an overall prohibition of the slave trade was proclaimed in 1745, although there would be recurrent mention of isolated incidents of abduction and slave trading during the subsequent decades.

Over the course of the eighteenth century, the sources repeatedly displayed the mission's concern with its own standing and the Tamil inhabitants' pragmatic adaptation and appropriation of the colonial setting. Their actions contributed to major changes in the institutional and legal framework, most prominently the prohibition of the slave trade. Matters of reputation fuelled developments that shaped the norms of slavery and the slave trade in Tranquebar.

Works Cited

Primary Sources

Archives of the Francke Foundations, Halle, Bio-bibliographical Register, https://digital.francke-halle.de/fsbio?lang=en (21.8.2023).

Archives of the Francke Foundations, Halle, Mission Archives [AFSt/M].

Der Königl. Dänischen Missionarien aus Ost-Indien eingesandter Ausführlichen Berichten, 9 vols., 108 "Continuationen" or issues (1710–1772) [HB], https://digital.francke-halle.de/fsdhm?lang=en (21.8.2023).

Huschke, Philipp E., ed. (1903). *Gai Institutionum Commentarii Quattuor.* Leipzig: Teubner. https://archive.org/details/gaiinstitutionu00huscgoog/page/n72/mode/2up (21.8.2023).

King James Bible (*Authorised Version*).

Lehmann, Arno, ed. (1957), *Alte Briefe aus Indien. Unveröffentlichte Briefe von Bartholomäus Ziegenbalg 1706–1719*. Berlin: Evangelische Verlagsanstalt. [AB]

Lehmann, Arno (1959). "Alte Indien-Post. Briefe der Maria Dorothea Ziegenbalg geb. Saltzmann." *Wissenschaftliche Zeitschrift der Martin-Luther-Universität Halle-Wittenberg* 8, 487–500.

Liebau, Kurt, ed. (1998), *Die Malabarische Korrespondenz*. Sigmaringen: Jan Thorbecke. [*Malabarische Korrespondenz*]

Neuere Geschichte der evangelischen Missionsanstalten zur Bekehrung der Heiden in Ost-Indien (1770–1848), 8 vols., 95 "Stück" or issues (1770–1848). [NHB], available in the digital library *Münchener DigitalisierungsZentrum*, https://www.digitale-sammlungen.de/de (21.8.2023).

Niekamp, Johann Lucas (1740). *Kurtzgefaßte Mißions-Geschichte oder Historischer Auszug der Evangelischen Mißions-Berichte aus Ost-Indien, Theil 1*. Halle: Waisenhaus.

Rigsarkivet, Copenhagen [RA], Sager fra den tidligere danske Mission i Tranquebar, Protocoll für Special-Conferentz 1725–74.

Rigsarkivet, Copenhagen [RA], Indkomne sager den ostindiske mission vedkommende (1738–1808), Missionskollegiet og Direktionen for Vajsenhuset (1738–1808), F39–1.

Rigsarkivet, Copenhagen [RA], Asiatisk Kompagni, Afdelingen i Trankebar: Trankebarsk rapportbog, 1695–1778, no. 1283.

Secher, Vilhelm A., ed. (1891), *Kong Christian den Femtis Danske Lov*. Copenhagen: J.H. Schultz.

Secondary Sources

Ahuja, Ravi (1999). *Die Erzeugung kolonialer Staatlichkeit und das Problem der Arbeit: eine Studie zur Sozialgeschichte der Stadt Madras und ihres Hinterlandes zwischen 1750 und 1800*. Stuttgart: Steiner.

Ahuja, Ravi (2002). "Labour Relations in an Early Colonial Context: Madras, c. 1750–1800." *Modern Asian Studies* 36, 793–826.

Allen, Richard B. (2014). *European Slave Trading in the Indian Ocean, 1500–1850*. Athens OH: Ohio University Press.

Bayly, Susan (1999). *Caste, Society and Politics in India from the Eighteenth Century to the Modern Age*. Cambridge: Cambridge University Press.

Brimnes, Niels (1999). *Constructing the Colonial Encounter. Right and Left Hand Castes in Early Colonial South India*. Abingdon: Routledge.

Cairns, J.W. (2012). "The Definition of Slavery in Eighteenth-Century Thinking." J. Allain (ed.), *The Legal Understanding of Slavery: From the Historical to the Contemporary*. Oxford: Oxford University Press, 61–85.

Campbell, Gwyn, ed. (2004). *The structure of slavery in Indian Ocean Africa and Asia*. London: Frank Cass.

Capogrossi Colognesi, Luigi (2016). "Ownership and Power in Roman Law." Paul J. du Plessis et al. (eds.), *The Oxford Handbook of Roman Law and Society*. Oxford: Oxford University Press, 524–36.

Chatterjee, Indrani, and Richard M. Eaton, eds. (2006). *Slavery & South Asian History*. Bloomington, Indiana University Press.

Eaton, Richard M. (2006). "Introduction." Indrani Chatterjee and Richard M. Eaton, eds., *Slavery & South Asian History*. Bloomington: Indiana University Press, 1–16.

Fenger, Johannes Ferdinand (1845). *Geschichte der Tranckebarschen Mission nach den Quellen bearbeitet*. Grimma: J.M. Gerbhardt.

Germann, Wilhelm (1868). *Ziegenbalg und Plütschau*, vol. 1. Erlangen: Deichert.

Gross, Andreas, Liebau, H. and Y. Vincent Kumaradoss, eds. (2006). *Halle and the beginnings of Protestant Christianity in India*, 3 vols. Halle, Franckesche Stiftungen.

Harrill, James A. (1999). "The Vice of Slave Dealers in Greco-Roman Society: The Use of a Topos in 1 Timothy 1:10." *Journal of Biblical Literature* 118, 97–122.

Jeyaraj, Daniel (1997). "Die Wechselwirkung zwischen Kirche und Kultur in der frühen Tranquebar-Mission." Dieter Becker and Andreas Feldtkeller (eds.), *Es began in Halle …* Erlangen: Verlag der Ev.-Luth. Mission, 136–45.

Jeyaraj, Daniel (1996). *Inkulturation in Tranquebar: Der Beitrag der frühen dänisch-halleschen Mission zum Werden einer indisch-einheimischen Kirche (1706–1730)*. Erlangen: Verlag der Ev.-Luth. Mission.

Kaarsholm, Preben (2020). "From abolition of the slave trade to protection of immigrants: Danish colonialism, German missionaries, and the development of ideas of humanitarian governance from the early eighteenth to the nineteenth century." *Atlantic Studies* 17, 348–74.

Krieger, Martin (2012). "Der dänische Sklavenhandel auf dem Indischen Ozean im 17. und 18. Jahrhundert." *Jahrbuch für Europäische Überseegeschichte* 12, 9–30.

Krieger, Martin (1998). *Kaufleute, Seeräuber und Diplomaten: der dänische Handel auf dem Indischen Ozean (1620–1868)*. Köln: Böhlau.

Lehmann, Arno (1956). *Es begann in Tranquebar. Die Geschichte der ersten evangelischen Kirche in Indien*. Berlin: Evangelische Verlagsanstalt.

Liebau, Heike (2010). "Die Dänisch-Englisch-Hallesche Mission (Tranquebarmission)", *Europäische Geschichte Online*, urn:nbn:de:0159-20100921291 (21.8.2023).

Liebau, Heike (2008). *Die indischen Mitarbeiter der Tranquebarmission (1706–1845): Katecheten, Schulmeister, Übersetzer*. Tübingen: Max Niemeyer.

Liebau, Kurt (1998), "Einleitung: die 'Malabarische Korrespondenz' als Beispiel indisch-deutschen Dialogs." *Die Malabarische Korrespondenz*. Sigmaringen: Jan Thorbecke, 7–36.

Larsen, Kay (1938). "Danmark og Sklavehandelens Ophævelse." *Historisk Tidsskrift* 10.4, 106–108.

Major, Andera (2012). *Slavery, Abolitionism and Empire in India, 1772–1843*. Liverpool: Liverpool University Press.

Manickam, Sundararaj (1993). *Slavery in the Tamil Country: a historical overview*. Madras, Christian Literature Society.

Mann, Michael, ed. (2008). *Aufgeklärter Geist und evangelische Missionen in Indien*. Heidelberg: Draupadi.

Mann, Michael, ed. (2006). *Europäische Aufklärung und protestantische Mission in Indien*. Heidelberg: Draupadi.

Mann, Michael (2012). *Sahibs, Sklaven und Soldaten: Geschichte des Menschenhandels rund um den Indischen Ozean*. Darmstadt: WBG.

Mentz, Søren (2017). "Handelsstationen Tranquebar 1630–1750", in: N. Brimnes (ed.), *Danmark og Kolonierne. Indien: Tranquebar, Serampore og Nicobarerne*. Copenhagen: Gads, 76–111.

Miers, Suzanne (2004). "Slavery: A question of definition." Gwyn Campbell, ed., *The structure of slavery in Indian Ocean Africa and Asia*. London: Frank Cass, 1–15.

Neill, Stephen (1985). *A History of Christianity in India: 1707–1858*. Cambridge: Cambridge University Press.

Nørgaard, Anders (1988). *Mission und Obrigkeit: die Dänisch-hallische Mission in Tranquebar 1706–1845*. Gütersloh: Gütersloher Verlagshaus Mohn.

Osterhammel, Jürgen (2010). *Die Entzauberung Asiens*. München, C.H. Beck.

Pearson, Michael (2003). *The Indian Ocean*. New York: Routledge.

Rajan, Rekha V. (2012). "Kontrapunktische Einlagen. Indische Stimmen in den Halleschen Berichten." *German Studies in India* 3, 23–38.

Reinhard, Wolfgang (2018). *Die Unterwerfung der Welt. Globalgeschichte der europischen Expansion 1415–2015*. München: C.H. Beck.

Roeber, Anthony G. (1998). *Palatines, liberty and property: German Lutherans in colonial British America*. Baltimore: Johns Hopkins University Press.

Yule, Henry and Arthur Coke Burnell (1903). *Hobson-Jobson. a glossary of colloquial Anglo-Indian words and phrases, and of kindred terms, etymological, historical, geographical and discursive*. London: John Murray.

Zeuske, Michael (2013). *Handbuch Geschichte der Sklaverei: Eine Globalgeschichte von den Anfängen bis zur Gegenwart*. Berlin: De Gruyter.

Edmund Burke and the Moral Struggle of the British Empire

André Kahl

Introduction

A study of Burke's imperial views quickly reveals a certain imbalance. Especially in the 1780s, he was a constant polemicist against the East India Company and its crimes. As a result, in 1785 his "colleagues shouted Burke down on the grounds that he spoke too much about India".[1] The abundance of moral invective in this context stands in contrast to the conspicuous absence of statements on the equally morally explosive issue of slavery. Not only that, but Burke's essentially rigorous position on the question of India corresponds to a distinct contradiction he reveals in relation to slavery. In what follows, I will explore the question of why Burke's moral condemnation of the events in India is so clear-cut, while his attitude to slavery remains ambivalent. In doing so, I argue that Burke's treatment of India must be read more politically. For Burke, events in India were not only morally problematic, but also posed a threat to the stability of the British Empire. Because moral and economic reasons are partly in tension, his position on slavery is less clear. Burke is not a staunch supporter of abolitionism, although he often makes clear that he finds slavery morally repugnant.

My first step will be a brief discussion of the self-image of the British Empire in the eighteenth century. Against this background, I will consider Burke's engagement with the East India Company. In a third step, I will clarify his ambivalent attitude towards slavery. In doing so, I will distinguish between three positions that Burke reveals over time.

The Imperial Self-Description of the British Empire in the Eighteenth Century

In her study *Britons: Forging the Nation, 1707–1837*, Linda Colley describes how, after the union with Scotland in 1707, the British "began to define themselves

---

1 Kramnick, *Rage of Edmund Burke*, 127.

© BRILL SCHÖNINGH, 2024 | DOI:10.30965/9783657796328_011

as a single people".[2] This process was a separation from the 'universal monarchies' of Spain and France, which were primarily seen as despotic, rather than a productive self-definition. In the process, an imperial self-understanding emerged in the 1730s that the British Empire was "Protestant, commercial, maritime and free".[3] In this context, the Royal Navy played an important role because, in addition to its primary task of fighting sea battles, it was also concerned with the secondary task of securing the trade routes. In this respect, the British Crown had at its disposal an effective means of controlling the flow of trade between the various colonies "of free, Protestant British citizens", who in turn enjoyed "the rights of Englishmen abroad".[4] In this context, talk of free and Protestant Englishmen is an indication of the extent to which transatlantic trade was constitutive of this self-image during the period of its genesis. It should be noted, however, that the term 'British Empire' was not used consistently throughout much of the eighteenth century. The Treaty of Union of 1707, for example, created a 'land empire' comprising Wales, Scotland and England. In addition, the British Crown had numerous dominions, for example in the West Indies, on the west coast of Africa, in India and in New England. But it was only after the Seven Years' War (1756–1763) that these came to be known as the single British Empire, having previously existed as many British Empires. Burke plays a significant role in this, for he was "prominent among those who began to use the term British Empire in what was to become its modern sense, as a single empire of rule throughout the world".[5] His entry into day-to-day politics in 1765 took place in a challenging situation. In the course of the Seven Years' War, its permanent rival, France, had been forced to withdraw from large parts of its territory, such as India, West Africa and the West Indies. At the same time, the British Empire was five times larger than it had been before the war.[6] In addition, the proportion of *freeborn Englishmen* in the total population of the Empire declined significantly as the population became more ethnically diverse, for example the 70,000 or so Catholics in Quebec or the Hindus and Muslims in Asia. The Seven Years' War is also seen as a pivotal event, because, from then on, the political relationship between the centre and the periphery began to change. The costly conflict led Westminster to involve parts of the Overseas Territories more financially, which in the case of New England was not well received. There were also rumours in England of large-scale smuggling

2 Colley, *Britons*, 6.
3 Armitage, *Ideological Origins*, 173.
4 Marshall, *Making and Unmaking*, 7.
5 Marshall, "Burke and Empire", 290.
6 O'Neill, *Conservative Logic*, 69.

off the coast of America and with France, a permanent rival. As a result, Westminster began to emphasise parliamentary sovereignty, a departure from the "wise and salutary neglect" doctrine typical of New England.[7] In addition, the "empire of the sea" was increasingly transformed into an "empire of conquest", which was less and less in keeping with the liberal self-description.[8] For Burke, too, parliamentary sovereignty is a core component of his concept of empire. According to his understanding, an empire is

> an aggregate of many states, under one common head; whether this head be a monarch, or a presiding republick. It does, in such constitutions, frequently happen (and nothing but the dismal, cold, dead, uniformity of servitude can prevent its happening) that subordinate parts have many local privileges and immunities. Between these privileges, and the supreme common authority, the line may be extremely nice. Of course disputes, often too, very bitter disputes, and much ill blood, will arise. But though every privilege is an exemption (in the case) from the ordinary exercise of the supreme authority, it is no denial of it. The claim of a privileges seems rather, ex vi termini, to imply a superior power.[9]

Richard Bourke specifies here that Burke's understanding of empire is "a diversified structure of subordination".[10] In this respect, not all parts of an empire are treated equally; rather, regional characteristics must be taken into account. According to this doctrine, a civilised people deserves more opportunities to regulate its own political affairs than those considered less developed. Although Burke repeatedly stressed the sovereignty of Parliament over the colonies, he believed that it would be politically unwise to depart from this principle too often. He was aware of the centrifugal forces associated with the overuse of power, as evidenced not least by his appeal to his countrymen, in connection with the tax controversy, to be cautious and not to let the conflict get out of hand. Here he prophesies that "if we go this far, the Americans will go further".[11] Burke was to be proved right. As a result of the loss of the American colonies, India became more central to the British national interest. There is another aspect to be noted with regard to the imperial self-image of the British, who claimed a special sense of mission for themselves. Colley summarises this in the following way "God, the British were encouraged to believe, watched over them with special concern. […] They had a mission, a special purpose".[12]

7 W&S III, 118.
8 Nechtmann, *Nabobs*, 19.
9 W&S III, 132.
10 Bourke, "Burke's Idea of Empire", 457.
11 W&S II, 426.
12 Colley, *Britons*, 20.

This kind of exceptionalist thinking is not really British; rather, all empires choose a "world-historical task" in order to legitimise their actions.[13] For the British, this task was to civilise the world, i.e. "to spread education, science, law and parliamentary government".[14] This self-description came to be increasingly at odds with political developments in the second half of the eighteenth century, most notably the actions of the East India Company in India, which Burke became increasingly critical of as his career progressed.

Burke's Criticism of the East India Company in India

Even in his own lifetime, Burke had already acquired a reputation as a connoisseur of India. Isaac Kramnick even claims that Burke was "obsessed with India".[15] Frederick Whelan, on the other hand, praises the later revolutionary critic as "one of the first major European thinkers to make a serious effort to understand a non-Western civilisation and to incorporate his findings into his general political thought".[16] It is no exaggeration to say that the Irish Whig had a great admiration for the Indian subcontinent. This is most evident in his scathing criticism of the actors in the East India Company, most notably Warren Hastings (1732–1818), the former Governor-General of the British East Indies. However, it should not be concluded from this that Burke represents a "postcolonialism avant la lettre"[17].[18] Throughout his life, Burke was convinced of the legitimacy of the British colonial empire. Arguably, one of the most pressing features of his legitimising the British colonies can be seen in his believing in Providence. Burke expressed this repeatedly, for example in 1783:

> All these circumstances are not, I confess, very favourable to the idea of our attempting to govern India at all. But there we are; there we are placed by the Sovereign Disposer: and we must do the best we can in our situation. The situation of man is the preceptor of his duty.[19]

---

13 Münkler, *Imperien*, 132.

14 Kumar, *Idea of Englishness*, 122.

15 Kramnick, *Rage of Edmund Burke*, 26.

16 Whelan, *Burke on Empire*, 44.

17 Becker, "Burkes Kritik an der englischen Kolonialherrschaft", 151.

18 Burke expert Richard Bourke sums it up as follows „From his earliest interventions into the debate on the legal status of the East India Company in the 1760s to his final, angry indictment of the conduct of Warren Hastings in the 1790s, Burke defended the legitimacy of the British conquest of Asian territories. He was, by extension, a defender of the rights of the British Empire in the east." (Bourke, *Empire and Revolution*, 365)

19 W&S V, 404.

Shortly before his death in 1797, he would reaffirm this in a letter in which he spoke of the "dominion of the glorious kingdom which has been given into our hands by an incomprehensible dispensation of Divine Providence".[20] This idea can even be generalised. In Burke's view, political rule is always to be regarded as a gift from God, which he summarises as follows: "All dominion of man over man is the effect of divine disposition. All power is of God and if it be, it is bound by the eternal laws of him who gave it, which no human authority can dispense".[21] What is important here, however, is that ruling is based on making each other better. The legitimacy of rule must therefore always be measured by the benefit to the governed, Burke argues, so that "[w]hen a British governor is sent abroad, he is sent to pursue, as far as possible, the good of the people in the spirit of the laws of this country, which in all respects contemplate their preservation, happiness, and prosperity".[22] At another point Burke even goes so far as to assert that the prosperity of the natives must be prior to the profit of the colonial power itself.[23] The greatest financial gain for the English treasury would thus be skimming off a flourishing trade through tariffs and underlining the company's solvency as collateral for London's further borrowing.[24] The British Crown, represented in India by the East India Company, failed to live up to the reciprocal betterment claimed. This is particularly true of the colonies in the East. Burke repeatedly complains that the colonised hardly benefited at all:

> Every rupee of profit made by an Englishmen is lost for ever to India. With us are no retributory superstitions, by which a foundation of charity compensates, through ages, to the poor, for the rapine and injustice of a day. With us no pride erects stately monuments which repair the mischiefs which pride had produced, and which adorn a country, out of its own spoils. England has erected no churches, no hospitals, no palaces, no schools; England has built no bridges, made no high roads, cut no navigations, dug out no reservoirs. Every other conquerer of every other description has left some monument, either of state of beneficence, behind him. Were we to be driven out of India this day, nothing would remain.[25]

Essentially, Burke uses two arguments to criticise the East India Company. On the one hand, he condemns the Company on moral grounds; on the other, he argues for a narrower interpretation of what it's supposed to achieve, arguing

20 Corr. 9, 62.

21 W&S VI, 470.

22 W&S VI, 345.

23 W&S V, 221.

24 Bourke, *Empire and Revolution*, 348, 356.

25 W&S V, 402.

that its very purpose is to trade. But this is precisely what it prevents by using its military power and overriding the free play of supply and demand. In this respect, the relations "between Britain and India [...] are not those of commerce, but of extraction based on the use of force, carried out by a nominally commercial corporation".[26] In this way, the employees of the East India Company act in a fundamental way contrary to the often-proclaimed liberal character of the British by resorting to coercion and violence.

The 1760s were a period of consolidation and expansion of English power in India. The *Treaty of Allahabad* transferred *diwani rights* to the Company, enabling it to collect taxes.[27] Bengal alone, with a population of 40 million, had four times the population of the whole of Britain, which in turn was governed by only a few hundred East India Company employees. In the eyes of many a young and venturesome Englishman, India was emerging as the promising 'Wild East', a place of danger for life and limb, but also of extreme wealth. The problem was that India was not being conquered by England, but by a trading company. Moreover, most of the revenue was no longer generated by trading, but by paying tribute and taxing.[28] In other words, England was now behaving in a similar way to Spain and France, whose primary source of power was land grabbing, and from whom the British counterpart mostly tried to distance itself, which Marshall summarises as follows: "In theory at least, the conquest of territory and the subjection of alien peoples had no part in any British empire".[29]

Burke's assessment of what the East India Company was doing cannot be understood without considering how he saw the Indian Subcontinent. In his view, India was already a civilised country and there was therefore a need for equal treatment of its people. With this perspective, he argued against the common cliché of the time that the Orient was, in the words of Bryan Turner, "all state and no society".[30] One of the most famous thinkers who helped popularise this stereotype, described by Edward Said in his famous Orientalism (1978), was Montesquieu (1689–1755). Although Burke held Montesquieu in high esteem, claiming him to be "the greatest genius that has enlightened this age", he accused him of propagating a distorted image of the Orient, and of India in particular.[31] In this context, Burke claimed that "every word that Montesquieu has taken from idle and inconsiderate Travellers is absolutely

26 Muller, *Mind and the Market*, 122.

27 Marshall, "Empire and Opportunity", 111.

28 Norman, *Edmund Burke*, 107.

29 Marshall, *Making and Unmaking*, 6.

30 As cited in in Mehta, *Liberalism and Empire*, 184.

31 W&S I, 445.

false".[32] Burke countered the contemptuous gaze of many Europeans by rejecting the assumption of an inferior East. At the same time, he insisted on the imperial mission of the British in India. To him, the degree of a country's civilisation was closely linked to whether it had an institutionalised religion and an aristocracy. Both, according to Burke, were present in India before the arrival of the British. The Irish member of the House of Commons pointed this out as early as 1783:

> This multitude of men does not consist of an object and barbarous populace; much less of gangs of savages, like the Guaranies and Chiquitos, who wander on the waste borders of the river of Amazonas, or the Plate; but a people for ages civilized and cultivated; cultivated by all the arts of polished life, whilst we were yet in the woods. There, have been (and still the skeletons remain) princes once of great dignity, authority, and opulence. There, are to be found the chiefs of tribes and nations. There is to be found an venerable priesthood, the depository of their laws, learning, and history, the guides of the people whilst living, and their consolation in death; a nobility of great antiquity and renown; a multitude of cities, not exceeded in population and trade by those of the first class in Europe; merchants and bankers, individual houses of whom have once vied in capital with the Bank of England [...] millions of ingenious manufacturers and mechanics; millions of the most diligent, and not the least intelligent, tillers of the earth. Here are to be found almost all the religions professed by men, the Braminical, the Mussulmen, the Eastern and the Western Christians.[33]

For Burke, the level of civilisation created equality. It was therefore not surprising that he saw India as a largely equal part of the empire.[34] For the British, he claimed that these "come from a learned and enlightened part of Europe" and this "in the most enlightened period of its time". With regard to the colonies in India, it was now a matter of advertising "the advantage of liberty and spirit of a British constitution".[35] However, a delicate touch is needed here, because the policy decisions that are made in England have to be based on the specific circumstances of the country. Burke condensed this to the following advice:

> it was our duty, in all soberness, to conform our Government to the character and Circumstances of the several people who compose this mighty and strangely diversified mass. I never was wild enough to conceive, that one method would serve for the whole; I could never conceive that the natives of *Hindustan* and

32 As cited in Pitts, *Turn to Empire*, 80.

33 W&S V, 389.

34 This is also emphasised by Marshall when he writes „what is particularly striking about Burke's sense of a British empire is the speed with which he incorporated India into it." (Marshall 1998, 290)

35 W&S VI, 315.

> those of Virginia could ordered in the same manner; or that the Cutchery Court and the grand Jury Salem could be regulated on a similar plan.[36]

In his criticism of the East India Company's employees, Burke echoed the existing narrative of an empire that sought to exert a civilising influence on the territories it ruled, arguing that the majority of local men had brought the British into disrepute through their barbaric behaviour overseas. It was also feared that the immoral behaviour of the periphery would spill over into the centre. Such autodestructive forces were prominently described by Montesquieu in his *Reflexions sur la monarchie universelle* (c.1727). Herfried Münkler sums up the idea in the following way "No power, however, can act barbarically in the distance without this having repercussions in its centre, where after a while the same forms of domination and oppression can be found as on the periphery".[37] The actors who embodied this tension in the second half of the eighteenth century were the so-called 'nabobs'[38], those who worked for the East India Company and were blamed by the British public for the company's misbehaviour and economic imbalance.[39] They moved at the interface between centre and periphery, or as Nechtmann writes "Nabobs were, thus, the visible footprint of the Indian empire on the island shores of domestic Britain".[40] Because of the pejorative undertone of the attribution, the term was often a source of protest among those affected.[41] Burke repeatedly expressed his concern about the nabobs. He accused them of enriching themselves unduly on the spot and returning with the wealth they had gained, rather than acting as moderate actors and representing the ideal of a gentleman. Once in England, they used their economic capital to gain access to political power. From then on, they determined the country's policies. The route via the East India Company can be understood here as a social shortcut, because the newly rich young men do not have the necessary education that is embodied in the gentleman who is oriented towards the common good. This educational aspect is a point Burke makes frequently. In his opening speech against Warren Hastings, he says:

> My Lords, the next circumstance which distinguishes the East India Company is the youth of the persons who are employed in the system of that Service. They have almost universally been sent out at that period of life to begin their progress

36 W&S III, 316–317.

37 Münkler, *Imperien*, 130.

38 The term 'nabob' originated from an incorrect translation of the term 'nawab'. This was used to refer to regional rulers in the Mughal Empire (Nechtman, *Nabobs*, 11, 14).

39 Nechtmann, *Nabobs*, 11–12.

40 Nechtmann, *Nabobs*, 21.

41 Nechtmann, *Nabobs*, 227.

> and career in active life and in the use of power, which in all other places has been employed in the course of a rigid education. They have been sent there in fact [...] with a perilous independence, with too inordinate expectations, and with boundless power. They are schoolboys without Tutors. They are minors without Guardians. The world is let loose upon them with all its temptations; and they are let loose upon the world, with all the powers that despotism can give.[42]

Accordingly, the young men sent to India are not morally stable and are corrupted by the power they receive in India. On the spot, they acquire a "taste for despotism",[43] which continues on their return home. This is accompanied by an increase in so-called *moneyed interests* in the British House of Commons.[44] This import of corruption in turn endangers the fragile constitutional structure. Burke claims: "I am certain that every means, effectual to preserve India from oppression, is a guard to preserve the British constitution from its worst corruption".[45] In the famous *Speech on Fox's India Bill*, the later revolutionary critic warns of a gradual and irreversible infiltration by the nabobs:

> Arrived in England, the destroyers of the nobility and gentry of a whole kingdom will find the best company in this nation, at a board of elegance and hospitality. Here the manufacturer and husbandman will bless the just and punctual hand, that in India has torn the cloth from the loom, or wrested the scanty portion of rice and salt from the peasant of Bengal, or wrung from him the very opium in which he forgot his oppressions and his oppressor. They marry into your families; they enter into your senate; they ease your estates by loans; they raise their value by demand; they cherish and protect your relations which lie heavy on your patronage; and there is scarcely an house in the kingdom that does not feel some concern and interest that makes all reform of our eastern government appear officials and disgusting; and, on the whole, a most discouraging attempt.[46]

Burke is not alone in this position, as William Pitt (1708–1778) argues in a speech from the year 1770, which has a similar meaning:

> The riches of Asia have been poured in upon us, and have brought with them not only Asiatic Luxury, but, I fear, Asiatic principles of government. Without connections, without any natural interest in the soil, the importers of foreign gold

42 W&S VI, 288.
43 Marshall, "Burke and Empire", 291.
44 Frederick Whelan describes this notion as follows "In the eighteenth century, 'monied interest' in the narrow sense could refer to financiers or investors in the public debt, a group- which would include the Arcot creditors- to whom Burke, unlike earlier Whigs, was always extremely hostile" (Whelan, *Edmund Burke on India*, 120).
45 W&S V, 383.
46 W&S V, 403.

> have forced their way into Parliament by such a torrent of private corruption as no hereditary fortune could resist.[47]

Another perspective seems important here. With regard to the establishment and organisation of great empires, the question arose as to which models could be emulated. For a long time, the *Imperium Romanum* was considered a relevant example.[48] Particularly in the aftermath of the Seven Years' War, the overriding question was how the phase of expansion could be transformed into a period of stability that would last as long as possible. Michael W. Doyle, referring to Emperor Augustus (63 BC-14 AD), calls the reforms that enabled this transition the "Augustan Threshold"[49].[50] In particular, the creation of a corruption-resistant elite within the administration is seen by Doyle as an effective measure to stabilise the Roman Empire at that time. As Doyle points out: "Rome in the first century B.C. was near collapse".[51] Accordingly, it faced a problem similar to that of the British Empire in Burke's lifetime "Each governor attempted to enrich himself, his family, and his clients during a short term of office".[52] Burke, too, was aware of the danger posed to the centre of a great empire by a peripheral administration which fails to function. He summarised this in relation to the *Imperium Romanum* as follows:

> The downfall of the greatest empire this world ever saw, has been, on all hands agreed upon to have originated in the mal-administration of its provinces. Rome never felt within herself the seeds of decline, till corruption from foreign misconduct impaired her vitals, and as an elegant commentator upon the orations of Cicero – Midianus says, *prevaricatione testimonii*, (by prevarication of testimony) the inroads of corruption destroyed the political frame, then were all things at stake.[53]

47 As cited in Dirks, *Scandal of Empire*, 12–13.

48 Ottow, *Edward Gibbon*, 163.

49 Doyle, *Empires*, 93.

50 Of course, this is not the only measure; Doyle summarises the catalogue of reforms as follows "The Augustan revolution rested on three achievements. Augustus rescued and thus won the full support of the Italian and provincial landed gentry who had suffered so directly and gained so little from the civil wars and predations of the urban oligarchy of Rome. He reformed the administrative system. And he acquired a special, charismatic influence over the polity which he was able to bequeath to his successors as a monarchy in all but name" (Doyle, *Empires*, 95).

51 Doyle, *Empires*, 93.

52 Doyle, *Empires*, 93.

53 W&S VI, 63.

Such a fate, Burke suggested, was also in store for the British if they did not treat the Indian colonies properly. To this end, he will use his celebrity to create a public event that will put pressure on the *men on the spot* in India. In 1788, a trial accusing Warren Hastings of various crimes began, in which Burke played a large part. However, it was less about Hastings as an individual than about the corrupt system he represented, and the trial signalled that the practices of governance in the colonies would henceforth be more closely scrutinised. In this context, it was particularly important for Burke that Hastings was not accused as just another person, but as a leading agent. As Burke argued:

> We have brought before your Lordships one of those poor, obscure, offenders, in an inferior situation, who when his insignificance and weakness is weighed against the power of the prosecution, gives even to public justice something of the appearance of oppression. No, my Lords, we have brought before your Lordships the first man in rank, authority and station; we have brought before you the head, the chief, the captain-general in iniquity; one in whom all the frauds, all the peculations, all the violence, all the tyranny in India are embodied, disciplined and arrayed.[54]

The message of the trial was twofold. The message to the British people was that there would be no tolerance of crimes in the name of the British Crown. It was intended to restore confidence in the moral character of the British Empire. With regard to the employees, it was intended to send out a signal that the trading company would be watched more closely in the future.

The impeachment trial was initially a great spectacle for the media and attracted the interest of the general public. Burke's impeachment trial took place over four days (15.02.1788–19.02.1788), during which he is estimated to have spoken for eleven hours. The trial was traditionally opened in *Westminster Hall*. It was attended by the social elite of the time, including the Queen and her daughters. Not least because of the length of the proceedings, interest in Hastings and his misdemeanours began to wane. Sara Suleri summarises this as follows: "The eight years of the Hasting's impeachment before the House of Lords provided eighteenth-century England with a spectacle first of political pageantry and then of boredom".[55] The acquittal of Hastings and the rapid decline of interest in the trial at the time was also a sign of a shift in public

54 W&S VI, 275–276.

55 Suleri, *Rhetoric of English India*, 49.

consciousness. By the end of the eighteenth century, the nabobs were no longer seen as the central threat to the British polity.

Three Burkes on the Topic of Slavery[56]

For a long time, the question of slavery was neglected in the study of Burke. The few comments that were made by Burke scholars on his relationship to slavery tended to suggest that the Irish member of the House of Commons viewed the practice of slavery with great revulsion. Only in recent years, and especially through the work of P.J. Marshall (2019), Daniel O'Neill (2020) and Gregory Collins (2019), Burke's statements on the subject have come to be more fully reappraised and, more importantly, reevaluated. While Collins emphasises Burke's abolitionist motives, O'Neill and Marshall stress that Burke can hardly be understood as a serious critic of slavery. In what follows, I do not aim to reconcile the various statements made by Burke throughout his career and to definitively clarify his relationship to slavery, but rather to sort out the existing references and make them plausible. To achieve this, I want to distinguish between a *Burke No. 1* who harbours moral misgivings about slavery. *Burke No.2* argues for slavery on economic grounds, while *Burke No.3* argues against slavery for economic reasons. All three Burkes will now be outlined briefly.

Recurrently, Burke condemns slavery, as he calls it "inhuman traffick" in his *Speech on Conciliation with America* (1775).[57] At least three times he criticises the practice of slavery during the 1770s.[58] But he condemns it particularly clearly in two speeches in close succession in 1789, calling for "that the African trade was a robbery that ought to be and could be abolished".[59] But what is the basis of Burke's critique of slavery? Basically, Burke assumes that

56 The talk of three burkes is reminiscent of Steven Lenzner, who published an article entitled Strauss's Three Burkes in 1991. In this article, he claims that Leo Strauss describes not one but three Burkes in his famous work *Natural Law and History* (1953).

57 W&S III, 131. However, as Daniel O'Neill has pointed out, this remark should not be overstated, for in the same scripture he advocates slavery in the following words "With regard to the high aristocratic spirit of Virginia and the Southern Colonies, it has been proposed, I know, to reduce it, by declaring a general enfranchisement of their slaves. This project has had its advocates and panegyrists; yet I never could argue myself into any opinion of it. Slaves are often much attached to their masters. A general wild offer of liberty, would not always be accepted. History furnishes few instances of it. It is sometimes as hard to persuade slaves to free, as it is to compel freeman to be slaves; and in this auspicious scheme, we should have both these pleasing talks on our hands at once" (W&S III, 131).

58 W&S IV, 272.

59 W&S IV, 277.

people are committed to a moral narrative of progress. Burke remained faithful to this throughout his life and is already to be found in his early aesthetic writing *A Philosophical Enquiry into the Origin of our Ideas of the Sublime and Beautiful* (1757). Human beings are fundamentally required to perfect their natural endowments. This does not happen individually, but in the political community. In order to establish a lasting political order, God has endowed us with three passions, namely sympathy, imitation and ambition. Sympathy means being able to share in the emotional world of other people. The need to imitate ensures that one imitates more or less critically and thus ties in with traditional knowledge. The last passion Burke mentions is ambition, whose role he outlines as follows:

> Although imitation is one of the great instruments used by providence in bringing our nature towards its perfection, yet if men gave themselves up to imitation entirely, and each followed the other, and so on in an eternal circle, it is easy to see that there never could be any improvement amongst them. Men must remain brutes do, the same at the end that they are at this day, and that they were in the beginning of the world. To prevent this, God has planted in man a sense of ambition, and a satisfaction arising from the contemplation of his excelling his fellows in something deemed valuable amongst them.[60]

Accordingly, it is in the nature of man to form virtues. This imperative of perfection is also of political significance, and is often found in the positions that Burke takes with regard to the legitimacy of the British Empire. As shown above, he does not question the legitimacy of the British Empire. However, it is not simply a zone of domination; rather, Burke emphasises the duties of imperial rule, which is ostensibly the civilisation of the dominated territories.

In more recent times, thinkers such as John Pocock and Daniel O'Neill have highlighted the influence of the representatives of the Scottish Enlightenment on Burke. These, in turn, became the "leading British and European exponents of the ideology of manners".[61] It was often assumed that manners were a valid and scientific criterion for the assessment of a society's civilisational progress.[62] Refined mores were thus a central feature of a civilised society, becoming the "common currency" of the moral discourses of the day and thus a common point of reference for subjects such as law, history or ethnographic research.[63] The stadial theory, which provides an analytical and interpretative framework for distinguishing human communities, is of central importance

60 W&S I, 225.
61 Pocock, "Political Economy of Burke's Analysis", 333.
62 Phillips, *Society and Sentiment*, 147–148.
63 Phillips, *Society and Sentiment*, 147.

in this context. According to this model, societies progress through a series of stages, beginning with hunting and herding and ending with agriculture and trade (Kohn/O'Neill 2006, 194). Burke was in contact with leading representatives of the Scottish Enlightenment; he corresponded with David Hume, Adam Smith and William Robertson. The latter is not only a major historian of the eighteenth century, but is even described by the Japanese Burke scholar Sora Sato as Burke's "favourite historian" (Sato 2018, 226).[64] The esteem was once mutual: Robertson sent Burke a copy of his *History of America* (1777). After reading it, Burke was enthusiastic about what he had read and replied to Robertson in a letter:

> I read many parts of your history with that fresh concern, and anxiety, which attends those who are not previously apprised of the Event. You have besides thrown quite a new light on the present State of the Spanish provinces, and furnished both materials and hints for a rational Theory of what may be expected from them in future. The part which I read with the greatest pleasure is the discussion on the Manners and character of the Inhabitants of that new World. I have always thought with you, that we possess at this time very great advantages towards the knowledge of human Nature. We need no longer go to History to trace it in all its stages and periods. History from its comparative youth, is but a poor instructour. When the Ægyptians called the Greeks children in Antiquities, I we may well call them Children; and so we may call all these nations, which were able to trace the progress of Society only within their own Limits. But now the Great Map of Mankind is unrolled at once; and there is no state or Gradation of barbarism, and no mode of refinement which we have not at the same instant under our View. The very different Civility of Europe and of China; The barbarism of Persia and Abyssinia. The erratick manners of Tartary, and of arabia. The Savage State of North America, and of New Zealand. Indeed you have made a noble use of the advantages you have had. You have employed Philosophy to judge on Manners; and from manners you have drawn new resources for Philosophy.[65]

As can be seen from the above quotation, Burke here is describing two perspectives that are offered by the stage model. In addition to the diachronic view, which can be used for a society's own historical self-understanding, there is also a synchronic view. This makes it possible to categorise the most diverse communities in other countries. In turn, this categorisation enables the justification of civilisational measures, if necessary.

According to Burke, there are two supporting layers which are the decisive reasons for the civilisational development of the whole of Europe:

---

64 Sato, *Edmund Burke as Historian*, 226.

65 Corr. III, 350–351.

> Nothing is more certain, than that our manners, our civilization, and all the good things which are connected with manners, and with civilization, have, in this European world of ours, depended for ages upon two principles; and were indeed the result of both combined; I mean the spirit of a gentleman, and the spirit of religion. The nobility and the clergy, the one by profession, the other by patronage, kept learning in existence, even in the midst of arms and confusions, and whilst governments were rather intheir causes than formed. Learning paid back what it received to nobility and to priesthood; and paid it with usury, by enlarging their ideas and by furnishing their minds. Happy if they had all continued to know their indissoluble union, and their proper place! Happy if learning, not debauched by ambition, had been satisfied to continue the instructor, and not aspired to be the master! Along with its natural protectors and guardians, learning will be cast into the mire, and trodden down under the hoofs of a swinish multitude.[66]

Churches, and the rules negotiated within them, provide concrete recommendations for action. The nobility – and Burke has the British landed gentry in mind here – cultivate a way of life that calls for imitation. Many representatives of the Scottish Enlightenment also emphasised the civilising effects of trade, a consideration decisively advocated by Montesquieu and more widely known as the *doux-commerce thesis*. In this context, Pocock is the first to point out that Burke inverts this idea, writing as follows:

> Hume, Robertson, Smith, Millar – we may add Gibbon – had all isolated the growth of exchange, production and diversified labour as the motor force which created the growth of manners, culture and enlightenment. Burke characteristically regards this as preposterous, as mistaking the effect for the cause. He insists that commerce can only flourish only under the protection of manners, and that manners require the pre-eminence of religion and nobility, the natural protectors of society.[67]

Accordingly, the process of civilisation is not favoured by trade; rather, the success of trade presupposes a sufficient degree of morality.

A core part of the civilising mission claimed by the British is therefore the education of morality. However, it must be said that no civilisation took place among the enslaved in the West Indies or on the east coast of Africa. But it is not only the training of virtues that does not take place sufficiently. Burke fundamentally assumes that slavery intellectually dulled those affected.[68] In a letter he sends to Henry Dundas – a Scottish statesman and lawyer – he claims that the minds of slaves are "crippled", which means that they "can do nothing

66 W&S VIII, 129–130.
67 Pocock, "Political Economy of Burke's Analysis", 337.
68 W&S III, 131.

for themselves; everything must be done for them".[69] For this reason, slavery is described as an "unnatural practice" because it prevents human emancipation. Burke specifies this idea as follows:

> Death is natural to a man, but slavery unnatural; and the moment you strip a man of his liberty you strip him of all his virtues: you convert his heart into a dark hole, in which all the vices conspire against you.[70]

For the most part, however, the Empire failed in this civilising mission. Indeed, as Burke pointed out in a speech in 1789, the practice of slavery was a contradiction in terms of the empire's claim to civilisation. It could also be said that the slave trade called into question the very self-image of the British Empire. In *The General Evening* Post, Burke aggravates the moral contradiction between the self-image on the one hand and the slave trade on the other: "Civilisation [...] and a traffic in men were utterly incompatible".[71] By engaging in the slave trade, Burke implied that one was behaving in a barbaric manner, which was one of the most vehement invectives of the time. The consequence of this is interesting, for although Burke has moral misgivings about slavery, he does not advocate the immediate emancipation of slaves. This becomes particularly clear in the following episode. On 7 November 1775, John Murray, the 4th Lord of Dunmore and governor of the colony of Virginia, offered slaves the prospect of freedom if they fought on the side of the Loyalists for the British Crown during the American War of Independence. For Burke, the idea that slaves, previously trained to obey, would now be allowed to enjoy freedom seemed horrifying. As Daniel O'Neill persuasively argues in this context, Burke finds the equation of 'savage' and 'civilised' problematic, which he expresses as follows:

> You will not, we trust, believe, that born in a civilized country, formed to gentle manners, trained in a merciful religion, and living in enlightened and polished times, where even foreign hostility is softened from its original sternness, we could have thought of letting loose upon you, our late beloved Brethren, these fierce tribes of Savages and Cannibals, in whom the traces of human nature are effaced by ignorance and barbarity. We rather wished to have joined with you, in

69 Corr. VII, 124.

70 Prior, *Life of the Right Honourable Edmund Burke*, 270. In a speech from 1789 with the title Speech on Abolition of the Slave Trade, he still says in this regard "He next adverted to the impossibility of a country being ever civilized, that was, thus, in the habits of slavery, as the Africans were. While we continued to purchase them, they must remain in a state of savage barbarity; for it was impossible to civilize a slave; it was contrary to the system of human nature. There was no country whatever in this state that was known to be in a state of civilization." (W&S IV, 278)

71 As cited in Collins, "Burke on Slavery", 16.

> bringing gradually that unhappy part of mankind into civility, order, piety, and virtuous discipline, than to have confirmed their evil habits, and encreased their natural ferocity, by fleshing them in the slaughter of you, whom our wiser and better ancestors had sent into the Wilderness, with the express view of introducing, along with our holy religion, its humane and charitable manners.[72]

It must be said, of course, that Burke's view of liberty was that it was a privilege that should be in the hands of those who were capable of its proper use. Accordingly, freedom is a privilege whose use must be learned. It presupposes a sufficient degree of self-control, as Burke pointed out: "It is ordained in the eternal constitution of things, that men of intemperate minds cannot be free. Their passions forge their fetters".[73] Through the process of civilisation described above, people learn to control their passions and thus practise the virtue of temperance. This is a central criterion for the exercise of freedom. Burke argued that abrupt emancipation was out of the question because most slaves in the British Empire had not yet developed this degree of self-control. Slavery should only be abolished when slaves are sufficiently civilized "until then, slavery was only prudent".[74]

Accordingly, the moral argument, which calls for abolition in the long term, is juxtaposed with a short- to medium-term perspective, which not only tolerates slavery for economic reasons, but also promotes it. The latter argument belongs to *Burke No. 2*. Already in an early writing entitled *Account of the European Settlements in America* (1757) – a text Burke wrote with his friend (and possibly even distant relative) William Burke – Burke insists that the high demand for labour in the New England colonies must be met, as the authors write "nothing could excuse the slave trade at all, but the necessity we are under of peopling our colonies, and the consideration that the slaves we buy were in the same condition in Africa, either hereditary or taken in war".[75] This meant that slavery had to be extended. Many towns and cities in England had close links with the slave trade. London, Liverpool and Bristol stand out. Between 1774 and 1780, Burke represented Bristol in the House of Commons.[76] The merchants

72 W&S III, 281–282.

73 W&S VIII, 332.

74 Kohn/O'Neill, *Tale of Two Indias*, 205.

75 As cited in Marshall, *Burke and the British Empire*, 23.

76 According to his self-image, Burke is a "philosopher in action" (W&S II, 317). In his role as a politician, he is accordingly required to make generally binding decisions in varying contexts and under the impression of time scarcity, whereas as a person with a philosophical claim he is oriented towards largely consistent thinking. Crawford Macpherson

operating in Africa and the West Indies were wealthy and politically influential players. They formed an effective community of interest with the plantation owners of Jamaica and other islands off the coast of America. There can be little doubt that Burke was a champion of their cause, and he was also a vigorous defender of the Royal African Company. This was partly his role as a representative of Bristol, but also his need to be seen as a friend of free trade, which had a distinctly progressive connotation at a time when a general "cult of commerce" prevailed.[77] In *Letter to a Noble Lord* (1796), written to justify a pension granted to him by the King based on his *Reflections on the Revolution in France* (1790), he claims that:

> If I had not deemed it of some value, I should not have made political economy an object of my humble studies, from my very early youth to near the end of my service in parliament, even before.[78]

Burke was instrumental in the drafting of the *Free Port Act* of 1766[79].[80] This was a partial departure from England's mercantile policy. Six British ports in the Caribbean were opened to foreign traders to facilitate trade. Among the goods to be traded were obviously slaves. Marshall writes: "The Free Port Act of 1766, for which Burke was largely responsible, could be interpreted as classifying slaves as 'articles of merchandise'".[81] A cynical point to be made here is that the Act was an extremely 'successful' one. If 1,258 slaves landed on the Caribbean island of Dominica between 1761 and 1765, the number had already increased to 1,353 between 1766 and 1770.[82] In this context, Marshall stresses that "the African trade had indeed been expanded by an act in which Burke had been deeply involved".[83] It could be argued that Burke, as an MP for the city of Bristol and thus a politician, felt compelled to champion political causes that he actually opposed. This is certainly not entirely wrong. However, this assumption is at odds with the way he sees himself as an MP. In a speech to his constituents in 1774, he self-consciously made it clear that he did not see his

---

will therefore claim about Burke in his role as MP that "Burke infused every particular issue with general principles" (Macpherson, *Burke*, 13).

77 Colley, *Britons*, 56.

78 W&S IX, 159.

79 Marshall, *Burke and the British Empire*, 155.

80 In his work *Edmund Burke and the British Empire in the West Indies*, Marshall devotes an entire chapter to the genesis of the *Free Port Act*, critically examining Burke's role in this context (Marshall, *Burke and the British Empire*, 105–124).

81 Marshall, *Burke and the British Empire*, 179.

82 Marshall, *Burke and the British Empire*, 122.

83 Marshall, *Burke and the British Empire*, 122.

role as representing the collective interests of Bristol in Parliament. He confidently asserted that "You chuse a member indeed; but when you have chosen him, he is not member of Bristol, but he is a Member of Parliament".[84]

Burke 3 also argues economically, but against slavery. There are two ways in which he does this, as I shall demonstrate. One way is more direct, the other more indirect. I shall begin with the more indirect argument. First, it is important to remember that "the ultimate reference point of Burke's political economy, both analytically and normatively, was the Scottish Enlightenment understanding of commercial society"[85]. The concept of commercial society is multifaceted, but can be understood with Donald Winch as follows:

> Commercial society is not merely one in which more people are engaged in producing capital goods, though this may be one of its concomitants; it is one in which more people are drawn into the wider circle of commercial relationships. It is the situation arrived at once the division of labour has been thoroughly established, and men can supply only a small part of their need from their own produce. It is that form of society in which 'every man [...] lives by exchanging, or becoming in some measure a merchant'.[86]

Thus, the development of a commercial society goes hand in hand with the development of cost-benefit analysis. The practice of slavery, however, being a largely inefficient system, did not fare well in Burke's view. This view, expressed in the 1750s and shortly before his death, has considerable continuity in Burke's thinking:

> It is an ill-grounded opinion, that by the labor of slaves, America may possible vie in the cheapness of manufactures with Great Britain. The labors of slaves can never be so cheap here, as the labor of working men is in Great Britain. Any one may compute it. I am the more convinced of the necessity of these indulgences, as slaves certainly cannot go through so much work as free men. When a man knows that his labor is for himself, and that the more he labors, the more he is to acquire; this consciousness carries him through, and supports him beneath fatigues under which he would have otherwise sunk.[87]

In the late *Thoughts and Details on Scarcity* (1795) he will reaffirm this idea in somewhat varied form:

84 W&S III, 69.
85 Ince, *Colonial Capitalism*, 93.
86 Winch, *Adam Smith's Politics*, 80.
87 As cited in Murphy, *Land without Castles*, 209.

> No slave was ever so beneficial to the master as a freeman that deals with him on an equal footing by convention, formed on the rules and principles of contending interests and compromised advantages.[88]

Free labourers are much more motivated than slaves, and therefore work harder and longer. This in turn makes their products cheaper than those produced by slaves. Regarding the relationship between employee and employer, to use today's diction, Burke paints a very harmonious picture. The parties to the wage contract are characterised by a high degree of congruence between their interests. For Burke, there is no contradiction here because the landlord can count on his workers being highly productive if they are properly fed and generally in good condition. Conversely, the worker's wage depends in the long run on satisfactory labour performance[89].[90]

Alongside these effects of expanding commercial society, Burke also proposed to gradually abolish slavery. These can be found in his *Sketch of a Negro Code*. This is a text written by Burke in 1780. The text then disappeared in a drawer for twelve years, Burke's explanation being that the time was not yet ripe: "At the time when I formed the plan which I have the honour to communicate to you, an abolition of the slave trade would have appeared a very chimerical project".[91] It was not until twelve years later that Burke saw the time had come to send the script to the aforementioned Dundas. By the late 1780s, it must be said, the debate over slavery had intensified. By way of illustration, between 1788 and 1792 there was a marked increase in the number of petitions that were strongly against the practice of slavery. On 2 April 1792, a week before Burke's dispatch of his sketch and accompanying letter to Dundas, agreement was reached in the House of Commons on the principle of the gradual abolition of slavery. Dundas had been one of the negotiators of this compromise, and it was now time for him to set out his ideas on the subject. In this respect, Burke's letter served as a template and aid to the meeting.[92] It is important to note that Burke was responding to public pressure and advocating gradual abolition. Accordingly, he was precisely not "one of the leading opponents of slavery in this early period".[93]

88 W&S IX, 130.

89 W&S IX, 124–125.

90 Burk writes in this context "It is the interest of the farmer, that his work should be done with effect and celerity; and that cannot be, unless the labourer is well fed, and otherwise found with such necessaries of animal life, according to it's habitudes, as may keep the body in full force, and the mind gay and cheerful" (W&S IX: 125).

91 Corr. VII, 123.

92 Collins, "Burke on Slavery", 10.

93 As cited in O'Neill, *Conservative Logic*, 203.

So what is significant about the Sketch of a Negro Code? First and foremost, it is a set of seventy-two measures for the regulation of the slave trade, the aim of which is "to diminish the inconveniences and evils attendant upon the said traffic, and upon the condition of servitude, until both shall be gradually abolished".[94] Thus, on the one hand, the conditions of the slaves were to be improved, and on the other, the civilising mission of the Empire was to be taken more seriously, which Burke explains as follows:

> And whereas, in providing for the second Object of this Act, that is to say, for the Trade on the Coast of Africa, it is just and prudent, not only to provide against the manifold Abuses to which a Trade of that nature is liable, but that the same may be accompanied, as far as is possible, with such advantages to the Natives, as may tend to the civilizing them, and enabling them to enrich themselves by means more desirable, and to carry on hereafter a Trade, more advantageous and honorable to all parties. And whereas Religion, Order, Morality and Virtue are the elemental principles, and the knowlege of Letters, Arts, and handicraft Trades, the chief means of such civilization and improvement. For the better attainment of the said good purposes, be it hereby enacted.[95]

Writing to the above-mentioned Dundas, Burke again emphasised that the sketch did not aim to abolish slavery immediately. Rather, freeing the slaves was a long-term goal that needed to be orchestrated. In addition, the many regulations were designed to reduce the incentive for the slave trade, as Burke summarized: "To make the abolition gradual, the regulations must operate as a strong discouragement".[96] To achieve this, the author drew up a catalogue of measures relating to housing and transportation, to the condition of the slaves and to educating them. These measures were to be carried out by officials:

> And for the better direction of the said Inspectors, no persons are to be sold, who to the best judgment of the said Inspectors, shall be above thirty five years of Age, or who shall appear on examination to be stolen, or carried away by the Dealers by surprize, nor any person who is able to read in the Arabian or any other Book, nor any Woman who shall appear to be advanced three Months in pregnancy, nor any person distorted or feeble, unless the said Persons are consenting to such sale – or any person afflicted with a grievous or contagious distemper – But if any person so offer'd is only lightly disorder'd, the said person may be sold; but must be kept in the Hospital of the Mart – and shall not be shipped, until completely cured.[97]

94 W&S III, 563.
95 W&S III, 565.
96 Corr. VII, 123.
97 W&S III, 568.

In addition to the minimum requirements that the slaves must fulfil and the specifications regarding their shipment, those remarks that are supposed to civilise the slaves are interesting for our context. In this regard it is said:

> And be it enacted that the African Directors or Committee shall appoint one sufficient Schoolmaster who shall be approved by the Bishop of London, and who shall be capable of teaching Writing, Arithmetic, surveying and Mensuration, at a Salary of [...] And the said African Committee is hereby authorised to provide for each settlement a Carpenter and Blacksmith with such encouragement as to them shall seem expedient, who shall take each, two Apprentices from amongst the Natives, to instruct them in their several Trades, the African Company allowing them as a fee for each Apprentice.[98]

There are also legal shifts, so slaves are allowed to own property and are formally not subjects of their owners but of the British government.[99] This argument can now be described as economic because "Burke is adding an endless series of regulations onto the back of the slave trade so that it would eventually groan and collapse under its own weight".[100] For Burke, slavery is "driven by demand" and the *Sketch of a Negro Code* aims to increase the costs corresponding to slavery to such an extent that it becomes unprofitable, while at the same time civilising it to release it into freedom.[101]

Conclusion

With the French Revolution, Burke's career not only ended in a historically significant phase, it also began in one, for when he entered the political arena in the mid-1760s, a metamorphosis was taking place. An empire that saw itself as largely mercantile, liberal, Protestant and maritime began to operate more and more on the land, becoming more religiously and ethnically diverse and shifting to a more extractive mode of rule.[102] However, this transition was not the result of deliberate change; rather, as the famous nineteenth-century British historian John Robert Seeley (1834–1895) pointed out "We seem, as it were, to have conquered and peopled half the world in a fit of absence of mind".[103] Seeley thus insinuates that there was no pronounced will to found a

98 W&S III, 567.
99 W&S III, 576–577.
100 Collins, "Burke on Slavery", 13.
101 Collins, "Burke on Slavery", 56.
102 Ince, *Colonial Capitalism*, 78.
103 Seeley, *Expansion of England*, 8.

world empire. Many questions remained unanswered for a long time, not least because of this, as Tillmann Nechtmann notes:

> The bonds, links, direction, and structures of political sovereignty were far from clear in these contexts. Did the crown, for instance, have absolute rights in the imperial world? Or, could chartered companies wield sovereignty outside Britain's official domestic borders? And, where exactly did Parliament fit in the relationship between these companies and the crown?[104]

Burke's tenure falls into this period of political self-confidence, but also political uncertainty about how to transform the empire's expansionary phase into a period of stability. His preoccupation with India and his intense debates about it ultimately serve to accompany this consolidation phase, for the purpose of stability the administrative elite, especially in India, must be reliable. In this respect, the highly moralistic debate about Hastings serves the purpose of stabilising the imperial political order, which is perceived as particularly urgent. Against this background, a clear prioritisation can be discerned: India, if mismanaged, can threaten the political order. This is because Burke saw the feedback effects of the corruption perpetrated there by the nabobs as posing a direct threat to England, with its mixed constitution. This is particularly clear in a letter Burke wrote to the lawyer and politician Alexander Wedderburn (1733–1805) a year before his death:

> Our Government and our Laws are beset by two different Enemies, which are sapping its foundations, Indianism, and Jacobinism. In some Cases they act separately, in some they act in conjunction: But of this I am sure; that the first is the worst by far, and the hardest to deal with.[105]

This statement may be particularly surprising in view of Burke's place in the canon of the history of political ideas as a result of his polemical pamphlet against the French Revolution and its ideas. Equating the threat Burke saw coming from France and India once again underlines the importance Burke attached to the colonies in the East. Against this background of threat, it is clear why Burke devotes far more attention to India than to slavery. Moreover, moral and political motives converge in relation to India, which is not the case with slavery. There is a tension here between economic and moral beliefs.

However, the concept of civilisation is a link between India and the issue of slavery. As mentioned above, the mission of civilisation was the central mission

104 Nechtmann, *Nabobs*, 19.

105 Corr. VIII, 432.

of the British in their dominions. This gives special significance to the question of the degree of civilisation of a country or region. Unlike many of his contemporaries, Burke regarded the Indian subcontinent as an already civilised entity, and this should be reflected in his behaviour towards it. This was not the case for the slaves that the British shipped along their transatlantic trade routes. He assumed that they did not yet have a sufficient degree of self-control to reject slavery, at least in the medium term. In the long term, however, it was necessary to enable slaves to become free through religion and education.

Works Cited

Armitage, David (2000). *The Ideological Origins of the British Empire*. Cambridge/New York: Cambridge University Press.

Becker, Michael (2021). "Burkes Kritik an der englischen Kolonialherrschaft in Nordamerika und Indien" Thomas Lau/Volker Reinhardt/Rüdiger Voigt, ed. *Edmund Burke: Vater des Konservatismus?* Baden-Baden: Nomos, 149–171.

Bourke, Richard (2000). "Liberty, Authority, and Trust in Burke's Idea of Empire." *Journal of the History of Ideas* 61.3, 453–471.

Bourke, Richard (2015). *Empire & Revolution: The Political Life of Edmund Burke*. Princeton/Oxford: Princeton University Press.

Colley, Linda (1992). *Britons: Forging the Nation, 1707–1837*. New Haven and London: Yale University Press.

Collins, Gregory (2019). "Edmund Burke on Slavery and the Slave Trade." *Slavery & Abolition* 40.3, 494–521.

Copeland, Thomas W., gen. ed. (1958–1978). *The Correspondence of Edmund Burke*. 10 vols. Cambridge/Chicago: Cambridge University Press. [Corr.]

Dirks, Nicholas B. (2006). *The Scandal of Empire: India and the Creation of Imperial Britain*. Cambridge Mass./London: Belknap Press of Harvard University Press.

Doyle, Michael W. (1992 [1986]). *Empires*. Ithaca/London: Cornell University Press.

Kohn, Margaret/O'Neill, Daniel I. (2006). "A Tale of Two Indias: Burke and Mill on Empire and Slavery in the West Indies and America." *Political Theory* 34.2, 192–228.

Kramnick, Isaac (1977). *The Rage of Edmund Burke*. New York: Basic Books.

Kumar, Krishan (2015). *The Idea of Englishness: English Culture, National Identity and Social Thought*. Farnham: Routledge.

Langford, Paul, gen. ed. (1981–2015). *The Writings and Speeches of Edmund Burke*. 9 vols. Oxford: Clarendon Press. [W&S]

Macpherson, Crawford (1980). *Burke*. Oxford/Toronto/Melbourne: Oxford University Press.

Marshall, Peter James (1995). “Empire and Opportunity in Britain.” *Transactions of the Royal Historical Society* 5, 111–128.

Marshall, Peter James (1998). “Burke and Empire.” Stephen Taylor/Richard Connors/Clyve Jones ed. *Hanoverian Britain and Empire: Essays in Memory of Philip Lawson.* Woolbridge: The Boydell Press, 288–298.

Marshall, Peter James (2005). *The Making and Unmaking of Empires: Britain, India, and America c. 1750–1783.* Oxford: Oxford University Press.

Marshall, Peter James (2019). *Edmund Burke and the British Empire in the West Indies.* Oxford/New York: Oxford University Press.

Mehta, Uday Singh (1999). *Liberalism and Empire. A Study in Nineteenth-Century British Liberal Thought.* Chicago/London: The University of Chicago Press.

Muller, Jerry Z. (2003). *The Mind and the Market: Capitalism in Western Thought.* New York: Anchor Books.

Münkler, Herfried (2005). *Imperien: Die Logik der Weltherrschaft – vom Alten Rom bis zu den Vereinigten Staaten.* Reinbeck: Rowohlt Taschenbuch Verlag.

Murphy, Thomas K. (2001). *A Land without Castles: The Changing Image of America in Europe, 1780–1830.* Boston/Oxford: Lexington Books.

Nechtmann, Tillman W. (2010). *Nabobs: Empire and Identity in Eighteenth-Century Britain.* Cambridge: Cambridge University Press.

Norman, Jesse (2014). *Edmund Burke: The Visionary Who Invented Modern Politics.* London: Harpercollins.

Ince, Onur Ulas (2018). *Colonial Capitalism and the Dilemma of Liberalism.* New York: Oxford University Press.

O’Neill, Daniel I. (2016). *Edmund Burke and the Conservative Logic of Empire.* Oakland: University of California Press.

O’Neill, Daniel I. (2020). “Edmund Burke on Slavery and the Slave Trade: A Response to Gregory M. Collins.” *Slavery & Abolition* 41.4, 816–827.

Ottow, Raimund (2011). “Edward Gibbon über die inneren Ursachen des Niedergangs des Römischen Reiches: Imperium versus Polyzentrik.” Harald Bluhm/Karsten Fischer/Marcus Llanque ed. *Ideenpolitik: Geschichtliche Konstellationen und gegenwärtige Konflikte.* Berlin: Akademie Verlag.

Pitts, Jennifer (2005). *A Turn to Empire. The Rise of Imperial Liberalism in Britain and France.* Princeton/Oxford: Princeton University Press.

Phillips, Mark Salber (2000). *Society and Sentiment: Genres of Historical Writing in Britain, 1740–1820.* Princeton/Chichester: Princeton University Press.

Pocock, John (1982). “The Political Economy of Burke’s Analysis of the French Revolution. ” *The Historical Journal* 25.2, 331–349.

Prior, James (1878). *Life of the Right Honourable Edmund Burke.* London: George Bell & Sons.

Sato, Sora (2018). *Edmund Burke as Historian: War, Order and Civilisation.* Cham: Palgrave Macmillan.
Seeley, Robert (2010 [1883]). *The Expansion of England: Two Courses of Lectures.* Cambridge: Cambridge University Press.
Suleri, Sara (1996). *The Rhetoric of English India.* Chicago: University of Chicago Press.
Whelan, Frederick G. (1996). *Edmund Burke on India: Political Morality and Empire.* Pittsburgh: University of Pittsburgh Press.
Winch, Donald (2008 [1978]). *Adam Smith's Politics: An Essay in Historiographic Revision.* Cambridge/London: Cambridge University Press.

Contributors

Turkana Allahverdiyeva
is a Research Associate and a doctoral candidate at the Bonn Center for Dependency and Slavery Studies at the University of Bonn, Germany. Her research project, titled "Non-Elite Household Slavery in the Early Eighteenth-century Crimean Khanate," is being supervised by Prof. Christoph Witzenrath, Prof. Suraiya Faroqhi and Prof. Stephan Conermann. Her primary areas of interest encompass slavery and dependency studies in the Crimean Khanate, slavery raids, and slave agency. Allahverdiyeva conducts her research using Crimean Court Registers, dating from 1700 to 1720, as well as travelogues and correspondences.

Bahar Bayraktaroğlu
graduated from History with a Double major in International Relations at Istanbul Medeniyet University, Turkey. After successfully defending her MA thesis titled "Children and Slavery In the Ottoman Empire" at Sabanci University in Turkey in 2021, she embarked on her journey as a young historian at the University of Bonn in Germany. She is a doctoral researcher at the Bonn Center For Dependency and Slavery Studies, focusing on enslaved and dependent children in the urban settings of Late Ottoman Constantinople. She has a scholarly passion for the abolition of slavery, human trafficking, and subaltern studies.

Rômulo Ehalt
(Max Planck Institute for Legal History and Legal Theory) is a historian with training in both Brazil and Japan. His research focuses on the history of the intellectual production and the presence of the Society of Jesus in Asia, particularly Japan. Currently, he is in the process of developing a book manuscript derived from his doctoral dissertation (Tokyo University of Foreign Studies, 2018), which explores how Jesuit missionaries in Japan perceived slavery as a theological and legal problem. Additionally, Rômulo is engaged in a project that delves into the development of moral theology and casuistry in the Iberian empires in Asia. His contributions include articles and chapters published in both Western and Japanese academic publications.

Christoph Haar
is Assistant Professor (Akademischer Rat a.Z.) of Early Modern History at the University of Würzburg, Germany. He earned his PhD from the University of Cambridge in 2015 and he has held research fellowships from the German Research Foundation (DFG) and the European Commission (Marie-Skłodowska-Curie Postdoctoral Fellowship). Currently, he is working on a book project on slavery in eighteenth-century Tranquebar. Haar's research interests include early modern cultural history and intellectual history.

André Kahl
is a Research Associate at the University of Halle-Wittenberg, Germany. He studied in Halle and at the Institut d'études politiques de Rennes (Sciences Po Rennes). His research interest revolves around political theory and intellectual history in general, especially in the early modern period. His PhD dissertation deals with the connection of sceptical motives and the role of providence within the thinking of the Anglo-Irish Member of Parliament Edmund Burke. Kahl was Fellow at the graduate school "Society and Culture in Motion" at the University of Halle-Wittenberg (2016–2018).

Eva Marie Lehner
is a postdoctoral researcher at the Bonn Center for Dependency and Slavery Studies in Germany. She completed her studies at the Free University of Berlin and earned her PhD degree from the University of Duisburg-Essen. Her dissertation, "Taufe – Ehe – Tod. Verzeichnungspraktiken in frühneuzeitlichen Kirchenbüchern"/"Baptism – Marriage – Death: Practices of Indexing in Early Modern Church Records" was published in 2023. Her research interests focus on the history of knowledge and record keeping, the history of gender, the body, and slavery during the early modern period.

Lionel Mira
is a PhD candidate at the University of Liège, Belgium. He received his BA in History from the same university in 2021. His thesis is carried out under the supervision of the prof. Annick Delfosse (ULiège) and Maria Laura Salinas (UNNE) and focuses on the study of the Jesuit missions of Paraguay in the seventeenth and eighteenth centuries. More specifically, Mira aims to analyse the connections that existed between Paraguay and Europe through transatlantic travels of Jesuit procurators.

Maximilian Rose
is a PhD candidate at the University of Hamburg. He studied History and English at the Technical University of Dresden and University College Cork. His PhD project investigates how themes of stereotyping, ethnicity and slavery relate to narratives of failure of Protestant missionary attempts in early modern West Africa.

Stefano R. Torres
is a doctoral assistant at the Institute of History and Anthropology of Religions (IHAR) at the University of Lausanne. Stefano is currently working on a dissertation supervised by Prof. Christian Grosse. His research compares descriptions of American Indigenous peoples in the accounts of the Spanish colonies in Austral America. Torres's research focuses on the representation of otherness from a European and Catholic perspective in the context of the early modern missions of the Society of Jesus. This research takes an interdisciplinary approach, combining global history and a decolonial perspective with textual and discourse analysis. In 2022–2023, Torres completed a fellowship residency at the Istituto Svizzero di Roma and conducted archival research in Chile, Spain, and Italy. Additionally, he is a member of the editorial board of *ASDIWAL. Revue genevoise d'anthropologie et d'histoire des religions.*

Index